THE QUALITY OF HURT

THE QUALITY
OF HURT

*The Autobiography of
Chester Himes*

VOLUME I

1972

Doubleday & Company, Inc., Garden City, New York

Library of Congress Catalog Card Number 71-151601
Copyright © 1971, 1972 by Chester Himes
All rights reserved
Printed in the United States of America
First Edition

The quality of mercy is not strain'd,
It droppeth as the gentle rain from heaven
Upon the place beneath; it is twice blest;
It blesseth him that gives and him that takes:
'Tis mightiest in the mightiest; it becomes
The throned monarch better than his crown;
His sceptre shows the force of temporal power,
The attribute to awe and majesty,
Wherein doth sit the dread and fear of kings;
But mercy is above this sceptred sway;
It is enthroned in the hearts of kings,
It is an attribute to God himself;
And earthly power doth then show likest God's
When mercy seasons justice.

THE MERCHANT OF VENICE, act 4/scene 1
Shakespeare

THE QUALITY OF HURT

Book I

1.

I suppose there were many reasons for my coming to Europe, but I don't remember them clearly. It was very like the many impressions my seven and one half prison years had made on me: I knew that my long prison term had left its scars, I knew that many aspects of prison life had made deep impressions on my subconscious, but now I cannot distinctly recall what they are or should have been. I find it necessary to read what I have written in the past about my prison experiences to recall any part of them. I have almost completely forgotten prison, what it was like and what I was like while there. The only impression it left absolutely and irrevocably is that human beings—all human beings, of whatever race or nationality or religious belief or ideology—will do anything and everything. And I think it has partly convinced me— at least I have tried to convince myself that it has convinced me— that I can never again be hurt as much as I have already been hurt, even though I should live one hundred thousand years.

It is like that with my reasons for coming to Europe. I am not certain that I remember clearly what they were. Race prejudice, of course. I know that was one even though I don't remember it. I am black and I was born and raised and lived in America, and the fact that race prejudice was one of my reasons for leaving it is inescapable. But I know there were many others as well. Perhaps one is that I had the money for it. Another is that I came very close to killing the white woman, Vandi Haygood, with whom I had lived; and I was both shocked and frightened. I suppose murder, and more, given America's sex and racism syndrome, when the potential murderer is a black male and his potential victim a white female. I had always believed that to defend my life or my honor I would kill a white man without a second thought. But when I discovered that this applied to white women too, I was profoundly shaken. Because by then, white women were all I had left.

I begin to realize I must tell you more of my life in the U.S.A.

I was born July 29, 1909 in Jefferson City, Missouri, the state capital, across the street from the entrance to Lincoln Institute, where my father, Professor Joseph Sandy Himes, taught black-smithing and wheelwrighting as the head of the Mechanical Department. Most Negro colleges in the South were known as "A. & M." colleges—agricultural and mechanical—in the Booker T. Washington tradition. As a child I often heard my father quote the famous saying of the great educator: "Let down your buckets where you are."

I was the youngest of three children, all boys. The only memory I have of my life in Jefferson City is of my brother Joseph and myself painting our hair with green paint left by the house painters. I also vaguely remember our mother instructing us to squeeze the bridges of our noses to keep them from becoming flat. My mother was an octoroon, or perhaps whiter. I remember her as looking like a white woman who had suffered a long siege of illness; she had hazel eyes, a sallow complexion, and auburn hair. Her family, the Bomars, were descended on their father's side from their white slaveowner and a slave, and on their mother's side from an Indian slave. I remember once seeing Grandmother Bomar when I was a child; she looked like a lithograph of an old, deeply wrinkled, pipe-smoking squaw from a Hollywood film. I saw only a picture of my grandfather; he was a tall fair white-looking man with a long blond beard, holding the reins of the horse of a Confederate cavalryman who was his master, and his half-brother, according to my mother. He was his master's body-servant and followed him to war.

My mother claimed that my grandfather's father was a direct descendant from an English noble family, and she was very proud of it. Much of her nagging and scolding and punishing and pushing us stemmed from her desire for us to live up to our "heritage."

All of the Bomars I ever saw were very fair, and some had moved into the white race. The only two I remember well were my mother's cousins, Mabel and Margaret Bomar, who had taught at Haines Institute in Augusta, Georgia, the year my mother went there to teach and took my brother Joseph and me. I remember them as being very animated and pretty; I was eight years old and I fell in love with them.

By then we had moved to Mississippi, where my father had taken a post as the head of the Mechanical Department of Alcorn A. & M., the Mississippi state college for blacks. Alcorn, formerly the white state school, named after Governor Alcorn, had been handed down to blacks when the white college moved to Oxford— the "Ole Miss" made famous by William Faulkner and James Meredith.

My father was the exact opposite of my mother. He was a short black man with bowed legs, a perfect ellipsoidal skull, and an Arabic face with a big hooked nose.

Now you can imagine what I look like. We all looked like that —like what you are imagining would be the combination of our mother and our father. Only I look more so. My hair is kinky, my complexion sepia, my features might be handsome were my nose not so tiny, and my skull is so flat and misshapen the students of my father used to say he had made it in the blacksmith shop.

My father's father was the slave blacksmith of a Jewish slave-owner, probably named Heinz, whose name he took when he was freed. That's how I came by the name Himes. I do not remember ever having heard any reference to his mother. He had two sisters,

Fanny and Leah, who migrated to Cleveland, Ohio, with their husbands, and one brother, Andrew, whom I knew, although I seem to remember hearing that he had another brother, named Tom, whom I never met. "Uncle Tom" was a joke of my generation.

Aunt Fanny was married to a "stationary engineer" who tended a boiler for the Standard Oil refinery in Cleveland; he was a huge, rawboned dark-brown man who would eat great quantities of food —he didn't care what, as long as there was plenty. I have seen Uncle Wade eat a platter of boiled rice, a dishpanful of boiled beef lungs ("lights"), a gallon can of string beans, and a loaf of white bread for one meal. They had a son, Gerald, a few years younger than me, a fat boy whom they spoiled by overindulgence because he was their only child. Uncle Wade was operated on for gallbladder trouble, and enough gallstones the size of marbles were taken from his gallbladder to fill a Bull Durham sack; he never recovered. Aunt Fanny died a couple of years later from cancer. And a short time afterward my cousin Gerald shot his sweetheart twice in the head and himself once; she lived and he died.

Aunt Leah married a former teacher, Rodney Moon, who became a federal meat inspector after they emigrated to Cleveland. When I knew them they were the only black family in a white neighborhood in the 105th Street–Superior Avenue district (which has since become a ghetto), and as a consequence had great social status. They had two children, both considerably older than myself. One, Henry Lee, graduated from Howard University in Washington, D.C., I believe, and became a journalist-cum-schoolteacher of a sort; and his sister Ella, who had also been a schoolteacher. To my knowledge Henry taught at Talladega University in Alabama, was city editor of the Harlem newspaper the *Amsterdam News*, an executive of Sidney Hillman's Political Action Committee when Franklin Roosevelt ran for his last term in office, and was one of the group of black writers and intellectuals who were invited to Russia by the Russian government in the 1930s to make a film about Lincoln freeing the slaves. These brothers and sisters, among whom were Ted Poston, Langston Hughes, Loren Miller, Arabel Thompson, Molly Lewis, one of the founders of the Urban League Guild and now my cousin Henry's wife, quarreled among themselves and were sent home, it may now be said. Henry Moon, along with Ted Poston, now a reporter for the New York *Post*, Robert Weaver, former executive director of H.U.D., and other soul brothers, were members of President Roosevelt's "Black Cabinet," a group of visible black faces in federal jobs. Now Henry is a member of the national executive board of the NAACP and editor of *The Crisis*.

My father's generation are all dead as far as I know: Uncle Roddy and Aunt Leah, Uncle Andrew and perhaps Uncle Tom, and my father. We three brothers are still alive, but none of us has any children, so the Himes family will die with us. Joseph is an internationally known sociologist, a professor in the North Carolina College in Durham, North Carolina, and Edward, my eldest brother, was a waiter at a chichi restaurant on midtown Lexington Avenue, the last I heard, and an executive of the waiters union. I've heard black waiters in Harlem address him as "Mister Himes" with great respect, which they never did for either Joe or me, so he must be important. The fact that he lives in Harlem doesn't have anything to do with it.

I can't say that I remember very much of Eddie from childhood. He is about nine or ten years older than me, and I don't remember seeing too much of him. I was too young to remember him from Jefferson City, Missouri, and for most of the time we lived at Alcorn, Mississippi, he was away—first at school at Atlanta University and later on the road as a dining-car waiter.

But Joe and I were inseparable, despite the year's difference in our ages. Our mother was horrified by the elementary schools for blacks in Mississippi, and she taught Joe and me herself, in our living room, year in and year out, until we finished the seventh grade, or its equivalent in the Southern black school system. Haines Institute in Augusta was the first school we attended; I was eight or nine years old, and we were enrolled in the eighth grade. We were so far ahead in our studies that from the start we were always in classes with students twice our age.

Aside from Miss Lucy Laney, the big black woman founder and principal of Haines, whipping my bare bottom with an inch-thick pine board, latticed by a number of dollar-size holes, while I ground the enamel from my teeth to keep from crying; and a great fire one night in the nearby slums which left a large portion of the community homeless; and falling in love with my cousins, Mabel and Margaret Bomar, who were more than twice my age at the time, I do not remember anything about Haines. Oh yes, the *geechee*, those descendants of runaway slaves and Indians who lived in the Georgia and Florida swamps; and Maud, the mule, who bit me seriously on the nose for stealing her corn, which I would roast and eat; and Pomp, the geechee mascot, startling the school one morning with, "O, Milaney, Milaney, de gote done dead." Yes, there was a goat, but he was "done dead." And fighting my cousin, Will Porter, at the instigation of the older boys.

My father bought a car, a secondhand Studebaker, in Memphis during the last year of the war and became the only car owner in our county in Mississippi. I learned to drive it but my legs weren't long enough to reach the pedals and I knocked down several picket fences in the school.

My mother used to take us for rides in the country with a student driving, but we got into so many controversies with the cracker farmers of the county by frightening their mule teams that my father was dismissed from the school and driven from the state. And I must confess I find white people just the same today, everywhere I have ever been, if a black man owns a big and expensive car they will hate him for it. Of course part of that was due to my mother's attitude; she always carried a pistol on our car rides through the country, and whenever a cracker mule driver reached for his rabbit gun she beat him to the draw and made him drop it.

My father got the same job in the Branch Normal College in Pine Bluff, Arkansas, which has later become known as the

Arkansas A. & M. I don't know where it derived its first name—evidently it was the black "branch" of a white "normal" college; anyway, it was the Arkansas state school for blacks.

Joe and I were enrolled in what was known as the first year of college. I was twelve and he was thirteen and our classmates were in their twenties. There was a roll call at the beginning of each class. A student named Jerry Ramsey told me that he wouldn't be to class the next day and when the professor called his name I was to say he'd gone to Memphis chasing whores. I didn't know what "whores" were, but I knew "hoers" were always needed to hoe the cotton and chop the corn. So when Jerry's name was called the following day I stood up and said loudly, "He's gone to Memphis chasing hoers." The ignorant professor, thinking I knew what I was saying, called me to the front of the class and attempted to punish me; and I began fighting him. He got me down on the floor and began beating me and my brother came to my help. It caused quite a scandal in the school.

A couple days later, when our botany class was taking a walk through the woods, the class belle, a girl of about twenty-five, fell in beside me and asked, "Didn't you really know what they were?" Blushing, I said, "Sure." I remember her looking at me curiously.

I remember that we lived in a house near the railroad tracks some distance from the school and we used to hop the freight trains and ride as far as the crossing just outside the school grounds if any should pass.

Joe and I almost died of smallpox the first year we lived there. We broke out in pustules all over our bodies, inside our nostrils, on the palms of our hands, the soles of our feet; our eyes became spotted. Our father was at school when it was discovered that our high fever was due to smallpox. Along with our mother we were quarantined in our house, and our father was not permitted to come beyond the front fence for the duration. Our mother saved us from permanent scars by tying our hands inside feather pillows and keeping us covered with carbolic salve. We had had chicken pox in Mississippi and had been vaccinated against smallpox, but it didn't help. When we recovered, mother burned all of the bedding, the mattress, and all of our clothing and possessions that had been in the room during the period of our illness.

Like all schools in those days, Branch Normal College covered a large area in the wide angle made by the crossing of the Southern and Yellow Dog Railroads. It was an Arkansas adage— *where the Southern crosses the Yellow Dog.* The school grounds were enclosed by various types of fences and all of the school buildings were built of wood. Only the president, whose name I have forgotten, lived within the campus. I have vague memories of baseball and football games and the older boys fighting the professors and throwing stones through the windows of the buildings in resentment, and vaguer memories of school rooms and classes. My father was required to conduct academic classes in addition to his mechanical classes; his subject was Negro history. He used a number of textbooks and reference books on Negro history which I have never seen since.

Each year, toward the end of the term, the school presented a rehearsed performance for the parents of the students, to demonstrate the various avenues of education it offered. Students with the highest grades were chosen to demonstrate their skills and special techniques in the school auditorium, so the parents could get an idea of what we were learning. Some recited parts from plays, speeches of great Negro educators, lines from Homer, etc.; others demonstrated the mixing of bread dough, how to chop the weeds from the young cotton, the proper way to hold the leg of a mule while shoeing it. Some discoursed on the future of the combustion engine, others on the stability of the horse; and no program was ever concluded without a debate on which was the more destructive, fire or water.

That year, 1922 or 1923, Joe and I were chosen to give the chemistry demonstration. We were permitted to choose whatever demonstration we wished. It was not too long after the end of the First World War, and we had discovered how to make "torpedoes" from a mixture of ground saltpeter (potassium nitrate), ground charcoal (carbon), and ground glass (silica), which we would put on the railroad tracks for the engines to run over and explode with a loud bang. The ingredients were pulverized separately with mortar and pestle and at the last stage carefully mixed and made to explode by carefully packing the powder into an empty shotgun shell and throwing it against a concrete wall.

I do not remember why we chose that particular feat; it had little to do with our chemistry course. It was probably my choice; I was always the showoff, the adventurer. However, as was customary, I did something naughty—perhaps said a "swear word" in my mother's presence, or was disobedient, or "sassed" her— and my mother punished me by forbidding me to take part. I had looked forward to the performance and she knew that no punishment would be greater than forbidding it. Years later, when I was serving time in prison and used to see the signs—*Spitting on the floor is forbidden . . . Talking at night is forbidden . . . Taking food from the dining room is forbidden . . . Whistling is forbidden*—I was reminded of this. It had been a mistake. My brother had needed me. It was a delicate and dangerous performance.

When he began to mix the ground glass into the other ingredients, working alone, the contents of the whole mortar exploded in his face.

That one moment in my life hurt me as much as all the others put together. It still does, a half century later. I loved my brother. I had never been separated from him and that moment was shocking, shattering, and terrifying. I vaguely remember the confusion. I leaped to Joe's aid and fell down a flight of stairs. Next, I remember, we were squeezed into the back seat of a Stutz touring car—my mother and father and Joe and myself— and were hurtling through the night. Lights of other cars followed. We pulled into the emergency entrance of a white people's hospital. White clad doctors and attendants appeared. I remember sitting in the back seat with Joe watching the pantomine being enacted in the car's bright lights. A white man was refusing; my father was pleading. Dejectedly my father turned away; he was crying like a baby. My mother was fumbling in her handbag for a handkerchief; I hoped it was for a pistol. Joe was strangely silent. We took him to the black people's hospital. No one there seemed to know exactly what to do. Finally his face and eyes were bandaged and he was put to bed. His face was not disfigured but he was blinded.

Five days later my mother took him to St. Louis so he could be treated in Barnes Hospital. My father and I moved from our home and took rooms close to the school entrance; I don't remember whether we had owned the house or not. Suddenly it was summer; the school term was over and the summer school for teachers had begun. My father was made acting president that summer while the president was away. He let me take turns in driving the Fordson tractor for the farm. I felt big and important driving the tractor. I became thirteen years old that summer. The young black women teachers eyed me appraisingly. I played tennis with them. I developed a great passion for one young mulatto woman, who let me take her to the movies. I fought my father when he tried to curb me. I fell in love with a young brownskin girl in town, but her family did not approve of my taking her out at night.

My father had the use of the school Ford, and each Sunday he drove us early to the Baptist church, where he taught Sunday school and served as a deacon. After Sunday school I would skip church if I could and go out and sit in the Ford in the shade of a tree and entertain my sycophants. I was a big shot to all the other little black children who went to Sunday school because I was from the college and drove the school tractor during the week, and sometimes the school Ford on Sundays. The little black girls offered their bodies. In the South, black girl children reach puberty at nine or ten years old and at thirteen they are mating like rabbits. They are not a bit ashamed of lying on their backs and opening their legs and offering their nappy pussies. They don't care who knows as long as it's kept from their parents and the "old folks." Church picnics were the best occasions for them to go off in the woods with the boys. The boys would return and show how "greasy" their penises were to prove their manhood. The girls would name each boy she had lain with. Strangely enough, it was not that summer I lost my virginity. Their shamelessness repulsed me; I felt disgusted by their casual fornication. I must have been a puritan all my life. Then as now, I consider the sexual act private. I do not want my sexual experiences to be made public. I do not care for women who discuss the sexual behavior of men in public, or vice versa. I don't want to hear about it.

My father bought a house in St. Louis on Taylor Avenue within walking distance of the one black high school, Wendell Phillips, and the Overton beauty products company known as Poro College, which made hair straighteners and skin lighteners and creams and scents for Negro women. He resigned in the fall and moved us to St. Louis. I was back in Missouri again. We had left Jefferson City when I was four years old. During the nine years which followed I had lived in Cleveland briefly, Alcorn, Mississippi, in Augusta, Georgia, and Pine Bluff, Arkansas.

I was assigned to the second year of high school in St. Louis. Joe was going out to Barnes Hospital daily for treatment—the doctors were attempting to remove the scar tissue from the corneas of his eyes—and he had enrolled in the Missouri State School for the Blind and was learning Braille and how to play the clarinet. Although the public schools in St. Louis were strictly segregated, both white and nonwhite males and females attended the school for the blind. Revealing, isn't it?

I remember St. Louis as a strange big city where I played football, baseball, soccer, basketball, any game that you can name, with suicidal intensity. The other boys on the playground either ganged up on me or refused to play with me; the gym teacher stopped me from playing all games in school. I broke my right shoulder blade, which healed out of place and still looks deformed; my left ear was half torn from my head; all of my teeth were chipped. I cut classes and roamed alone through the strange big city, spending hours in the railroad station watching the trains come and go. I was unpopular with my teachers, dis-

liked by the students; I was lonely, shy, and insufferably belligerent.

The first winter in St. Louis was very cold; it was said to be
one of the coldest winters on record. The Mississippi River, which
flowed through St. Louis, dividing East St. Louis from St. Louis
proper, froze over that winter, and the big drays drawn by broad-
beamed Percheron horses crossed on the ice. I have never met
anyone who believes this. I know it sounds very like the school of
whales that Hemingway sighted off the coast of Cuba. But I
distinctly remember standing on the bridge and seeing the brew-
ery carts passing on the ice beneath me.

We had hot-air central heating in our house, but the coal was
delivered to a back shed fronting on the alley, and it was my job
to bring it into the basement. I didn't mind the cold. I used to
take Joe bobsledding down the hill from the museum in Forest
Park; once we stayed out so long my toes were frostbitten and I
barely escaped losing them; thick layers of dead tissue peeled off
eventually.

I do not remember my father having any particular job at
that time. We were all so concerned with the welfare of Joe that
the significance of his unemployment entirely escaped me. Later
I learned that he had been working as a waiter in one of the big
beer halls.

After two years the doctors at Barnes Hospital said they could
do no more for my brother's eyes. Scar tissue completely covered
the cornea in one eye, but in the other he still retained a little
vision; he could tell light from dark and he could distinguish
large objects—such as people—in motion at short distances, and
he could read the large numerals on a wristwatch if he held it
about two inches from his eye. They said there was a danger of
completely destroying his vision and even his eyes if they attempted to remove more scar tissue.

For a time my parents entertained a wild idea of fitting Joe's
"good eye" with some sort of telescopic lens, but that proved im-
practical. My father was suffering from the frustrations of unemployment and Jim Crow, and as there was no longer any

benefit to be had for Joe in St. Louis, he took us to Cleveland, Ohio, where he had two married sisters and a brother.

In 1913, when we left Jefferson City, Missouri, he had parked us for a half year with his sisters while he secured the post in Alcorn, and I had vaguely pleasant memories of Joe and me in kindergarten. And once, before I was born, he had worked for a firm in Cleveland that built Pullman cars, and on the whole his reminiscences inspired hope. But when we returned he soon discovered there was little difference from living in St. Louis.

Cleveland was the first city in which I lived that was in the "North." I do not remember any legal segregation in housing or education, but most blacks lived in ghettos and sent their children to the public schools in the ghettos. Most of the unskilled jobs in the factories and steel mills were taken by imported foreign labor from Poland, Hungary, and other European countries.

First we lived with Aunt Fanny and Uncle Wade Wiggins. Their son, Gerald, was about a year younger than me, but he was a "mamma's boy" and I couldn't tolerate him. Uncle Roddy was a federal meat inspector and lived out in a white neighborhood; his job had great status among blacks.

My mother didn't get along with my father's people. While my father was a professor in various black state colleges in the south, he had helped his sisters and brothers-in-law to go North and get established, and my mother felt they owed him a debt of gratitude. Instead they patronized him because he was unemployed. Then there was the question of color. Even during slavery, the light-complexioned house slaves, who were sired by either their masters or their overseers, considered themselves superior to the black slaves who worked the fields, partly because of their superior "white" blood and partly because they considered themselves more beautiful, more intelligent, and of a higher class. This color class within the black race prevailed long after the slaves were freed, and there are still remnants of it left among black people. The "light-bright-and-damn-near-white" blacks were offered the best jobs by whites; they maintained an exclusive social clique, their own churches, their own manners and morals. A marriage between a black man and a light-complexioned woman had the status of an interracial marriage with legal consent.

My father's people suspected my mother of looking down on them because they were black. Maybe she did. They hated her. She hated them. My father was in the middle. Poor Dad.

The Wigginses lived in a mixed neighborhood off Hough Avenue, near the Cleveland Indians' baseball park. I remember my cousin Gerald hustling tips parking cars in his front yard during the Indians' home games.

I entered East High School, which was located a great distance from the Wiggins house, but it must have been the high school for the district. Strangely, although other black families lived in the neighborhood, there were only three other black students at East High while I was there; perhaps the other black families didn't have any children eligible for high school. One of the black students, Billy Williams, was not only the star quarterback for East High but the star football player for all Cleveland.

My mother took Joe away from the Wiggins house and found living quarters with a stranger in a distant part of the city. I don't think my father ever forgave her for that; that was the beginning of the ill feeling which led to their divorce.

My father began doing carpentry and small construction jobs. Then he and mother bought a house jointly way out in the white neighborhood of Glenville, not far from Uncle Roddy's and right across the street from Glenville High School. It's a black ghetto now, but at that time it was a middle-class Jewish neighborhood.

We moved into our house in the fall. I was in my last term in high school and wasn't required to change schools. I was sixteen years old and still a virgin. I remember standing behind the curtains of the parlor windows and masturbating at the sight of the big-tittied Jewish girls when they came out of school.

Joe was attending a school for the blind, preparatory to entering a public high school the following term. Readers for him, paid by the hour, were employed by the state.

I made only a grade of 56 in my final examination in Latin, but through a clerical error 86 was given as my grade; I was passed and graduated in January 1926, and had received my high school diploma before the mistake was discovered. My parents received an urgent letter from my Latin teacher requesting that I return the following term and review the course, but I refused and nothing was done about it.

Any graduate of a public high school in Ohio was eligible to attend Ohio State University. I planned to matriculate in September and study medicine. To earn money for my matriculation fees and other expenses over and above what my parents could afford, I took a job in the Wade Park Manor—a chichi hotel overlooking Wade Park—as a busboy. The dining-room staff was black. Mr. Smith, the headwaiter, was a small, quick, elegant brownskinned man who attended the same church as my father and was perhaps of the same age. He was extremely well liked by all the white guests; perhaps he was an Uncle Tom. I didn't think about such things in those days. Perhaps my father was one too.

My job was to go up to the rooms and suites and collect the wheel trays when the clients had finished breakfast or lunch. I rolled them into the service elevator, two or three at a time, and brought them back to the kitchen, which seemed as large as the waiting room in the Cleveland railway station.

Two young women sat in a glass booth facing the elevators and checked the trays of the room service waiters before they went upstairs. The young women were good-looking and white. Most of the young black waiters flirted with them; they returned the flirtation to a select few. One good-looking brownskin boy, a busboy like myself, was their favorite. I don't know whether any of the waiters had ever scored with either of them, but if not, it wasn't because they didn't try.

From the first day the girls began flirting with me. Other waiters noticed. Their previous favorite was furious.

It was during that week that I lost my virginity. They got me so excited that I was no longer satisfied with masturbation; I went to the black ghetto and paid money to an old fat ugly whore sitting on a stool outside her hovel on Scovil.

Scovil Avenue ran from Fifty-fifth Street to Fourteenth Street on the edge of the black ghetto and was the most degraded slum street I had ever seen. The police once estimated that there were fifteen hundred black prostitutes cruising the forty blocks of Scovil Avenue at one time. The black whores on Scovil for the most part were past their thirties, vulgar, scarred, dimwitted, in many instances without teeth, diseased, and poverty-stricken. Most of the black men in the neighborhood lived on the earnings of the whores and robbed the "hunkies." They gambled for small change, fought, drank poisonous "white mule," cut each other up, and died in the gutters. It was nothing unusual to see a black man lying in the gutter, drunk and bleeding and dying. "Don't touch him, man, don't touch him! They might think you did it," everyone warned. "They" generally meant the police, but it could mean his whore, his relatives, his friends, if he had any.

I must explain how Scovil happened; otherwise it's unbelievable. With the beginning of the steel mills in the Cuyahoga River Valley, which was to become one of the most despicable industrial ghettos in the world, foreign labor was imported from the underdeveloped countries of Eastern Europe—Poland, Rumania, Hungary, Czechoslovakia, and others. Years later when I wrote the history of Cleveland for the Cleveland Guide compiled by the Ohio Writers' Project (WPA), I came across a news item from a daily newspaper in the 1860s or 1870s describing how the owner of the "Newstead" Steel works drove to the freight station in his "elegant" buggy to pick up a freight-car load of immigrants to work in his mills, which he herded through the city like cattle. These foreign steel-mill workers, who could not speak a word of English, were quartered in shacks bordering on the black ghetto. They had left their women behind. A large section of Cleveland was inhabitated by these squat, thick, foreign men unattended by women.

But those immigrants, although ignorant and quite often de-based, who did not speak a word of English, earned money and eventually sent for their families and some of their children and grandchildren became ranking politicians and millionaires, while the blacks—many of whom were descended from runaway slaves dropped off in Cleveland by the Underground Railroad and had been educated and accepted members of the community for several generations—were totally unemployed by industry. From all the research I did on Cleveland history, I never discovered any reason for this except that they were black, and foreign white labor objected to working with black men whose ancestors had been slaves.

These foreign laborers invaded the black ghetto in search of women and food in such great numbers that a majority of the black women either became whores or lived with the foreign men as mistresses-housekeepers-cooks. The laborers became known as "hunkies"—whether it was a diminutive of "Hungarian" I never discovered. Anyway, the majority of the foreign laborers in the steel mills were Polish.

The black men did not object to their women being whores; black slave women had always been whores of a kind, or at least always vessels for the white man's lust. When the hunkies bought the black women for sexual purposes they were called "Johns." The black men simply preyed on the hunkies for their livelihood, robbed the hunkies, beat them, sometimes killed them, and lived on the money their women made as whores.

This became the absolute and irrevocable sociological pattern for Scovil Avenue, called the Bucket of Blood.

And that was where I went to lose my virginity when I became so excited by the playful flirtations of the white girls at the Wade Park Manor.

I had been with the hotel a couple of weeks and had just gotten sufficiently adapted to the job so that I wasn't always tense and nervous and afraid I'd drop a tray or do something wrong, when one morning I stopped in front of the closed elevator doors to kid with the "checkers," as the girls were called, trying to screw up my courage to ask one for a date. Realizing what I wished to do, they laughingly steered the conversation to topical chitchat, and began recounting the happenings when the famous Hollywood dog star Rin Tin Tin had had a suite there. It was with a sense of let-down that I turned away and pulled open the elevator doors and, looking at them accusingly, stepped inside.

I fell past the floor below and the high-ceilinged basement, between thirty and forty feet. I landed upon the heavy steel plate of the springboard that is at the bottom of every elevator shaft. I didn't lose consciousness. I remember the sensation of falling through space and landing on a solid platform with the feeling of my body spattering open like a ripe watermelon.

I remember calling for help in a tiny voice. My mouth felt as though it were filled with gravel. Later I discovered that it was only my teeth.

My chin had hit something that cut the flesh to the bone, broke my lower jaw, and shattered all my teeth. My left arm hit something and both bones broke just above the wrist so that they came out through the skin, dead white with drops of blood in the bone fractures. My spine hit something and the last three vertebrae were fractured.

The waiters came to pull me out, peering over the lip of the shaft with the flattened planes and whitened eyes of black faces in shock, and I remember crying out when they seized my broken arm. Then several jumped down into the shaft and lifted me out as tenderly as though I were a newborn baby. I remember seeing Mr. Smith's shocked face and tears flowing down the faces of the two white girls; then the ambulance came and I was rushed to the nearest hospital—a big, new, modern hospital—on 105th Street, facing the park.

I remember the expressions of regret on the aquiline faces of the two staff doctors who walked slowly toward the ambulance, shaking their heads while the red-faced driver expostulated dramatically. It occurred to me that a scene was being re-enacted, that I had seen it all before in the white hospital in Pine Bluff, Arkansas, when my brother was rushed there and the white staff doctors had turned him away. So in Cleveland three years later, in 1926, I too was turned away, because there was no space, no empty bed, but I was given a massive injection of morphine.

Then I was taken to Huron Road Hospital on Euclid Avenue, near Eightieth Street, and given a bed in a large crowded ward, and the Ohio State Industrial Commission doctors were sent for.

I was bleeding internally but my broken bones took precedent and I was wrapped in a body cast; my left arm was put in a cast and my broken teeth were anesthetized and my jaw wired. I still remember the names of the three Industrial Commission doctors: Steele, Castle, and Eisenbray. Dr. Eisenbray was the bone specialist, Dr. Steele the diagnostician, and Dr. Castle the internist, if I remember correctly.

My mother arrived shortly after I was put into my cast. I was too filled with morphine at the time to notice the ravages of her hurt. And I was asleep when my father came.

That night I discovered that I could not urinate. My bladder swelled dangerously and Dr. Castle was summoned. He operated on me at 4:00 A.M., when the rest of the hospital was asleep; he opened my urethral canal where it had been ruptured and inserted a rubber tube to my bladder which emptied into a bottle beside my bed. The casts for my broken bones were not touched.

Joe came with my mother several days later. He knew all about accidents; he was cheerful. Mr. Smith and waiters from the hotel visited, and various executives whom I had never seen before.

The Ohio State Industrial Commission paid all of my hospital and medical expenses and put me on a pension of seventy-five dollars a month for total disability until such time as the doctors might designate my disability as partial. The hotel promised to continue my busboy's salary of fifty dollars a month.

It was determined by investigators for the Industrial Commission that the Wade Park Manor was entirely responsible for my accident because the elevator doors were defective; state law required that elevator doors should lock automatically and remain locked until the elevator became level with the floor;

and on no account should it be possible to open the doors when the elevator was on another floor. Later I discovered that had I rejected the pension given me by the Industrial Commission I could have sued the hotel for a considerable sum of money. But when the Industrial Commission offered the pension and the hotel promised to continue paying my salary, my father persuaded me to sign the waivers to all rights for additional claims. My mother felt that I should have rejected the pension, and that became another topic of disagreement between my parents.

My father was born and raised in the tradition of the Southern Uncle Tom; that tradition derived from an inherited slave mentality which accepts the premise that white people know best, that blacks should accept what whites offer and be thankful, that blacks should count their blessings.

My mother, who looked white and felt that she should have been white, was the complete opposite. My mother was a fighter. She was a tiny woman who hated all manner of condescension from white people and hated all black people who accepted it. That much I inherited from her: I hate all manner of condescension from white people of whatever nationality —Americans, Frenchmen, Germans, Spaniards, Italians, Danes, Swedes, English, Dutch, whoever—all white people who are condescending toward me because I'm black.

But I respected my father and I did not consider him an Uncle Tom. I loved my mother with a strange fierce love which survived everything; but my father I respected. And while I loved my mother I obeyed my father. On his advice I signed away my rights.

I feel certain that my doctors did not expect me to ever walk again. But I fooled them all by getting out of the bed one morning without permission and walking as far as the window. Then I was measured for a back brace of leather with stainless steel supports, and the rubber tube was removed painfully from my urethral canal; it had become thickly encrusted with yellow crystals from leaking urine.

At the Huron Road Hospital, patients were not segregated by race, but the help was mostly white and resented attending black patients. The building was old and ugly, but the grounds, when I saw them, were lovely and green.

The patient beside me was a tall gaunt man who vaguely resembled my uncle Wade Wiggins. He was recovering from pneumonia and his wife, a pleasant woman, visited him daily. I had loaned him some of the blood-and-thunder books I had collected from visitors.

One morning his wife brought his clothes and informed him he could leave that afternoon. After lunch he finished reading a borrowed book before dressing to leave. Suddenly he died from a heart attack. One instant he was alive and the next he was dead. That shocked me.

The patient on the other side, also a black man, had blood poisoning, and his left arm was terribly bloated. It was threaded with strips of cloth to drain the poison, and was kept in a glass vat containing some sort of medication. The day following the death of the pneumonia patient a blood clot broke loose in a vein and began a slow journey to his heart. The doctors couldn't stop it. Perhaps nowadays they could have performed a transplant. But in those days he knew he was going to die. He began reciting the Lord's Prayer about nine o'clock that night in a husky anguished voice and the next morning before dawn he died. It wasn't his death that affected me so much that time; it was the sound of his voice reciting the Lord's Prayer through the night.

I was happy to leave that hospital. I was happy to return to our new house—new to us—in the white neighborhood. Joe had enrolled in East High School, which I had just left. We didn't live in the district but I suppose he was permitted to attend the public school of his choice because of his blindness. I didn't see much of him. I spent most of my time massaging my left wrist to restore its articulation and learning how to walk again with my harness. My brace consisted of two long bars of stainless steel, which flanked my spine and were held in place by straps that passed beneath my crotch and armpits and around my neck and shoulders and were buckled to a leather plate down my chest and stomach. I felt like a trussed fowl when I put on my brace. At the same time I began having my teeth filled, crowned, and repaired entirely by the Industrial Commission dentist.

The doctors employed by the Industrial Commission had private practices also; it was similar to socialized medicine. They accepted Industrial Commission patients for a prescribed fee paid by the state. The dentist to whom I had been assigned had formerly been a professor at the state dental college; he was conscientious and highly skilled. He began using gold in my fillings and crowns, but the cost was more than the state would pay, and he was ordered to use amalgam, which he refused to do, so I was transferred to another dentist. But the work he did lasted many years.

I was saving my money to enter Ohio State University that fall, father was working at odd jobs, and Joe was attending East High, when suddenly Mother became angered by my signing away my right to sue the hotel; she felt they had taken advantage of my youth and inexperience and race. She went to the hotel and created a considerable row; the hotel stopped paying me my fifty dollars a month salary. She and my father had a furious quarrel over this. She called him spineless and a bootlicker, which doubtless he was, but it created an intolerable atmosphere in our house. I was happy when September came and I could go off to college.

I entered Ohio State University in Columbus in September 1926. A high school diploma from any high school in the state was all that was required to matriculate. We were given quite extensive examinations to determine our intelligence quotients. I was later told that I had the fourth highest I.Q. of that year's entrants, and I must confess I felt proud.

Black students could not live in the school dormitories, and all the fraternity houses within the environs of the campus were strictly Jim-Crowed. The nearest a black student came to getting inside one of them was as a waiter or dishwasher. But many of the black householders in the environs took black students as roomers, and some also furnished board. I boarded in a rooming house several blocks away which also boarded a few coeds.

There were two fraternities and two sororities for the six hundred or so black students, but they met in the city's black neighborhood bordering on Long Avenue, which was several miles from the campus.

I bought a coonskin coat for three hundred dollars, a knickerbocker suit, a long-stemmed pipe, and a Model T Ford roadster, and I became a collegian. Because of my injury I was exempted from ROTC, which was compulsory for two years, and I did not have to buy the ROTC uniform, which other freshmen wore. Freshmen were also required to wear felt beanies with the school colors, but the white upperclassmen who enforced this rule could not tell that I was a freshman because I never wore a uniform, so I didn't have to wear a beanie either; many students thought I was an upperclassman.

I would have been a great success with the pretty black coeds if I had had more experience. Also, having to wear a backbrace humiliated me. It wasn't long before I discovered the whores in the ghetto.

In Columbus the whores were quite different from those I had known in Cleveland. Some of the whores in Columbus were young and beautiful, or so I thought. One in particular, a girl named Rose with whom I was trying to win a home, as the saying went, used to say, "You got an awful lot of steam for a li'l boy." And it was true.

One of the freshmen in my class was Stanton DePriest, son of Oscar DePriest, the black congressman from Chicago. He was a tall, light-complexioned, languid boy who tried for the basketball team, but didn't make it, although he could play well enough. I felt important to be considered Stanton's friend, and I used to lend him my car. Naturally he took advantage of me and sometimes used to keep my car for weekends, when I needed

it myself, and drive down to the black A. M. E. college, Wilber-
force, to see the girls.

Of the two black fraternities, Alpha Phi Alpha and Omega
Phi Psi, the Alphas were more popular in the North, the Omegas
in the South. I became pledged to the Alphas and was initiated
by being blindfolded and thrown into the lake in the park
at the end of Long Street in the upperclass black neighborhood;
then, with the others, I became a Sphinx; the following year I
would become a lifetime fraternity brother.

The sororities were the Kappas and the Deltas; they pledged
all the stylish, light-complexioned girls, and their older members
were noted for their enviable marriages and distinguished works.

However, the fraternity and sorority circle was the arbiter of
all the social functions of the black students. There were lots
of house parties, and most of the black girls were experienced
and willing, and with my roadster and coonskin coat I could
have scored on all occasions. But I had developed an inferiority
complex and felt shy in their company. I preferred older, amoral
women.

I went to see all the black musicals on Warren Street, which
was the next street over from Long and ran through the worst
of the black slums. So many soul brothers killed each other for
one reason or another on Warren Street that it was known as
The Burma Road. There were two movie theaters in the ghetto,
the most pretentious on Long Street. I will always remember
a tall brown-skinned man with slicked-down hair who used to
sing *Moonlight on the Ganges* during the intervals, and the
students who patronized that theater would try to imitate him.
All the movie theaters in downtown Columbus and the white
neighborhoods either segregated blacks in the upper balconies
or did not receive them at all. And no white restaurants served
blacks anywhere in the city, not even those near Ohio State
University. I always tightened up inside whenever I passed one
of them.

The white students didn't know exactly what to make of
me. I dressed and behaved like the "Yes We Are Collegiate"

students; I wore my coonskin coat and smoked my pipe and drove my Model T roadster, and yet I was black, a member of the inferior race. I rarely spoke to white people, and never unless I was addressed first by them, and yet I would find them always looking at me. I ignored them. I didn't hate white people then; I simply didn't need them, didn't want to know them, and always felt that they couldn't reject me any more than I could reject them.

I took pretty black coeds for drives in my car, driving so fast the manifold became white-hot; and went to see the slim black girls in the black musicals—Josephine Baker and Ethel Waters in *Running Wild* and others, now deceased who became rich and famous. I always sat in the front row. Sometimes I went backstage after the show to look into their muddy, sexy brown eyes up close and smell their musky femininity. I saw Greta Garbo and John Gilbert in *Flesh and the Devil*, and helped to pull down the stadium gates before the Ohio State–Michigan University football game in 1926. There had been famous black players on Ohio State's football team in the past, but there were none that year. Black students could star in any of the school athletic activities, but they could not live in the school dormitories on the campus, nor eat in any of the restaurants near the campus, nor attend the movie theaters, nor visit or become a member of the white fraternity houses. Yet this was Columbus, Ohio, where all forms of racial discrimination were prohibited by state laws.

I did not do very well in my studies. I was depressed by the white environment. Ohio State had quarter terms, and the first ended shortly before Christmas. I had already been in a fistfight with my laboratory instructor and no longer went to the lab; I turned in a blank form for my German examination; I had failing grades in all my other courses; my attendance was poor, my attitude was wrong, my interest was lacking. Freshmen who failed the first quarter were generally dropped from the university. As I prepared to return to Cleveland for the Christmas holidays, I fully expected to be dropped. But for reasons which

I have never known, I passed. And now I had to go back. But by then I was tired of Ohio State University and its policy of discrimination and segregation, fed up with the condescension, which I could never bear, and disgusted with myself for my whoremongering and my inability to play games, my instinctive withdrawal from intimacy, and my schizophrenic impulses to be inconspicuous and conspicuous at the same time. It was much later in life that I came to understand I simply hadn't accepted my status as a "nigger."

Christmas was disastrous. My parents quarreled bitterly; Joe went to visit friends; Eddie hadn't been at home in five years. Our house was gloomy and unbearable. My mother felt that she was suffering a divine punishment through her children.

I had no intimate friends in Cleveland. I had lost contact with the few "nice" girls whom I had known. Mr. Smith, the headwaiter at the Wade Park Manor, was courteous but embarrassed because the hotel had cut off my salary and he couldn't do anything about it. I scarcely knew my cousins, Henry Lee and Ella, and I despised my cousin, Gerald, as a fat mama's boy. I paid duty visits to my aunts and uncles, but they talked so venomously about my mother I dreaded seeing them. As an escape I sought out the night life in the Cleveland ghetto.

Between Central and Cedar on Fifty-fifth Street there was first the high school, where the student body was almost entirely black; and then a night club, called the Elks' Cabaret, in the basement of the house occupied by the Cleveland chapter of the black Elks Lodge. Bud Jenkins' Cotton Pickers were playing there at the time, and I will never forget the effect the trumpet player's solo in the *Bugle Blues* had on the women. They leaped atop tables and pulled up their dresses showing their strong black legs and black pussies as though on the slave block.

Black women were easy to pick up and made exciting bedmates; maids were the easiest and good-looking whores were the hardest. I liked black women; black black women. I always have. I liked the velvet black sheen of their skin. I liked the boneless cushion of their pubic hair and the tight demanding suction of their pussies. I was entranced by the dumb passion in their shallow muddy eyes. And I liked them because they liked me. Practically every night during the holidays I wound up with some black woman in the Majestic Hotel.

My mother was furious with me for staying out all night, but my father, looking tired and defeated, defended me, accepting the stories I offered to cover my activities. My mother said I needed to rest, that I would make myself ill, that I would injure my back. I was sullen and resentful. They quarreled so bitterly I was glad to leave and return to college.

The holidays and the quarreling had left me exhausted and listless. I lost all interest in academic study; I resented the cliques, pretensions, and discriminations within the black student body. I suppose I shouldn't have; I was one of the chosen. My skin was brown enough to be acceptable in a male, I was from a "good" family, I possessed the superficial manifestations of affluence—coonskin, English-type clothes, Model T roadster, I smoked a pipe and was an Alpha pledge. But even then I despised the in-group class distinctions based on color and the degree of white blood in one's veins. In those days light-complexioned blacks were more prejudiced toward darker blacks than were many white people. But I liked dark black people, I was accepted by them as just another person, I was at ease with them. Among them, I felt as black as the next person and as good as anyone. The "light-bright-and-damn-near-white" social clique got on my ass.

I probably wouldn't have been dropped from the university if I had kept up my studies.

The Alpha pledges—the Sphinxes—gave a formal dance just before the end of the second quarter and the Easter holiday. This dance was held on Warren Street because the only ballroom of any size was located in the heart of the ghetto and served the public dances and other events. I had come in my tuxedo and had brought a girl whom I hardly knew and whom I quickly lost. I was bored and my teeth were set on edge by the very proper behavior of these very proper young black people who were trying so hard to ape white people.

I thought it might be a good idea to take a bunch of these innocent young things to George's house, where Rose worked, which was only a block and a half from the ballroom. George had a two-story brick house on a side street between Warren and Long, and besides his wife and the three whores, all of whom lived in the house and turned tricks, he sold home brew. The johns sat in the parlor and drank home brew and listened to the record player while they got their courage up.

I got six couples together, promising to take them to a nice quiet house where we could drink home brew and listen to re-cordings. George was surprised to see us but he became the polite and obsequious host. All the whores had gone to bed, his wife stayed out of sight. Fortunately there were no visitors. We sat around the ornate parlor and drank a little home brew and be-came gay, and we began playing records and dancing. They all thought it was a respectable house of a friend of mine. Everything was going well until Rose suddenly appeared in the doorway dressed in her nightgown, rubbing sleep from her eyes and staring at the young people with a jaundiced expression. Then she saw me and suddenly realized it was my party. She threw a wing-ding. I couldn't imagine her being jealous of me, she was a professional whore. I supposed it was the sight of the young girls frolicking innocently on her territory which infuriated her. She began scream-ing the foulest curses and snatched the record from the turntable and broke it and began hurling other records from the stack at the shocked and frightened young people.

George didn't know she had come downstairs until he heard her; he had been keeping out of our way, remaining discreetly in the kitchen. He rushed out and clutched her from behind and tried to subdue her. But the young couples rushed from the house in a panic-stricken flight. I felt sick; I looked at Rose accusingly. She looked vicious and vindictive. "I fixed your little red wagon, you snotty motherfucker!" she shouted. George hit her in the face and knocked her down. I shook my head. "Don't hurt her," I begged. It was already done; no need of beating her up then.

"Come on," she said. "I'll give you some good pussy." I got my hat and went home.

Some one, or perhaps all, of the girls reported the incident to the dean of men the next day. I was called to his office. He said he was going to permit me to withdraw for reasons of "ill health and failing grades." He did not mention the incident of the night before, but I understood.

When I returned to Cleveland I was really sick, physically sick. My back froze up and Dr. Eisenbray prescribed lying in hot baths twice daily. My parents still quarreled. The atmosphere in our house was depressing. Thoughts of myself were depressing. I didn't think. I passed the spring in a daze.

But when summer came I got up and out.

I ran into a young busboy named Ramsey from the Wade Park Manor who took me to Bunch Boy's. Bunch Boy had converted the top floor of a two-story house on Cedar Avenue near Ninety-fifth Street into a gambling club. In the big front room he had installed a specially made kidney-shaped blackjack table which could accommodate ten players, and in the back room a billiard table with a chain across the middle for the dice players. He used another bedroom equipped with blackboards and telephones for horserace bets, getting the results from a betting syndicate downtown which had financed the entire establishment.

There were three well-known gambling clubs in Cleveland's black ghetto at the time. The biggest was on Central Avenue, not far from Fifty-fifth Street, and there was another across the street from Bunch's, run by a gambler called "Hotstuff" Johnson, where only craps were shot. Hotstuff had a guard on his door who used to take the guns and knives of the players before they were allowed in the gambling room, and who also signaled when the police raided by pressing a loose nail in the door frame, which blinked the lights in the back room. I heard there was another club for big-time pimps on Short Scovil, north of Fourteenth Street, but I never saw it.

Bunch had one man to run his crap game and another named

Johnny Perry, who generally ran the blackjack game. Most of the time Bunch took charge of the horserace bets himself. Bunch wanted his club to appeal to blacks who worked in service and liked to gamble: hotel employees, bellhops and waiters and janitors—servants in private families, chauffeurs, housemen, butlers, railway waiters and porters, building employees, elevator operators, porters—all blacks in any sort of legitimate business and employment. He was strictly opposed to rough stuff. He didn't have any guards; the blacks who patronized his club were the "nice" fellows, the "good" blacks, who were employed in some manner or other for the white man. He barred pimps and professional gamblers and criminals. Johnny Perry was soft-spoken, handsome, married, a pleasant-appearing man with a soft voice and a superficial air of culture.

Bunch was an old, very small, dried-up-looking, light-complexioned man with straight hair, strange washed-out blue eyes, and a cynical expression. He was not what you would call elegant, but he wore very expensive clothes: silk shirts, English-tailored suits, and Stacy Adam shoes. When I first went there he drove an open Cord touring car, but later he turned it in and bought one of those very expensive Packard coupés with very high suspension.

Bunch Boy's true monicker was Gus Smith. He lived with his wife out in an exclusive white neighborhood bordering Rockefeller Park. He had reportedly come to Cleveland from Chicago, where he had operated a big policy house and had been kidnaped by the Al Capone mob and held for eighty thousand dollars' ransom. He had paid his ransom and left. Prior to that he had lived in Seattle, where he was known in the ghetto as a hard-betting gambler.

I liked Bunch. I began going there every day and hanging around until they closed. Ramsey and I were almost always together. Bunch called us the "Katzi Kids" after the Katzenjammer Kids in the comic strip; Ramsey was big Katzi and I was little Katzi. He liked us; he was amused by us, I think. When he learned that I was drawing a pension from the Ohio State Industrial Commission he would lend me money any time I asked.

Ramsey had the job I had held when I'd had my accident. Both of us were compulsive blackjack players and quite often we started off the games, which I think was another reason Bunch Boy liked us. As a rule Johnny Perry ran the blackjack game and worked on the stick, changing the money and banking the game when there was no one else available. Bunch ran a game with a walking deal; whenever someone caught blackjack he could take the deal and bank the game if he wished; otherwise Johnny Perry took over.

After a time Johnny used to let me handle the money sack and sit at the stick and bank the games, too. There was a big snaggled-toothed red-brown man with stained muddy eyes named Val who used to lookout for the game. The "lookout" passed the cards along from the dealer, saw that the bets were placed, collected the bets from the losers, and paid off the winners out of the bank, and if the bank made money he asked for a tip saying "good lookout, the bank made money."

I loved it there. To silence my mother's constant nagging I told her I had got a night job in the Hotel Gilsy on Ninth Street relieving the night clerk and taking ice water to the rooms, and I was saving money to go back to college. I warned her against coming around investigating lest the Industrial Commission discovered I was working and cut off my pension like the Wade Park Manor had done. I never knew whether she believed it but she accepted it, and my father didn't question it. Neither of them had any knowledge of Bunch Boy's club or the slightest knowledge of that kind of life-style. I said my job was from five in the afternoon until two next morning. I would leave home in the early afternoon and return about three or four next morning.

At that time my father had a temporary job as janitor for a nightclub on Euclid Avenue. He worked from midnight until eight or nine in the morning, cleaning up the club after it had closed. Occasionally when I left Bunch Boy's I would stop by his nightclub to eat from the refrigerators. My father thought I had come from my job.

I enjoyed that summer around Bunch's and the blackjack game as much as any summer I can recall. I discovered a love for gambling. I learned fast and well and became a good blackjack player. Val helped me out; he never let anyone cheat me.

As a consequence of my connection with the club, I discovered a new life. Ramsey and I would make the rounds with Val and his friends and meet successful pimps and madams, and I learned something of the inside of the hustling life. There was a madam on Scovil Avenue, a big rawboned black woman with short straightened hair and a scarred face, who offered Val five thousand dollars if he could get me to come and live with her. She always wore ankle-length black satin dresses and black straight last Stacy Adam's men's shoes. I was repulsed by the sight of her, but she treated me with the tenderness of a black mammy fondling a white baby. Val offered to split the five thousand with me if I went to live with her for a month. "Then, Katzi, all you's gotta do is leave," he urged. She was an important and respected "land-prop" in the ghetto, but I wouldn't do it.

I learned to drink the illegal whiskey of the prohibition era: the white lightning and the white mule. One could go into any whorehouse and order it by the pitcher. Half-blind, diseased, ragged and smelly whores and their equally repulsive mates used to chew a kind of root when drinking to keep from being poisoned. A root-man would appear every so often among the drinkers and hawk his roots; perhaps they had definite rounds they covered. Occasionally the white mule was colored with burned sugar to give it an authentic whiskey look.

My brother Joe began his senior year at East High School in the fall. I hadn't seen my eldest brother, Eddie, since we lived in Mississippi. I no longer saw any of my aunts and uncles and cousins on my father's side and never thought of them.

During the winter an acquaintance of mine who worked at the Gilsy took sick and I filled his job for him. The Gilsy was one of those hotels known from coast to coast as a good pitch for prostitutes. Roving prostitutes stopped there to work a week and moved on. Others took their place. Their pimps booked them in as man and wife and gave the nod to the bell captain. The girls were not allowed to "entertain" any men in their rooms; they had to be taken to the rooms of their clients by a bellhop. The bellhop collected two dollars; the prostitute could not charge less than five, but as much more as she could get. The time limit was one half hour; over that the bellhop charged a dollar every fifteen minutes. Most of the time the tricks lasted much less than a half hour. The bellhop would then be called to take the whore back to her room. It was well organized and ran with clockwork precision; there was seldom any controversy. If we ran across a whore unwilling to pay us we reported to the desk that there was a whore in the hotel trying to work and had her put out. It seems incredible that the hotel management and the various desk clerks were unaware of the prostitution, as it was famous as a prostitution hotel all over the United States. But from the manager to all the desk clerks, prostitution was treated as though it weren't countenanced or even heard of. The Gilsy advertised itself as a convention hotel, and most of its legitimate clients were men attending one or another of the thousands of conventions held in Cleveland.

In addition to our income from prostitution, we sold whiskey to the johns that was manufactured and bottled by the head porter, or bell captain as he was sometimes called. The whiskey was his racket. We bought whiskey from him for a standard price of two-fifty for a pint, five dollars a quart. We were required to sell it for five dollars a pint and ten dollars a quart. If we were caught selling any whiskey other than his we were fired on the spot. Before my time a couple of boys had been arrested and convicted for selling narcotics; but that was strictly forbidden by the bell captain and chances were he had ratted to the police. Our salary was sixty dollars monthly, all of which we turned over to the bell captain to pay for our jobs. There were six of us, and with our combined salaries and his whiskey racket he did quite well.

The shifts rotated; some days we were on days, some days on nights. Of course nights were better. But on days one had a chance to room a whore when she arrived and keep her hidden from the rest of the boys for one's own profit. But it was risky because one had to keep her busy or she would contact the bell captain.

I worked there for about a month, and as I remember I never made less than fifty dollars a night, or twenty dollars a day.

With so much money pouring in, I began to shoot dice across the street from Bunch's at Hotstuff's. I bet hard and high because I didn't know any better, and quite often I'd win as much as five hundred dollars in fifteen minutes. But everyone stole from me, I forgot side bets and left stacks of money lying around for anyone to pick up, and whatever I won I'd lose it back just as quickly if I didn't quit.

Some of the regulars were Abie the Jew, Red Johnny, Four-Four, Chink Charlie, Dummy, and other characters I've used in my detective story series.

Sometimes I'd walk away a winner and the next day I'd go downtown and buy clothes. I was ridiculously vain. I kept my hair pasted down with white pomade (defined by Webster as "a fragrant unguent for the hair or scalp") which I had learned to use during my last term in high school. And I don't know exactly where I got my taste in clothes; it was partly influenced by the collegiate style and partly by the clothes Bunch Boy wore. I bought very expensive suits, shirts, ties, shoes, and coats— stylish but not outlandish. I never went for any of the way-out fashions like peg tops, zoot suits, bell-bottoms, box-backs, etc. I liked tweeds, Cheviots, and worsteds. I remember my most daring venture was a pair of square-toed yellow pigskin bluchers by Florsheim, which today in Paris would be the height of fashion. I got to know the expensive men's stores where blacks rarely ventured.

I don't know what effect my appearance had on women in general; I hadn't met a woman whom I remembered more than a few days.

When spring came I bought a secondhand Nash touring car, which I didn't dare take home. I parked it several blocks away when I went home. Through one of my friends, I think it was Big Katzi, I met two sepia-colored sisters who had originally come from Georgia. Mary, the elder, was married to a black man who worked in service, and Maud lived with them in a house they

rented off of Cedar Avenue on Eighty-eighth Street. I liked Maud
from the first; she was one of those soft, pleasing, flat-featured
mulatto women with a big cushiony mouth, bedroom eyes, and a
thick caressing voice. I began taking the family for rides to nearby
cities—Akron, Warren, Sandusky, Youngstown—to get a chance at
her. Soon I was lending my car to Mary and her husband so
Maud and I could have their house on Sunday afternoons. She
was the first healthy, passionate woman I'd ever had.

I think I loved Maud. I know she loved me. But after she told
me she was pregnant I avoided her. I was afraid she'd try to
marry me and I knew my mother would object. I did not love
Maud enough to face my mother. Someone told me later she had
gone back to her home in Georgia. I wonder if my life would have
been happy if I had married her.

After she left, I began to grow very restless. Bunch Boy sent to
Chicago for a former associate called Cateye, and with him as
manager opened up a policy house which he called the Tijuana
house. Before then the only policy house in Cleveland was the
Green House, run by an illiterate black man named Rufus Jones,
who sent his daughter to school in Paris. Years later Rufus was
sent to the Atlanta federal penitentiary for income tax evasion.
But in the summer of 1928, when Bunch opened his house, the
legal precedent for sending criminals to the federal pens for income tax evasion when all else failed had not been established
by the Al Capone case.

As soon as Bunch opened his policy house, a number of other
black hustlers, gamblers, pimps, club owners like Hotstuff, and
businessmen like the Richardson brothers, got in on the act and
opened houses of their own. Policy began booming in the ghetto
to such a degree that the Italian mob who controlled the alky
racket, headed by Big Angelo and Little Angelo, began to muscle
in on it.

It was an unusual period of my life. I seemed to be in a trance.
I think it was the result of so many emotional shocks. My parents'
quarreling had entered its final stage; sometimes my father would
strike my mother and she struck back. I would separate them

when I was at home. Shortly after Maud left, I ran my car into a concrete stanchion underneath the railroad bridge over Cedar Avenue and wrecked it.

The city of Cleveland presented Joe with a gold medal for scholastic honors when he graduated that spring, in lieu of the valedictorianship for which he was ineligible for lack of having been enrolled long enough. He was preparing to enter Oberlin College in the fall.

We had not heard from Eddie for years.

I seldom saw my father's people at that time, my aunts and uncles and cousins Wiggins and Moon. When I think back on them today I realize they were pioneers in a way; the Wigginses were among the first black families who lived in what later became known as the Hough Avenue ghetto, where the riots occurred in 1967. And the Moons were the first black family to move out to Glenville beyond 105th Street in what is now known as the Superior Avenue ghetto, where the riots occurred in 1968.

Suddenly the world had changed again for me. It had always been changing as far back as I could remember, but in 1928 at age nineteen I was more vulnerable.

I think what most affected me was when Bunch Boy moved his policy house downtown to Central Avenue in the heart of the ghetto, and left Johnny Perry in charge of his "club." I suppose I must have considered Bunch something of a father figure. I depended on him; and the blackjack game, for all of its inherent evil, had been a steadying influence.

It left me at loose ends. Big Katzi seldom came by anymore and there were few pickings for Val. I went back to the Elks Cabaret and hung around landprops I had met.

Then, I don't remember where or when, I met a sneakthief named Benny. Benny was a big-framed, light-brown-skinned, simpleminded boy who elected me as his hero, and I did a lot of things I might not have otherwise done to live up to this picture. I learned to smoke opium and steal cars. I used to take Benny into swank men's stores I had patronized and he would steal the cigarette lighters or a pair of cufflinks on display while I engaged the clerk in conversation. Benny had a two-room basement flat somewhere in the Eighties off of Cedar Avenue, and he would always get girls in for a party. At one of these I met the most beautiful brownskin girl I had ever seen, Jean Johnson. Jean looked vaguely similar to Lena Horne in her youth, but her complexion was a darker brown. Her skin was the warm reddish brown of a perfectly roasted turkey breast the moment it comes from the oven. She had a heart-shaped face, thick hot lips, and brown eyes. What there was about me that attracted her so I never knew, but she fell desperately in love with my immortal soul. I know that sounds puerile and exaggerated. Eight years later I was to marry her and live with her for fourteen years, but at that time I treated her in the most casual manner; sometimes I would leave her standing on a corner waiting for me hours on end; and other times I would leave her in rooms we had rented for the night, in lieu of room rent, which I didn't have, and wouldn't see her again until several days later.

I introduced her to a landprop down on Short Scovil named Margaret, whom I had met through Val. Eventually Margaret persuaded me to run her whiskey joint in the alley back of Bunch Boy's out on Cedar Avenue, and put Jean to work selling whiskey; then we could live together, Margaret argued, and whenever I got hard up I could put her to tricking. I moved her into the house but I never made her a whore. Living with her in that house with all the rough belligerent customers who wanted to buy her infuriated me to such a degree that I bought my first pistol, an Owl's-head .32; and I was fortunate that it didn't shoot straight, because I shot at quite a number of people. It served its purpose so well that Margaret put us out. I was broke. I tried to borrow some money from Bunch, but he wanted Jean to go with him on a trip to Detroit.

I was so desperate for money that I let Benny talk me into a burglary he had planned with an older friend. His friend, who owned a relatively new Nash sedan, was employed in some capacity in the central offices of the Ohio State National Guard, and had information that a certain amount of arms and ammunition were stored in the Negro Branch of the YMCA on Cedar Avenue and Seventy-sixth Street. Their plan was to steal a case of .45-caliber Colt automatics and ammunition. John—I'll call him John because I don't remember his name—would furnish the car and Benny and I would burgle the Y and steal the guns.

We had planned to sell the guns in Warren and Youngstown, where blacks employed in the steel mills would buy them. The actual robbery went smoothly but before we reached Warren the two rear tires went flat and we had to walk into the nearest village and catch the early bus to Warren and find a garage to send a tow truck to fix the tires. They left me in Warren to see about getting rooms while they went back to get the car.

It was payday in the steel mills and the dice games in the pool rooms had begun by eleven o'clock in the morning. I had been to Warren before with Val and a friend who used to make the payday crap games and pick up some good stakes sometimes. I knew that most of the itinerant black workers lived in rented rooms in the ghetto; one just knocked on any door and asked if they had a room to rent. As I was coming from one house a pretty mulatto woman stopped me and asked if I was looking for a room. She wore the usual gingham dress but her Mongoloid features were unscarred and she had very sexy-looking eyes and long crinkly greasy black hair. At first I thought she was a whore and I was beginning to regret that I didn't have any money, but she said I could sleep with her for a few hours if I wished because her men would be at the crap games. Men? I asked. She explained that she lived with a man from each of the three shifts, who took turns in sleeping in her bed and a sweet man about my age. She said her three working stiffs wouldn't mind me but her sweet man could cause trouble.

Later I was lucky enough to get a room in the one black hotel, and I took John and Benny there when they arrived in the car. It was a back room on the second floor overlooking a shingle roof, which sloped down to the back yard. As soon as we had taken the boxes up to the room, John left and went back to Cleveland. I broke open the boxes and got one of the automatics and loaded it and, sticking it in my belt, went out to watch the crap games while waiting for the party. I was supposed to have been watching out for winners whom I could approach with an offer to sell them a gun, which Benny was doing. But I had been thinking all the while of the young woman.

Later that night I met her at a drinking party where I mingled with the blacks drinking white mule as though it were water, and whispered with her every chance I got. I showed her my .45 and it seemed to make her nervous. The men and women kept looking at me curiously, when all of a sudden I noticed the room had emptied. No one was left but the two of us. Then suddenly a tall brown-skinned young man with straight black hair and softly molded features stepped in from the front porch. He was wearing blue sneakers, denims, and a bright-red silk shirt. He had a long-barreled .38 dangling from his right hand. I felt a cold contraction of my scalp. The woman ran forward and wrapped her arms around him and began explaining hurriedly she was helping me find a room for myself and my friends. I took the advantage to get my Colt in my hand. He stood glaring at me. I glared back at him, I suppose. I had slipped the safety off and if he had made a move I was going to start pumping .45 slugs in his direction; I didn't feel anything but the absolute necessity to start shooting first. I didn't think of his life, or my life, or the act of murder, of the law, or the woman; just the pure and simple necessity to beat him to the trigger.

She wrestled him out onto the porch and evidently several men held him while the landprop rushed me out the back door and through the back gate down a dark alley until I got away.

That night Benny and I were arrested. It was about three o'clock in the morning. Benny was sleeping on a cot by the door, and I was sleeping on a cot beneath the window that opened onto the sloping roof.

We were taken back to Cleveland that morning with a police escort. The Cleveland dailies had already run the story about the theft of the pistols, which they had suggested had been committed by one of the "alky" mobs; they had warned there might be a gang war in the makings. That was the only funny part of the whole incident.

My parents were informed and my mother visited me. She was shocked. I told her I hadn't known about the theft, that I had just gone along with Benny and his friend for the ride. My mother suffered far more than I did, yet she did not excuse me. On the one hand she felt I should be punished, and on the other she was afraid that severe punishment might be injurious. She blamed my father for not disciplining me and she felt that his indifferent attitude toward my behavior was the root of all my troubles. Perhaps she was right, but in the final analysis she didn't want me to go to jail. I don't remember seeing my father at all.

I was taken to court alone. I hadn't seen or heard of Benny since our arrest, and I hadn't seen the owner of the car, John, who had masterminded the caper, since he had left us in Warren.

The judge was a woman. My mother testified that I had been led astray by bad influence because my father didn't exercise the proper influence. The judge questioned my mother about my father's position and background and learned about my brother's accident and my father giving up his job as a Southern "professor" to bring his son North for treatment. She learned about my own accident and my withdrawal from college and was extraordinarily moved by the predicament of our family. Because the guns had been recovered and no harm had come from the theft she gave me a suspended sentence, over the vehement protest of the prosecuting attorney.

My mother took me home and I went to bed. I didn't learn until much later that Benny had been given thirty days in jail, and only that little because I had got off with a suspended sentence. I never heard what happened to John, whether he'd been apprehended and sentenced or whether he'd escaped and left the city.

But I couldn't stand it at home because of my parents' violent quarrels. First my mother tried to get control of my pension, and then she tried to have me sent to some sort of institution for incorrigible youths, but for that she needed my father's permission, which he would not give, and no institutions of the kind she had in mind existed in Cleveland at that time.

In desperation she sued my father for divorce. By that time my father had been defeated by the cold indifference of the North. I loved my mother desperately and I was very close to her; I had always been her favorite and there was a cord of emotion linking us that was never broken. But I had this understanding with my father that he would never discipline me, resulting as it had in my brother's blindness.

One night, disturbed by a loud commotion, I had rushed downstairs to find my parents fighting in the dining room. My father, bleeding from a gash on the forehead where my mother had struck him with a flat iron, had my mother backed against a wall, throttling her. I separated them. My mother slumped into a chair and began crying. My father went upstairs to pack his suitcase. I wasn't angry with them, I was just so goddamned, desperately ashamed. Poor Joe was hovering in the background, incapable of doing anything, overcome by sympathy for my mother. I think he hated my father then.

My father left home that night and never returned. I left home the next day and found Benny back in his basement apartment after his thirty days in jail, with Jean occupying one of his rooms. I moved in with Jean.

I went home once to see my mother. My brother was packing to leave for Oberlin College. I realized it was September. I would not be going to school ever again.

A week later Benny and I stole a car and drove down to Columbus. We borrowed a car from a gambler, and went over to the white residential neighborhood beyond Euclid Avenue in the Eighties to find a car to our liking. I got in it and steered while Benny pushed it back to the ghetto, where we could work on the ignition in comfort. There was a moment of tension when we had to pass a traffic cop on Euclid, but he merely stopped traffic for a moment to let us pass.

The first term was in its second week at Ohio State University when we arrived in Columbus in our stolen car. I took Benny out to the dormitory near the campus where I used to take my meals. The upperclass students were amazed to see me in a big new car with a gangsterish-looking friend, but the freshmen didn't know me. I arranged with the landlady for us to share a room, but Benny contended that we should go into the ghetto and get a hotel room and try to sell the car as soon as possible. But I was excited by the college atmosphere and being in the company of the students again. The night we arrived a dance was being held in a barnlike roadhouse in an unpaved black hamlet several miles beyond the university campus, and all the black students were excited. We met several girls at dinner and I made a date to take one to the dance. I tried to get Benny to date one of the other girls but he was self-conscious; the school atmosphere was alien to him. He decided to visit in the ghetto instead.

While the car was parked in front of the rooming house a white driver ran into it and dented a rear fender, and the students stopped him before he could get away. Those were the days before compulsory automobile insurance and one had the offender arrested on the spot and took him to court. When the white man learned that we were all Ohio State University students, he offered to pay for the damages then and there if I wouldn't call the police, and of course I accepted payment; I don't remember how much it was but a number of five-dollar bills changed hands and the black students were impressed.

While getting into the car to drive to the dance (there were three couples) I lost the money I'd just received along with what little I'd had of my own, and when I went to buy the tickets discovered I had no money. I jumped in the car and rushed back the five miles or so to the dormitory and found the wad of money lying in the street where I had dropped it. I began to feel arrogant and lucky.

When I went back to the dance I had an aura of excitement. I'm sure I must have given off an odor of sensuality, such as I have smelled in other people at times. The girls responded to it. We charlestoned and belly-rubbed.

When I got back to the dormitory the next day there was a note from Benny saying he'd gone back to Cleveland. As I was standing there I noticed that one of the freshmen had left his identity card on the dressing table. The university issued these identity cards to each student on matriculation, and they were accepted all over Columbus as positive identification for cashing checks, establishing credit or any other business transaction where identification was necessary. I have forgotten what they were called but they were small green cards with the bursar's seal over the holder's signature and were required to be carried by the students at all times and presented to officials on demand. On sudden impulse I stole the card and drove over to the ghetto and stopped by George's to change the signature and substitute my own. He was surprised to see me, but after noticing the card and thinking it was mine congratulated me on being back in school; he said Rose had become ill and had to leave.

When I left George's with my false identity card proclaiming I was a student of Ohio State University, I noticed that the gas tank of my stolen car was leaking as a result of the collision the night before, and I put it in a garage on Warren Street for repairs.

Then I went to a branch bank on Long Street and cashed my first bogus check. It was only for twenty dollars, and I had to use one of the blank courtesy checks left on the desks for the customers' convenience, writing in the name of a bank in Cleveland. When I presented my identity card, the teller accepted it without question.

Emboldened by my success, I went downtown on High Street, the main shopping street in Columbus, and began going from store to store patronized by university students, buying small items such as ties, cufflinks, fountain pens, and socks and paying for them with checks of sufficient size to give me fifteen or more dollars in change. I worked my way out toward the university. I had stopped in fifteen or twenty stores—I don't recall the exact number. I had not been refused in any of them, which in itself should have made me suspicious of my success, for Columbus was a racist city.

I was near the campus when I got into trouble. I had bought

a pair of expensive woolen socks in a chic men's store from a nice-looking young white woman clerk. Something about me must have annoyed her, for she immediately questioned whether I had an account in a Cleveland bank. I argued that every other store had accepted my checks and what was wrong with her? I was losing my temper, which delighted her, it seemed. "Which stores?" she wanted to know. "The one across the street," I shouted angrily. She said just a moment and went into the back and telephoned the store across the street and while I was standing there a clerk came over from the store with the check which I had just cashed.

I could have run. I should have run. But, unfortunately, I never did run. Maybe that was the inspiration for my book *Run Man Run*, which I wrote thirty-two years later.

I stood there while they compared checks and telephoned for the police, who came and took me away. I was locked in the county jail until the first day of November, when my case went up for trial. That time it was my father who came down to Columbus for the trial. I pled guilty. Because of all the mitigating circumstances, the judge, a man this time, gave me a two years suspended sentence and put me under a five-year bench parole; if I committed another crime, even a misdemeanor, in the state of Ohio within the next five years I could be taken back to Columbus and sentenced to two years in prison. I never learned what happened to the stolen car.

My father took me back to Cleveland. He and my mother had been divorced and moved into rented rooms in widely separated sections of Cleveland, and our house was up for sale. Joe had opted for mother, but at that time he was at Oberlin College. My father had taken my clothing to his rented room on Eighty-ninth Street off Cedar Avenue, where we were to share a double bed. I kept away from the room as much as I could from the moment I saw it, but my father never reprimanded me. I learned that Benny was in the workhouse for another crime and Jean was living with his girl friend in his old basement flat. I stayed with Jean and hung around Bunch's old gambling club on Cedar

Avenue, although it had deteriorated since he had opened the policy house. I ran around with Val and occasionally Big Katzi; wandered in and out of whorehouses on Scovil and Central and off Fifty-fifth Street. I always carried my Owl's-head .32 revolver. Anything to keep away from that room that stank of my father's fear and defeat.

I discovered that I had become very violent. I saw a glimmer of fear and caution in the eyes of most people I encountered: squares, hustlers, gamblers, pimps, even whores. I had heard that people were saying, "Little Katzi will kill you." I can't say what I might have done. I swapped my .32 for a huge, old-fashioned .44 Colt frontier revolver that looked like a hand cannon and would shoot hard enough to kill a stone. I remember once being refused service at the counter of a restaurant at 105th Street and Cedar Avenue, on the very fringe of the ghetto and just two blocks from the Baptist church my father attended. I jumped to the top of the counter and kicked everything movable onto the floor—people's half-filled plates, glasses, pie bins, coffee cups, everything —and then struck the white girl behind the counter on the shoulder with my .44-caliber revolver and beat the white proprietor repeatedly across the head. The customers fled. I walked out and walked away. I was never arrested, never charged; as far as I know there was no inquiry.

I had left Columbus about the first of November 1928, and at the end of November I was arrested in Chicago for armed robbery in the first degree.

One night at Bunch Boy's I listened to a chauffeur bragging about the large sums of money his boss always kept in his house, which was located in an exclusive rich white neighborhood in Cleveland Heights at the top of Cedar Hill. I have forgotten the chauffeur's name but I recall that he was a somewhat vain and handsome mulatto man in his forties. Like many blacks still possessed of a slave mentality, he boasted of his employer's possessions as though they were his own, or as though he at least had a vested interest in them. His boss was named Miller. He boasted of Mr. Miller's platinum watch and diamond-studded

watch chain, of the stacks of hundred-dollar bills Mr. Miller kept
in his wall safe cunningly hidden at the back of the hat shelf
in his bedroom clothes closet, of all the fantastic jewelry Mrs.
Miller wore when she went out, of the two Cadillacs Mr. Miller
kept in his two-car garage, the small Cadillac, which he drove
himself, and the Cadillac limousine the chauffeur drove. Val
cautioned him not to talk so openly. But he was a compulsive
talker and I learned all there was to know about Mr. and Mrs.
Miller's money and jewels and habits. I both envied and resented
their wealth and their life.

In addition I wanted to get away; I wanted to leave Cleveland
and Ohio and all the United States of America and go somewhere
I could escape the thought of my parents and my brother, somewhere black people weren't considered the shit of the earth. It
took me forty years to discover that such a place does not exist.

The winter season of racing had opened at Tijuana, Mexico,
or was soon to open, and there was much talk around the club
about Tijuana as a city, inhabited by Mexicans who were a
mixture of Spanish, Indian, and Negro. I could envision the
dark-skinned caballeros, the black-eyed señoritas, a wild gay life,
and the hot southern climate. More than anything else I wanted
to go to Tiajuana to employ the gambling skills I had learned,
play the races, and sleep with the hot-bodied señoritas.

One night shortly before Thanksgiving I heard the Millers'
chauffeur say he would be off Thanksgiving eve, as he would have
to work on Thanksgiving day. I decided instantly that I would
go to Tijuana. Like many families of their class, the Millers had
only two servants who lived in, the black chauffeur-cum-butler-
cum-houseman and the black maid. The gardener, laundress, and
occasional footman (for when they entertained) came in by the
day.

The day before, I went out to Cleveland Heights and cased
their house. It was a large old-fashioned white-brick and clapboard house sitting far back from the street behind an immacu-
late garden in a corner lot. Trees and shrubbery screened the

front, which was approached by a long tree-lined walk, but the main entrance was a circular driveway from the side street that passed beneath a portico at the rear. Beyond the entrance was a two-car garage with doors paneled with small glass panes. There was a thick growth of shrubbery in the semicircle formed by the driveway, which effectively screened the back entrance and the garage doors from the street.

It was in there that I hid the following night waiting for their return. I had appeared at the house at about ten-thirty and rung the back doorbell. I was dressed in a blue suit, blue overcoat, and black hat and shoes. I was carrying the revolver in my right overcoat pocket. It was a double-breasted overcoat with patch pockets. When the maid answered the door, I had planned to ask for the chauffeur, who I knew would be absent, and then draw my pistol and force my entrance. But the maid was alone in the house and afraid to open the door. She was a big black suspicious woman who looked like any Hollywood mammy of the time. She snapped on the outside light and stood behind the glass and scrutinized me. She decided I didn't look like the type who would be asking for the chauffeur or like any of his friends she had ever seen. She said he was off and for me to come back next day. I thanked her and walked away. I don't know what it was about me that made her instantly suspicious, because I walked directly down the driveway into the street and she could not have seen me when I ducked into the clump of shrubbery and squatted down out of sight. But maybe there was someplace along the street where I should have appeared to return to the ghetto, or else there should have been the sound of my car starting and driving away.

She telephoned for the police, evidently following her employer's instructions: "When in doubt, call the police." That was the purpose of the police in Cleveland, to protect the persons and the property of the rich.

It is worth noting that in rich white neighborhoods there is an altogether different interpretation of the term "law enforcement" than in the poor black ghettos. In the black ghettos, "law enforcement" means whipping the heads of the inhabitants and making them obey the law; in the rich white neighborhoods it means protecting the inhabitants' privileges, property, and privacy and defending them against the lawless, which is to say, everyone outside of that neighborhood.

In any event, a car filled with policemen arrived and the maid let them into the house. I remained hidden in the shrubbery, where I had a bird's-eye view of all the activity. All the lights in the house and the garage were turned on and then the outside floodlights which revealed every possible hiding place on the entire estate with the exception of the one I had chosen by pure accident. I could see the police when they searched the house and then the grounds. One passed along the drive only several feet from me. I held my breath. Finally they gave up the search, the lights were turned off and they departed.

I remained in my hiding place. Several times I saw the maid's face appear in the window above the garage. I didn't dare move. I had pulled on a pair of gloves and I had turned up the collar of my overcoat. After a time it began to snow. Lazy fat white flakes of snow filled the air and slowly covered the landscape. By the time Mr. and Mrs. Miller returned in their Cadillac coupe, the night was cloaked in a mantle of white.

They drove straight into the garage, from which there was an entrance to the house, for soon afterward I saw the buxom black maid greeting them in the back hall with much gesticulating and head shaking, and I knew she was telling them about my visit and the subsequent search by the police. The Millers didn't seem to put much store in her suspicions for shortly they moved toward the front of the house and disappeared from view. I quickly left my hiding place and crossed to the garage. Both doors were locked. I took out my pistol, broke a pane, unlocked the door from within, and crossed to the back entrance to the house in the dark. I found the door unlocked and entered a lighted back hall. I went forward quickly and came out into the sitting room, where the Millers had thrown their coats across the sofa and were standing; she was standing by the fireplace and he was mixing a drink at the bar. He was wearing white tie and tails and she a brocaded evening gown.

"Stick your hands up," I said. Their heads wheeled about; their eyes stretched; and they turned as white as the outside snow. There was no doubt of their race then—they were white.

For a moment the only sound was that made by the maid moving about and humming to herself somewhere in the back of the house. And then she came into the room with a cup of Ovaltine, I suppose, on a tray. At the sight of me with the pistol in my hand the black drained from her skin, leaving it a mud-spattered gray. She opened her mouth to scream and I turned the pistol in her direction. It was a very large revolver of the kind used by gunmen in the Westerns, and it must have been a frightening sight. She dropped the tray and ran.

"Don't nobody move," I shouted and ran after her. I caught her in the back hall and quickly locked her in a handy toilet. When I returned to the sitting room I saw the Millers running up the broad carpeted stairs.

"Halt!" I yelled and they stopped and stared down at me from their white faces. I found a telephone on a stand at the foot of the stairs and ripped it from the wall. Then I followed the Millers up the stairs and forced them into their bedroom. They were trembling from fright. I stripped off all the jewelry she was wearing, necklaces, bracelets, rings, and took his platinum pocket watch and diamond-studded watch chain, his money and a key ring with a number of keys; then I opened the clothes closet and removed the hat boxes to reveal the safe and ordered him to open it. He looked stunned.

It contained five or six stacks of hundred and twenty dollar bills still wrapped in the bank bands. I stuffed all of my loot, the jewelry and money all mixed together, into the left patch pocket of my overcoat; then I locked them in the bedroom and went down the stairs and back into the garage. They probably had several ways of getting free, and the maid could have pushed open the door with her shoulder, but all of them were too frightened to move. I think that by pulling the telephone cords out from the wall I had alerted the police, or perhaps they were just cruising by again to see if all was well.

I started the Cadillac coupe and backed it out of the garage. It was still snowing heavily, and visibility was very limited. When I pulled out into the side street I saw that the snow was piled atop the hedges and the curbs were invisible. I saw the vague shape of a car making a U turn in front of the house beyond the intersection. I had to pass that way and I noticed the car skidding across the street as it attempted to accelerate, and then I heard the shooting. Suddenly I knew it was a police car; flashes of pistol fire spouted from its side, and its siren slowly began to scream. The street I was on went straight as far as the eye could see, and I thought it might go all the way to Shaker Heights, where I knew my way about. I had worked one summer as a bellman at the Shaker Heights Country Club and had driven the members' cars all about town when they were on the links.

So I just stepped on the gas and drove the Cadillac in a straight line down the snow-covered street. I remember it being exceedingly pleasant in the softly purring car moving swiftly through the virgin blanket of snow and the white translucent falling curtain. Soon the sound of shooting died away and the sight of the pursuing car disappeared in the snowscape of the rear-view mirror, and I was moving swiftly through the completely deserted, almost silent night. There was not a sign of life in sight. Falling snow refracted the headlights and shortened the perimeter of visibility and I had the illusion of hurtling silently through an endless cloud.

Suddenly I felt the car run over something; its movement became slower and bumpier as though it had entered a different terrain. A high hedge loomed suddenly in the milky brilliance of the headlights, and a moment later I was through it and the car came slowly to a stop. When I stepped out to investigate, my foot sank deep into the spongy mud beneath the snow. I looked back at the hedge and it dawned on me that I had run off the road and gone some distance through a snow-covered pasture.

Cleveland's suburbs were still underdeveloped in 1928, and cow pastures were not rare.

When I tried to drive on, the car sank into the mud. I put the floor carpets under the rear wheels, and then the seats, but they simply sank into the mud. I gave it up and turned off the lights. There were no houses or buildings of any kind in sight. But the glow of the city's lights formed a pale pink halo in the distant sky, and with that as a beacon I trudged through the mud in that direction. Hours later I came to an all-night restaurant-bar. My shoes were caked with mud and my coat and hat white with snow. I cleaned some of the mud from my shoes, shook off some of the snow, and went inside. A bald man stood behind the bar playing cards with his single customer, a half-drunk uniformed city policeman. "Where's the phone? I want to call for a taxi," I said. Both the barman and the policeman slowly looked me up and down. Neither spoke. "Well, I suppose I can buy some whiskey," I said, reaching into my side pocket for some money as I stepped up to the bar. When I brought out my hand, Mrs. Miller's four-carat platinum-banded diamond ring dropped to the floor. The policeman picked it up and examined it curiously. I held my breath. He passed it to the bartender who also examined it. "Zircon?" The policeman shook his head. "Zircons cost money." I put out my hand. The policeman held on to it to annoy me. "Why didn't you leave it wid her?" he said. I felt a laugh bubbling up inside of me. You cracker motherfucker, you don't know how funny you are, I thought. "I got it from her," I said. "You chickenshit pimp," he said contempuously. "If I catch you out here screwing these maids 'n' taking their money I'm gonna beat the shit outa you." I let out a guilty-sounding laugh. "You gotta catch me first," I said. He threw the ring onto the bar and and turned back to the bartender. I put the ring in my pocket and walked out.

Throughout the whole thing, I hadn't felt any conscious fear. I had suffered a moment of breathlessness when I felt myself in danger. But not once had I felt the cold fear of panic that I should have felt. I suppose that's why I behaved so stupidly.

I walked miles to Kinsman Road and found a taxi. I rode downtown to Clark's coffee counter on the ground floor next to the Gilsy Hotel. Why there? It was a familiar scene, but the chances were I wouldn't run into anyone who knew me, and I wanted some coffee. Also, it was near enough to the Union Station for me to walk.

It was 5:25 A.M. by the electric clock over the counter when I arrived and still black dark outside, but the snow had stopped. There were no other customers. I sat at the counter and the waitress came from where she had been sitting in the rear. Many of the coffee counters in Cleveland didn't serve blacks. But this particular Clark's, next door to the Gilsy, was patronized by the black bellmen and was therefore accustomed to black faces.

The waitress who came to take my order was young, white, and pretty with brown hair and a greasy face, the kind of young white girl black hustlers called "jailbait" or "Ohio Pen Pullet." I ordered coffee and doughnuts and since she was lonely she stood nearby and we looked across the counter at one another. "You wanna go to Chicago with me?" I said. "No, I'm not that kinda girl," she said. I pulled out a handful of banknotes. "I don't want you to work, I got plenty money," I said. I saw her eyes widen at the sight of the money and various emotions pass over her face. She licked her lips. Most of the lipstick had worn away and she hadn't put any more on. She was young enough not to need any. "When?" she asked. "Now," I said. "Oh, I couldn't," she suddenly decided. And suddenly I thought of Jean and felt guilty. I finished my coffee and doughnuts and paid her and left a dollar tip. Her eyes filled with conflicting emotions as she watched me go. Black pimps had taken thousands of white girls like her from the coal-mine towns of West Virginia and the little steel-mill towns of Ohio and put them to work as prostitutes in the ghettos. They liked it; they made the best whores. I suffered a vague sense of regret for leaving her.

I walked down Ninth Street to the Union Station on Lake Erie and bought a coach ticket to Chicago. I was still carrying all the jewelry and money in my outside overcoat pocket. On the platform I was stopped by a boy named Ralph who had been a classmate at Ohio State University. He was employed as a Red-cap, and he was working the graveyard shift, from midnight to eight. It was a really chickenshit job for a boy who had been to the university, and I was embarrassed to see him. But he got me a vacant seat all to myself and I felt embarrassed again when I gave him a tip. The coaches in the United States have chair seats, two on each side of the center aisle, all facing the engine; and one was assured of the greatest possible privacy if one could keep two adjoining seats, which Ralph had got for me.

I went to the toilet and transferred all of my loot to the inside pocket of my suit coat. I took off my overcoat, folded it and put it on the seat beside me, adjusted my own seat to a reclining position, and lay back and went to sleep. It was about ten hours to Chicago. Night was just falling when we arrived at about 4:30 P.M.

I went to a "nice" black hotel on the edge of the South Side ghetto that was run by either a relative or a friend of Stanton DePriest—I don't remember which—but I had heard about it from Stanton. By then it was dark and too late to do anything but eat and go to bed. I had been up all the night before and I had thought I would be sleepy, but I discovered I was too excited to sleep. I called the night bellman and told him I wanted a mulatto whore and afterward a white whore, and after I had finished with these two I decided I wanted the very best and most elegant black whore available to spend the night with me. When she came she told me she didn't usually do that; she had a job as a secretary and was engaged to be married. I can't imagine what impulse struck me to show her the jewelry I had stolen, but suddenly I took it from my pocket and spread it all out on the bed. She picked it up and began looking at it. She knew jewelry and she became terrified. I told her to take any-thing she wanted but she refused and hurriedly began dressing. She promised not to tell anyone about it and warned me not to show it to anybody else. But I only laughed. She begged me to be careful and left. The bellman appeared shortly afterward and asked what was the trouble. I told him I had just changed my mind and wanted to sleep alone and gave him a tip and locked the door behind him.

The next morning I was arrested while trying to fence the jewelry at a pawnshop near the Loop run by a notorious fence called Jew Sam. I had heard Bunch Boy and Cateye and other characters talk of Jew Sam with high praise, and I had planned to sell him the jewelry and keep on to Tijuana with only cash.

I had begun with the four-carat diamond ring, for which I asked five hundred dollars. Sam said give him a few minutes to examine it and took it into the back room. I suspected he was calling the police. I should have let him keep the ring and escaped. But I couldn't run; I never could run. I have always been afraid that that one stupid mental block is going to get me killed.

Two plainclothes detectives arrived, as I had suspected. They searched me and found the remainder of the jewelry and money and took me to the Detective Bureau, where four or five detectives interrogated me. They asked me who I had robbed. I maintained that the jewelry belonged to me, and they began hitting me. A captain of detectives arrived and interrupted the interrogation to speak to me privately. He said a woman residing in the Blackstone Hotel had been robbed the previous night and she had just come in and identified the jewelry as hers but she had consented to my receiving a light sentence if I confessed so she could claim her jewelry and depart. I said I could prove that I was in my hotel room all the previous night. "You'd better not try," the captain warned. Then he left me with the other detectives, telling them he needed a signed confession. They handcuffed my feet together and my hands behind my back, hung me upside down on an open door by the handcuffs about my ankles with my handcuffed hands hanging down along my spine past the back of my skull. Then they stuck the butts of their pistols inside their felt hats and began beating me about the ribs and testicles. I wanted to faint but I remained conscious. There was too much pain and not enough hurt. Finally, I mumbled that I would confess.

There was great consternation when I confessed that I had robbed a couple in Cleveland Heights, Ohio. They did not want to accept it. They wanted me to confess to robbing the woman from the Blackstone Hotel. I suspected that she was the mistress of the captain and they were going to split the loot, which was considerable. But there was a "reader" out from Cleveland Heights on the robbery, and the Chicago detectives were forced to honor it. They sent to Cleveland for someone to identify the jewelry, and one of the executives of the firm that insured it arrived. His name was Frieberg. Later he became a friend.

A detective from Cleveland Heights had come with him to take me back. I waived extradition and the three of us returned together. The total insurance for the jewelry amounted to twenty-eight thousand dollars, and there was a little over twenty thousand in cash. Mr. Frieberg paid for a drawing room for the three of us.

During the ride back he asked me a number of questions: Who was my accomplice? Who planned the job? Who gave us the inside information about the house? Was it my first robbery? I told him I had done it alone, no one else helped or gave me any tips of any kind; I just picked out a likely-looking house to rob, and I returned and robbed it. He shook his head unbelievingly.

He was surprised to find me so young and absolutely astounded to learn I had attended Ohio State University. It seemed he expected robbers to be uneducated, if not downright illiterate. He asked why I had committed the robbery and had I ever robbed anyone before. I told him it was my first time and I had done it because I wanted to get away. Away from what? he asked. Away from here, I said. He looked at me curiously and asked was it that bad. I said yes. When we parted at the Cleveland Union station he said he was sorry I had done it.

I was taken first to the Cleveland Heights police station to be questioned. The detectives asked much the same questions Mr. Frieberg had: Who was my accomplice? Who tipped the job? Who gave me the inside dope? How did I know where the safe was located? How did I know the chauffeur would be off duty on that particular night when more than likely he was the only chauffeur in all Cleveland Heights who was off then? Had I ever worked for the Millers or any of their neighbors?

I gave them much the same answers I had given Mr. Frieberg: I didn't have an accomplice, I did the job alone, no one had told me anything, I had just picked out their house by chance as a likely one to rob.

They didn't believe me either, but they didn't ask me whether I had ever committed another robbery before. They knew if I had been arrested it would be on record and if I hadn't I wouldn't admit it. But they wanted to know how I had gotten away if I didn't have an accomplice. They had found the abandoned car way out in nowhere. It had snowed heavily that night and I couldn't have gotten away unless I had a rendezvous with my accomplice.

They tried to get me to implicate the chauffeur. Who else could my accomplice be but the chauffeur? I said I didn't know the Millers' chauffeur; I wouldn't know him if I saw him.

They had the chauffeur in jail and they brought him in to confront me. He was yellow with fright. I looked him in the eyes and said I had never seen him before. He probably dirtied his pants from relief.

The one good thing I can say about the residents of Cleveland Heights is that they didn't permit their policemen to beat up suspects. The detectives appeared as though they would have enjoyed beating my eyes out, but finally they had to give up questioning me and let me go. I was turned over to the Cuyahoga County jail to be bound over to the grand jury.

My mother visited me and cried and said, "My poor boy, you were so brilliant," already speaking in the past tense. But it was my father who got the attorney for me. When he visited me he brought my back brace, which I hadn't worn for months. I was glad that Joe did not visit me. There were banner headlines and lead stories about the robbery in all the Cleveland dailies, but if by chance my brother Eddie ever noticed them, he gave no sign. He had completely disappeared.

At first I was taken out several times to be interviewed by probation officers, and my lawyer was optimistic; he thought I might be put on probation.

I refused to think about it, or to think about anything; I refused to think. Somewhere along the line I had ceased entirely to think, probably when I was being tortured in the Detective Bureau in Chicago. I had sealed my thoughts against all reality, against all contemplation of anything past, present, or future. I refused to think of the hurt I had inflicted on my parents, on my relatives, on myself. I did not think of Bunch Boy or any of the people I had met around his club; I did not think of any of the people I had met in school or at play. I withdrew. No one visited me except my mother. The only incident I remember vividly from that month in the county jail was a furious argument I had with a guard about a newspaper.

On the 27th of December, Christmas week of 1928, I was taken into court to be sentenced. It was in the morning of a cold gray day. The snow in the streets, seen from the courthouse windows, was already turning black. Except for Mr. and Mrs. Miller, wrapped in heavy dark coats, sitting to one side of the courtroom, their faces as white as painted masks, I don't remember anyone else being present. Neither of my parents was there; later I learned they had been given no notice. If my lawyer was there, I don't remember, for I don't remember him or anyone else speaking except the judge. The judge was named MacMahon; he was an old man with flinty gray eyes and a merciless expression. There were no spectators, I am certain.

I had never really hoped to be put on probation; I was already on probation. But when Judge MacMahon sentenced me—"I sentence you to twenty to twenty-five years of hard labor in the Ohio State Penitentiary, because you have taken ten years from the lives of each of your victims"—I was shocked. At that instant I suddenly knew that this motherfucking bastard had hurt me as much as I could ever be hurt if I lived a hundred thousand years; he had hurt me in a way I would never get over, I thought. Someday, I thought, I would get even.

2.

I grew to manhood in the Ohio State Penitentiary. I was nineteen years old when I went in and twenty-six years old when I came
out. I became a man, dependent on no one but myself. I learned
all the behavior patterns necessary for survival, or I wouldn't
have survived, although at the time I did not realize I was learning
them. On occasion, it must have seemed to others that I was bent
on self-destruction.

During my seven and a half years my father visited me once,
although he lived in Cleveland, and then only to get money.
The Depression began shortly after I arrived in prison, and I was
the most prosperous member of my immediate family.

My mother visited me often after I asked her to come and live
in Columbus to protect me. I had developed a paranoiac fear
that the prison doctor wanted to kill me. I had infuriated him by
cutting off the cast the Ohio State Industrial Commission had
ordered him to give me. I cut it off with a rusty nail. My mother
also kept house for my blind brother, Joseph, who was taking his
doctorate in sociology at Ohio State University. I assigned my
pension to her to help pay my brother's expenses, and also to
compensate for my guilt at having given my father so much of
my income from gambling.

THE QUALITY OF HURT

I forgot my resolution to get even with the judge and society for sentencing me to twenty years. That was to be revived later, long after I had been released, when society began punishing me for being black. In prison, at one point, I became indifferent about returning to the world as I had known it. I would serve my time and the outside world could fuck itself.

Yet, despite all these inconsistencies and outright contradictions, the seven and a half years I actually served did not seem to hurt me at all. I don't remember ever really hurting. It was all anticlimax.

Nothing happened in prison that I had not already encountered in outside life. Gambling was the chief pastime and principal hustle of the convicts, and I soon discovered that I had learned more than most of them knew during those years I had hung around Bunch Boy's club. Aside from masturbation, all sex gratification derived from sodomy, and I had encountered homosexuals galore around the Majestic Hotel and the environs of Fifty-fifth Street and Central Avenue in Cleveland. The pansies had called it "pussy without bone" when soliciting in Cleveland. But I had always preferred my pussy with all of its pelvic bone intact, whether it was sharp or cushioned. In prison the female of the species, known as "boy-girls," were not much different in behavior patterns and emotions from their counterparts outside, the black prostitutes, only their anatomy was different. The "wolves" in prison, the male of the species, would have been pimps, "sweet men," or just some bitch's "old man" outside. And the "wolverines" of prison who were neither one nor the other but practioners of both were similar to that class of free men known as bisexual. "You do it to me and I'll do it to you," they suggested. Nothing was new.

The boy-girls offered me their "boneless pussy" free: the wolverines suggested "swapping up," and the wolves advanced all the usual propositions. All because I was young and good-looking. But no one tried to rape me. Perhaps because I was too educated, and ignorant men, which most convicts are, are afraid of education. Perhaps it was because of the great capacity for vio-

lence I had developed. I could never bear to be used against my
will in any capacity. In comparison with most of the black convicts
in the Ohio Penitentiary my five feet nine inches in height and
one hundred and sixty-five pounds in weight made me practically
a midget. But I had such violent seizures of rage that I made men
twice my size quake with fright. In my fits of insensate fury I
would have smashed the world, crushed it in my hands, kicked
down the universe. I became blind, defenseless; many times I
would have been killed except for the aura of violence surrounding
me and the incredible distortion of my face. Many times others
saved my life; in a way I was indispensable: I was the syndicate
boss, I helped the gambling to be accepted, I could talk, I kept it
clean, headed off fights, stopped the cheating, protected the
"chumps," and personally paid off arguments before they erupted
into violence.

I survived, I suppose, because I knew how to gamble. It takes
a certain amount of intelligence to be a skilled gambler, and a
certain amount of nerve. I had both. I drew my seventy-five-dol-
lar monthly pension from the Ohio State Industrial Commission
for total disability all the time I was in prison, so I had money
and couldn't be forced to work.

Thanks to my gambling skill and pension money, I soon became
the boss of the gambling among the black convicts. I had an education, so I was always chosen to negotiate with the screws and
pay them off. I found the convicts like idiot children, like the
idiot giant of Steinbeck's *Of Mice and Men*, intensely grateful
for small favors and incomprehensibly dangerous from small
slights; they had to be watched every moment and handled with
utmost care. I was celled with the crippled convicts off and on
throughout my term, and I got along with them well enough,
although they were known to be extremely treacherous; but then
I was a cripple myself. Other convicts tried to take advantage of
the cripples and got themselves killed; but I have never wanted to
take advantage of a person's handicap, as so many people in the
free world love to do.

I found the convicts of the Ohio State Penitentiary as violent as myself, if not more so. I always carried a knife with blades of various lengths, depending on where I got it made, but never less than six inches. I used it primarily as a deterrent.

Convicts stabbed, cut, slashed, brained, maimed, and killed each other almost every day for the most nonsensical reasons. Two black convicts cut each other to death over a dispute as to whether Paris was in France or France in Paris. I saw another killed for not passing the bread. In the school dormitory a convict slipped up on another while he was sleeping and cut his throat to the bone; I was awakened by a gurgling scream to see a fountain of blood spurting from the cut throat onto the bottom of the mattress of the bunk overhead. And yet they were capable of attaining high degrees of heroism, as in the Easter Monday fire of 1930, in which three hundred and thirty-odd convicts were burned to death in their cells. Given freedom of the yard when the fire got out of control, convicts from other blocks braved death, asphyxiation, and injury to climb the steep steps of the burning cellblock through the dense black smoke, scorching heat, and leaping flames to rescue those convicts locked in the infernos of their cells. In my short story *To What Red Hell* published in the October, 1934, issue of *Esquire*, I wrote, "Someone bumped his shoulder, knocking him to his knees. He felt the side of his head strike the railing by the sidewalk. Then a heavy sound filled his ears like a roar. But it was only a voice yelling: 'Gangway! Live one!' Four men swept by into the stream of light up the hospital stairs. They carried a writhing body—a live one . . . Men working overtime at their job of being heroes, moving through the smoke with reckless haste . . . something to do—a lurid break in the dull monotone of routine." Later I wrote of the dead, "Whatever they had been or had ever dreamed of being—whatever their race or background or nationality—that foot of green vomit hanging from their teeth made them all alike." The Ohio Penitentiary fire was in the headlines of all the major newspapers in the world. I just escaped being one of the victims myself by a week; until the previous week I had been in a punishment company which comprised a large number of the dead.

The advantage I had over other black convicts was that I knew my own mind. I could influence them to do things the reason for which they didn't understand. Most of the black convicts in the Ohio State Penitentiary were dull-witted, stupid, uneducated, practically illiterate, slightly above animals. For the most part, black robbers and murderers were the least intelligent. Most black murderers had killed in a senseless rage, and most black robbers had robbed with even greater stupidity than I had. No wonder Mr. Frieberg had been so astounded to learn that I had been to college. But I have been a misfit all my life.

However, there are exceptions to every rule. I met one black murderer of great intelligence; he was just violent. He had been a jeweler in private life, and had killed his wife and her lover in a fit of jealous rage.

But I've never seen a convict who was a professional gambler on the outside lose his temper inside. Only me. Of course, I had never really been a professional gambler outside; I had merely played at it. Inside I became a professional gambler. But I lost my temper constantly. It's a wonder I stayed alive.

I began writing in prison. That also protected me, against both the convicts and the screws. The black convicts had both an instinctive respect for and fear of a person who could sit down at a typewriter and write, and whose name appeared in newspapers and magazines outside. The screws could never really kill a convict who was a public figure, or else convicts like Malcolm X and Eldridge Cleaver would never have gotten out of prison alive.

My first short stories were published in weekly newspapers and in magazines published by blacks: the *Atlanta World*, the *Pittsburgh Courier*, the *Afro-American*, the *Bronzeman*, *Abbott's Monthly*, and other similar publications. I sold my first short story, *Crazy in the Stir*, to *Esquire* magazine in 1934, and followed that same year with *To What Red Hell*, my story about the prison fire. I think *Esquire* had just begun to publish fiction the first of that year; before then it had been a men's-fashion magazine. After that, until I was released in May 1936, I was published only by *Esquire*.

I must admit that the convicts were unimpressed by my stories; anyway most of them never read them. But they were impressed by my name appearing in a national magazine which the prison newsboy, a lifer named Mack, was permitted to peddle about the prison. The screws could not kill me after my name began appearing in national publications, and they could not make me work as long as I drew compensation from the Ohio State Industrial Commission for total disability. But they punished me enough in other ways: Collectively I spent many months in solitary confinement—once I was in so long on starvation rations that my hair started coming out, my nails began falling off, and my body became weightless—I still bear the scars of the head whippings. They punished me in many more subtle ways which I have discovered to be peculiar to the white race. During my last year, when I was at the farm, the deputy warden, a sick man with a paralyzed arm, used to stand beside the dining-room door when we went to meals and wait for me so he could lean forward and grit his teeth at me. I then lost a year and a half of "good time" for "insubordination."

My first short stories, those I wrote in prison, were not racially orientated; I did not write about the lives of blacks in a white world. That was to come. In prison I wrote about crimes and criminals, mostly about the life in prison—*Crazy in the Stir, To What Red Hell, The Visiting Hour, Every Opportunity, The Night's for Crying, Strictly Business*, and such.

I gambled and captained the crippled convicts' softball team to a prison championship and wrote short stories. I didn't have time to think of my hurt. I didn't realize at the time that I was being hurt. "It's just costing the state and isn't hurting me a bit," I used to think of my imprisonment.

It is nonsense, even falsehood, to say that serving seven and a half years in one of the most violent prisons on earth will have no effect on a human being. But as far as I could determine at the time, and for a long time afterward, the only effect it had on me was to convince me that people will do anything—white people, black people, all people. Why should I be surprised when white men cut out some poor black man's nuts, or when black men eat the tasty palms of white explorers?

I was paroled to my mother in Columbus and went to live with her and my brother Joe. My compensation was stopped a few weeks previous to my being released, as though the directors of the Ohio State Industrial Commission had thought that freedom would make me well and strong. When I went to live with Mother and Joe I was broke and without income for the first time in my adult life. For some reason, perhaps the effect of freedom of movement, I became more hysterical than I had ever been before.

I wanted women, women, women. Good women took too long to make so I went with whores, all kinds of whores. I didn't have any money so I had to look for whores I could have for free. There were numerous white whores in the black ghettos of Columbus at the time, and I had success because I took them out, so long as they paid. Of course I had to keep out of the way of their pimps. Several times landlords had to intervene to keep me from being shot.

Once I met a group of ex-cons who persuaded me to go with them to "Georgia" a young black whore, which means to promise her payment and then renege. The leader of the group was an extremely tall, uncouth young man with pockmarked black skin, named Storey. It was to his room we took the fat, stupid girl, promising her five dollars in advance to service us all. She couldn't have been more than fifteen, but she was willing enough. The first two promised the next would pay and it was not until after she had slept with the third one that she became aware she was being "Georgiaed." I was the fourth and I found her crying, so I refused to take advantage of her. But she didn't appreciate my quixotic gesture, she just thought something was wrong with me. The only satisfaction I derived from the gesture was when I learned afterward that all the others had caught gonorrhea from her.

I made my mother frantic coming home late at night with my whorish smell. She threatened to report me to my probation officer and have me sent back to prison. We had such dreadful rows Joe had to intervene. But the incident which finally convinced my mother to send me away stemmed from my smoking marijuana.

Coming from church one Sunday with Mother and Joe some dude I knew slightly called me aside and suggested that we go someplace and smoke some "gauge," I said, "Okay," although I had never heard marijuana referred to as "gauge" and didn't really know what he meant. I told mother I had to go see about a job.

I got my first surprise when he took me to a private house that looked so much like the old home-brew joints I thought he was suggesting we drink some bootleg whiskey, even though whiskey had been legal for several years. But the *modus operandi* had changed while I had been in prison, I discovered. Instead of ordering a half pint, he asked for a couple of sticks, bomber size.

We sat on a sofa across a well-furnished room from a slick black joker playing a baby grand piano for a flushed white woman leaning on its top.

"Looka, looka, looka," he mumbled as though to himself, rippling the light fantastic on the treble keys. "Look at that motherfucker run, can't no white motherfucker run like that . . . look at that mother jump that fence . . . go, man, go . . . must have a big white titty waiting . . ."

The white woman giggled all over and slapped the backs of his hands.

"What's the matter with them?" I asked; I thought they were nuts.

He looked at me curiously, but before he could reply the land-prop brought in two hand-rolled cigarettes on a silver tray which she placed on the cocktail table in front of us. He gave her a dollar bill and didn't get any change. I felt foolish not knowing what to do. So when he picked up one of the cigarettes and lit it, I was eager to do the same. I heard him sucking in his smoke, like a snake hissing in reverse. I didn't see any sense in that so I just took deep lungfuls until my cigarette was finished. It smelled and tasted a great deal like the cubebs for the relief of catarrh but I didn't feel a thing. I called the landprop and ordered two more. He put his in his pocket but I smoked mine. Afterward I felt sober as a judge. I was disappointed; I hadn't known what to expect but I had expected some kind of sensation.

"Let's go to a movie," he suggested.

"Okay," I said.

When we began walking down the side street toward Warren Street, I noticed that the day was hot and brilliant and I felt good. We passed a well-dressed black couple obviously coming from church; the man was a big laborer type, but the woman was slender and beautiful, with sloe eyes and smooth black skin in a softly molded face. My friend tipped his hat. I noticed for the first time that he was wearing one of those hard straws we called caters. The woman looked startled. The man bunched up his shoulders belligerently and turned toward my friend, who banged his hat onto his head and hurried on.

"You know those people?" I asked.

We were hurrying down a brick-paved sidewalk past a white picket fence. I don't know whether my friend replied for suddenly I was distracted by the fence suddenly moving straight across my path. But the next instant it straightened itself out.

"You see that?" I asked in amazement.

But my friend was rapidly turning the corner into Warren and I heard him mumbling to himself ". . . getting away from them people . . ."

Warren Street was a microcosm of all the slum streets in the world; it was drab, dreary, dirty, depraved, and repulsive. Its façades were grimy or unpainted; its pavements full of loose street car tracks and deep potholes; its sidewalks crammed with black Christians, black workers, black drunks, black whores, black thieves, black cripples. Its ugliness was an affront. But when I looked up after turning the corner, all the grimy façades seemed to be a blaze of bright colors, gold, scarlet, blue, green, like an array of peacocks. The sky was boiling with suggestive figures and frenetic movements like a psychedelic nightmare. The black people in their bright summer cottons looked like exotic tropical flowers on a riverbank.

Suddenly the sidewalk began to undulate, sometimes it came almost up to my face and at other times it just rose high enough to make me stumble. I knew then that I was reeling for I had experienced the same sensation when a guard struck me across the back of my skull with his loaded stick and the concrete range came up and touched me on the nose. I realized I shouldn't be on the street, I would disgrace my mother and brother. "Gotta go home," I muttered to my friend and turned up our street. He went on toward the movie house; I never discovered whether he had heard me, for I never saw him again.

Our street had young trees spaced about thirty yards apart flanking the sidewalk. In time those trees became stations of my slow trek homeward. I was progressing so slowly that each tree became a separate station to be reached before setting out for another. I must have passed people but I don't remember seeing anyone, I was so "gauged," as they used to say.

But when I reached the steps to our house I became as sober as I had ever been, and I remained sober long enough to go around the house to the back door and negotiate the kitchen, where my mother sat reading to Joe, glancing up sharply as I passed through. I went up the stairs to my room and opened the door and closed it behind me without the suggestion of a stagger. But when I flopped down on the bed to sleep it off, I suddenly became as gauged again as I had been before. When I closed my eyes, circular saws began buzzing in my nose, sawing upward toward my eyes, which popped open in alarm. I looked at the rose patterns of the wallpaper to banish the saws from my nose, but the clusters of red roses on the pale ivory background began turning slowly in concentric circles, increasing in speed as they changed in appearance, first into red-painted upright kitchen chairs, then, unbelievably, into bleached cow skulls on a blinding beige desert, which so frightened me I quickly shut my eyes again.

I leaped out of bed and stood up and suddenly I was cold

sober again long enough to see the room and the rose pattern of the wallpaper in perfect perspective. But when I lay down again it began all over. I went out into the hall and called Mother. I told her I thought I was having a heart attack, everthing kept going and coming. She became alarmed and sent for our doctor. I don't remember whether we had a telephone or whether she had to send a neighbor's child, but the doctor arrived shortly and I asked to speak to him privately. When he took out his stethoscope and told me to strip to the waist, I confessed I had smoked some marijuana and I thought it had affected my heart. He put away his stethoscope and gave me a handful of small white pills. "Dissolve one under your tongue every fifteen minutes," he instructed me. "They're nitroglycerine." Then he went downstairs to the kitchen to talk to my mother.

I knew he would tell her and she would give me hell, and I swore I'd never smoke marijuana again.

My mother did not say one word to me, but she dressed and went to see my parole officer at his home. I never learned what she told him, but the next week I was paroled to my father in Cleveland.

When I returned to Cleveland that summer of 1936, I was on parole for the duration of my maximum sentence, a period of a little more than seventeen years. I found Jean, my sweetheart before I went to prison, and, obtaining the consent of my parole officer, married her. She was still in love with me, and I grew to love her too, desperately and completely. At the time I was living with my father in a couple of rented rooms on Ninety-third Street off Cedar Avenue, but after our marriage we went to live by ourselves in a series of shabby rented rooms.

Until then there had been nothing racial about my hurt, unbelievable as this may seem. But marriage made a difference.

Jean was an extremely beautiful brown-skinned girl, and I wanted to support her like any other man.

I worked in a country club as a part-time waiter, and as a temporary bellhop in the big hotels when there were openings. I tried desperately to write for popular magazines, but I only sold a few short stories to *Esquire* and *Coronet*. I did not want Jean to work and mostly we went hungry. She didn't seem to mind too much, she was loyal and loving and she believed in me. But I began to feel cornered in a black world.

No one in my immediate family could afford to help. My father was working on WPA as a teacher, and down in Columbus my blind brother was employed by the local branch of the Urban League. My uncle, Roddy Moon, who was a federal meat inspector, was in the best position in the family, and he and Aunt Leah had us out to their house for dinner and gave us food to take home whenever they could. But they had an ill daughter, Ella, who was unemployed, and their son, Henry, now the publicity director for the national NAACP, who needed help.

Eventually I was employed by WPA, at first as a laborer, digging sewers and dredging creeks in the snow and ice of the Cleveland suburbs, miles from where I lived, and then as a research assistant in the Cleveland Public Library, writing vocational bulletins for the Stevenson room, and lastly as a writer on the Ohio Writers' project.

It was while I was on the Writers' Project that I wrote a series of descriptive vignettes to "brighten up" the editorial page of the Cleveland *Daily News*, as the editor, N. R. Howard put it. Mr. Howard did not give me a by-line for these pieces, which were signed only CH, and accepted them personally, paying me one dollar each, for fear of difficulties with the union. At that time the Cleveland daily papers did not employ blacks, no doubt because there were no vacancies. As Louis B. Seltzer, editor of the Cleveland *Press*, put it, "I could not hire you if you were Jesus Christ reincarnated." But I have always considered Mr. Howard one of my best friends. He knew all about my prison record and he had read several of my stories in *Esquire* and knew I wanted to write fiction. And we talked of writing, among other things. We both liked Faulkner and we had both read Richard Wright's *Uncle Tom's Children*. I remember best Mr. Howard saying, "I am appalled at the number of mistakes I make each day." And it was Mr. Howard who said to me, "Chester, you have paid the penalty for your crime against society, now forget about it. You don't owe any more." That has been my attitude ever since; but there are some who think my debt should never end, and that I should pay it until my death.

While on the Writers' Project I did not feel the racial hurt so much. My supervisor assigned me to writing the history of Cleveland for the Cleveland guide, and the challenge occupied me.

My domestic life was happy and we were all, black and white alike, bound together into the human family by our desperate struggle for bread.

But the war in Europe commenced. American industry came to life, the Depression was over. WPA ceased. And I joined the long lines queueing up for jobs in private industry, at Warner & Swasey, American Steel & Wire, the Aluminum Company of America, and the other great industries in the Cuyahoga Valley. It was then that I learned what racial prejudice is like. My hurt became violent. Each day, a thousand times, I had to exert the greatest self-control to keep from smashing the face of some white personnel director.

I needed desperately to leave Cleveland. I persuaded my parole officer to apply to Governor Harold Burton for the termination of my parole and the restoration of my citizenship; and when I got my sheepskin, making me a citizen for the first time, I registered with the Democratic Party in Cleveland. But before I had a chance to vote I left to work on Louis Bromfield's Malabar Farm in Pleasant Valley, Ohio.

The Jeliffes, a white couple who ran the Karamu settlement house and theater in the black ghetto, had interceded for me, and Mr. Bromfield knew of my past and my ambition. He took the trouble to read a long novel based on my prison observations, which I had entitled *Black Sheep*, and offered to help me to get it published.

This novel was the outcome of my personal hurts, which I have briefly documented, and did not contain any reference to my racial hurts. The publishers didn't want it. I have since learned that American publishers are not interested in black writers unless they bleed from white torture. I was beginning to bleed, but I had not bled enough by the time I wrote that book. This attitude might also apply to the white American readers of novels. I have never heard the phrase "It's a beautiful book" applied to a book written by a black writer unless the black characters have suffered horribly. I have heard scores of white people say of Richard Wright's books *Native Son* and *Black Boy* that they were "beautiful books." Of course, this does not mean the same thing to me as it does to these white people. The suffering of others does not fill me with any spiritual satisfaction. Nor do I revel in the anguish of my fellow human beings. I am not uplifted by other people's degradation. Perhaps in this respect I am not a good Christian. The suffering of Christ affects me with abhorrence, and I look upon his crucifixion, as upon all crucifixions, as a sadistic brutality.

I had thought that Malabar Farm might soothe the tensions that were overwhelming me from my new experience of the horror of racial prejudice. But I soon discovered that I was merely hiding. So I had my wife rejoin me in Columbus, Ohio, and we took a Greyhound bus to Los Angeles.

I have written graphically in my first published novel, *If He Hollers Let Him Go*, about how Los Angeles affected me: ✓

"It wasn't being refused employment in the plants so much. When I got there practically the only job a Negro could get was service in the white folks' kitchens. But it wasn't that so much. It was the look on the people's faces when you asked them about a job. Most of 'em didn't say right out they wouldn't hire me. They just looked so goddamned startled that I'd even asked. As if some friendly dog had come in through the door and said, 'I can talk.' It shook me."

Los Angeles hurt me racially as much as any city I have ever known—much more than any city I remember from the South. It was the lying hypocrisy that hurt me. Black people were treated much the same as they were in an industrial city of the South. They were Jim-Crowed in housing, in employment, in public accommodations, such as hotels and restaurants. During the filming of *Cabin in the Sky*, starring Ethel Waters, Bill "Bojangles" Robinson and Lena Horne, the black actors and actresses were refused service in the MGM commissary where everyone ate. The difference was that the white people of Los Angeles seemed to be saying, "Nigger, ain't we good to you?"

The only thing that surprised me about the race riots in Watts in 1965 was that they waited so long to happen. We are a very patient people.

Los Angeles hurt me racially. The war hurt me racially. The armed services hurt me racially. I didn't serve during World War II; I was too old at the beginning, and when I was finally called for a physical, in 1943, it was discovered I had an "un-united fracture" of one of the vertebrae I had broken in 1926, and that my entire pelvic structure was twisted out of place. However, I met many Negroes who had served. My wife's older brother, Hugo Johnson, was a chief machinist's mate in the Navy when the war broke out, with twenty-four years of service, but the Navy assigned him to shore patrol on the Embarcadero in San Francisco and Seventh Street in Oakland, two "buckets of blood," during the war. And her younger brother, Andrew Johnson, was a chaplain in the Army with the rank of captain, and served out the war on the heavily contested Pacific Islands. I knew others who had served in the war, among them Reverend Grant Reynolds, Andrew's superior officer. All of them told me at one time or another that race prejudice was rampant in an armed forces dedicated to fight against racism in other parts of the world.

To briefly sum up my attitude toward industry on the West Coast I can say that I had twenty-three jobs during the first three years of the war, and all in essential industries. Since my father had been the head of the Mechanical Departments of various Southern agricultural and mechanical schools for blacks during the first fifteen years of my life, I had picked up certain mechanical skills. I could read blueprints; I understood, at least partially, most of the necessary skills of building construction—carpentry, plumbing, electric wiring, bricklaying, roofing; I understood the fundamentals of combustion engines; I could operate a number of machine tools—turret lathes, drills, milling machines, etc; and I was a fairly competent typist. But during those three years I had only two jobs that required any skill: as an apprentice ship-fitter in Henry J. Kaiser's Shipyard No. 1 in Richmond, California, where we built Liberty ships; and as a shipwright's helper in the Los Angeles Shipyard in San Pedro Harbor, helping to install the ventilation system in a floating drydock for the Navy. Both jobs I had to leave for domestic reasons. Otherwise I was employed as a laborer, shoveling gravel and sand for the California Rock Company, hammering sand into pipes for bending for the Crane Company, moving two-ton rolls of towel paper for the California Towel-Saver Company, laboring in the warehouse of the Hughes Aircraft Company—to mention only a few. Federal law permitted me to change my job unless I was employed at the highest skill for which I was fitted; therefore I could change at will.

My wife was employed as co-director of women's activities for the Los Angeles Area USOs. Her co-director was a white woman, and they supervised all of the entertainment provided by the USO units in the area, including the Hollywood Canteen.

It hurt me for my wife to have a better job than I did and be respected and included by her white co-workers, besides rubbing elbows with many well-to-do blacks of the Los Angeles middle class who wouldn't touch me with a ten-foot pole. That was the beginning of the dissolution of our marriage. I found that I was no longer a husband to my wife; I was her pimp. She didn't mind, and that hurt all the more.

It was from the accumulation of my racial hurts that I wrote my bitter novel of protest *If He Hollers Let Him Go*.

My cousin's wife, Molly Moon, used her influence to get me a fellowship from the Julius Rosenwald Foundation, and I went to New York City for the publication of my book by Doubleday, Doran and Company.

During that time I encountered the experiences which I later put into my novel *Pinktoes*.

Up to the age of thirty-one I had been hurt emotionally, spiritually, and physically as much as thirty-one years can bear: I had lived in the South, I had fallen down an elevator shaft, I had been kicked out of college, I had served seven and one half years in prison, I had survived the humiliating last five years of the Depression in Cleveland; and still I was entire, complete, functional; my mind was sharp, my reflexes were good, and I was not bitter. But under the mental corrosion of race prejudice in Los Angeles I had become bitter and saturated with hate. And finding myself unable to support my black wife, whom I loved desperately, I had become afraid. My wife deserved the support of her man. She was as beautiful and as feminine as a woman can be. I was thirty-one and whole when I went to Los Angeles and thirty-five and shattered when I left to go to New York.

New York hurt me in a different way—by accepting me. That sounds like a contradiction, but it's the truth. I knew that, as much as I had been hurt by then, I was sick. But New York accepted me as normal, and that made me sicker.

When I arrived in New York in 1944, President Roosevelt was running for his fourth and last term. I found myself caught up in a movement that was vaguely political but also strangely religious. The people in New York who worked for Roosevelt's reelection were not politicians, but disciples. The flood of humanity that worshiped at his shrine transcended party and political lines, racial and religious lines, class lines and caste lines. You were either for Roosevelt—no matter whether you were a communist, a unionist, a fascist, or a spy, black or white, gentile or Jew, old or young, male or female—or you were against him. Everything was used to garner votes: sex, white women, black women, married women, single women; money, eloquence, and intrigue.

In New York at that time there were many white women who wanted to give me their bodies, and I took them. And they were not from the lower classes, either. All of those whom I slept with at the time were from the middle or upper classes, a few intellectuals but mostly socialites.

I lost myself in sex and drunkenness and I didn't even vote for Roosevelt after all. I wasn't registered in New York State. I almost lost my wife, too. She came to New York and found me deeply involved in so many affairs that she tried to take her life. I was shocked back to normalcy, what was normalcy to me, and when I came to, *If He Hollers Let Him Go* had been published and well received. The book was considered by the editorial committee for Doubleday, Doran's *George Washington Carver Memorial Award* of twenty-five hundred dollars, but it was rejected because one of the women editors said it nauseated her. Instead a novel called *Mrs. Palmer's Honey* was given the award. To add insult to injury, the advertising copy that appeared in the *Saturday Review of Literature* for *Mrs. Palmer's Honey* referred to my novel, *If He Hollers Let Him Go*, as a *"series of epithets punctuated by spit."*

The whole episode left me very bitter, so when I was invited as one of five authors in 1945 to contribute to the feature in the *Saturday Review of Literature*, "The Author Talks Back," I flayed the carping white critics. To those who had complained about the objectionable language of my book, I wrote that they reminded me of the prostitute who, after employing every variety of her trade all night, went into the Chinese restaurant next morning and complained about a fly in her rice. And to those who complained that I had offered no solution for the problem my book presented, I wrote that I belonged to a nation which, coming from a severe depression, had had its fleet sunk at Pearl Harbor and had been caught in a war totally unprepared, without army or weaponry, but which had mustered its will and its energy and its ability and in five short years had amassed the greatest Navy and the greatest Army in the history of the world and had learned to split the atom as a weapon more powerful than could then be conceived by the average intelligence, and to ask me, an incidental black writer with a limited education and no status whatsoever, to solve its internal race problem, was preposterous. "Let the white people solve it their own goddamn selves."

I had become so bitter I wished to change publishers. Carl Van Vechten, whom I had met a short time before through Richard Wright, learned of my desire to find another publisher and persuaded his dear friend and editor, Blanche Knopf, to buy my contract from Doubleday, Doran and Company.

My wife and I decided to go live on her brother Hugo's ranch in northern California while I wrote my second book. We bought a Mercury coupe and drove across the United States from New York City to San Francisco via the Lincoln Highway. There was no other way I could have learned how brutal and vicious is American race prejudice in the North, although this certainly was not my purpose. Undoubtedly we could have found food and shelter in the black ghettos of the larger cities, but we passed mostly through towns too small to have self-supporting ghettos and we were at the mercy of white people, many of whom were from immigrant stock. We passed through Pennsylvania, Ohio, Indiana, Illinois, Iowa, Nebraska, Colorado, Utah, and Nevada, and literally none of the white people en route who operated hotels, motels, restaurants, or even local YWCAs or YMCAs would serve a clean, respectably dressed black couple in a new Mercury car. I had bought a 303 Savage rifle in New York because I had read that the Ku Klux Klan was active in the region of northern California where we were headed; but I found race hatred so frightening that I kept it loaded and within easy reach from the time I entered Illinois. Until we had passed through Donner Pass and entered California, we had found no place where we could sit down to a table and have a meal. California itself was certainly no "land of the free."

Hugo Johnson, my wife's brother, was chief of the shore patrol for San Francisco's Embarcadero at that time, and we found him in a café on the waterfront. He got a few days' leave and we took him with us back to his ranch on Honey Lake, which was on U. S. Route 395, seventy-five miles directly north of Reno, on the California side of the Nevada state line.

His ranch consisted of about six hundred acres of arable land bordering the lake and about ten thousand acres of mountain land on the other side of the highway, rising to an elevation of six thousand feet. On the mountain side of the highway there were a two-story house with peeling paint in a neglected state of repair and a small three-room shack with unpainted clapboards badly warped, in which lived thousands of sand lizards of varying sizes. Numerous field rats also lived in the attic and gnawed in the walls all night.

The unused barns and water trough were on the lake side, but the land had not been farmed nor the barns used for several years.

The tenant, a Portuguese man named Joe Mello, who had been leasing the farm on a sharecropper's basis for a number of years, had moved away upon learning that black people, his proprietor's sister and her husband, were coming to live on the property; and a white couple who had been living on state charity in an abandoned shack nearby had moved into the big house. The man was an old senile Texan who claimed to be over ninety (and looked it), and the woman, in her forties, was the local tramp, known as "Fertile Myrtle" because she had had eleven children, each sired by a different father. But ten of them had gone away: two of the boys were in the Army, I learned. At that time she and the Texan had only a small delicate child of about five with long red hair, obviously anemic, whom the old man claimed was his. They lived in incredible filth, unwashed and on the verge of starvation. There was a spigot for water in the kitchen but no sanitation, and the yard was littered with a pile of rubbish and garbage, cans, bottles, and all the filth that had been thrown from the house during all the years of Joe Mello's tenancy.

Although our shack was in worse repair, it was at least cleaner, simply because no one had lived in it for years. We learned that Joe Mello had rented it from time to time to itinerant families, but without Hugo's knowledge or consent. Our chief concern was that it was dangerous. There were no locks on the rickety doors, most of the panes were missing from the windows, and there were numerous holes in the walls, ceilings, and floors through which rats, snakes, and lizards could enter. Separating the two houses was a valley, in which Hugo had planted some fruit trees, but they were all dead by then from lack of care. Fortunately the other house, some distance away, was screened from our view by several huge oak trees overshadowing our shack and a grove of pine trees on the edge of their garbage dump.

We went with Hugo and met the old Texan, who said he didn't mind living next door to "buggers" as long as he didn't have to pay for it. They were paying no rent, but Hugo had been in the Navy for twenty-four years and had a strange sympathy for indigent people and let them stay.

When he went back, I drove into Susanville, seventeen miles north, which was the nearest town of any size, and bought screens for the windows, a heavy screen door for the kitchen; a new lock for the old door, and tools and sheet metal to cover the numerous holes. In a short time we got the shack shipshape. I sank an old fencepost near the huge oak tree which shaded the sandy patch of back yard beyond the kitchen porch and made a quite comfortable hammock with strong rope and the iron bed springs and a thin mattress from a single bed.

When our shack became functional, we went shopping for food in Susanville at the A & P supermarket, and even bought ice, which we kept beneath newspapers in a washtub. But it was completely isolated. The outhouse was about fifty yards from the house, reached by an almost imperceptible path through knee-high sagebrush, which shook and rustled with the movement of the sand lizards whenever we passed. The highway in front of us was out of sight, and behind us the badlands climbed through barren rocky terrain, scattered with stunted trees, lightning-scarred pines, gullies, boulders, and ravines, up to the little reservoir that had been constructed to catch the water from a spring and pipe it down to the two houses. Mule deer and big cats abounded. The old Texan and Fertile Myrtle were our nearest neighbors within five miles.

I made a gun rack with tenpenny nails at the head of my bed to hold my Savage rifle, and I slept with it loaded and cocked within hand's reach. It's a good thing that no innocent tramp approached that house after dark while we were there, or I would have blown him off the face of the earth.

I wrote the first draft of my second novel, *Lonely Crusade*, while we were there. We were so disturbed by the rats that I put a ladder up to the attic door outside and went in to scatter some poison grain. I found several dried veal heads, bits of hide, and numerous leg bones, left there by the various tenants who had been rustling the neighbors' cattle, along with beer and whiskey bottles, motor-oil cans, and all manner of rubbish. I had to clean it out before putting down the poison for the rats.

We only had water in the kitchen tap; the sink drained into a shallow trench someone had dug beneath the house and flowed down through the high dry grass toward the highway. Poison grain contains cyanide, which burns the rats' insides and makes them search frantically for water. Once they drink the water they die instantly and become bloated and begin to rot. Shortly after I had put down the poison grain, the foul odor of rotting rats became so strong that I had to crawl beneath the house and rake out the carcasses, and gather them from all about the house, and burn them.

We got rid of the rats, temporarily at least, but shortly afterward the rattlesnakes began coming out of hibernation. The first one I saw was coming from beneath the house and crossing the sandy patch of yard. I ran for my rifle, and my first shot cut him half in two; I finished him with a long-handled spade. Fertile Myrtle had heard the shot and had come across to learn the cause. When she saw the remains of the snake she said we must burn it or its mate would come back looking for it. We burned it, but its mate came back looking for it anyway.

Jean was sitting barelegged on the back steps and I was sitting on the side of the hammock talking to her, when the snake came out from beneath the house and began to cross the steps underneath her legs. She didn't see it and I couldn't let her know I saw it for fear she would move. It seemed as though it took seventeen thousand years for that snake to pass beneath her legs; then I ran and snatched her into the yard.

Beside the back porch was a lean-to that had been used to house a wagon or some farm machine, but there was nothing in it then but an old wooden door and various rusty hand tools. I snatched the same long-handled spade I had used before and the snake had started across the wooden door, leisurely and unconcerned, when I struck at it with the rounded blade of the spade. I missed it, and the sound of the spade hitting against the wooden door shattered my emotions. I was standing at the edge of the porch, about two feet above the snake. I had never seen a rattlesnake strike and I had thought they always struck out of a coil, but this snake came up like the letter S, standing on a minimum of tail, until he stood as high as my waist, and he struck the hickory handle of the shovel nearly at the middle, so fast and with such force he made a scar in the wood as though an ax had chopped it, and he broke one fang off at the root. Then he leaned back and hissed, blood flowing from the corner of his mouth where the broken fang protruded, and looked me dead in the eyes. Whether it was the sound of its hissing or the hynoptic glitter of its black lidless eyes that paralyzed me, I'll never know. But for an instant the strength went out of me and I sank into a void of dread. The next instant I had come out of it, striking blindly at the snake as it struck back at the shovel and I could hear its good fang pinging against the blade until it caught him in the middle and chopped him in two. I chopped the snake again and again in hysteria and fear until I had chopped it into tiny pieces, and then I built a fire and burned it with the nauseating scent adding to my hysteria. And I took Jean into the house and searched it and locked the doors and checked my rifle and took her to bed and didn't get up until next morning.

This experience was the basis for my short story, *The Snake*, which was published in *Esquire* magazine in 1955.

I killed ten other rattlesnakes after that, and three got away to my knowledge. They averaged about six feet which seemed much longer, with twelve to sixteen rings in their tails. I was told they were timber rattlers. I heard several of them rattle; to me it sounded like a note on a rusty horn. I never got near enough to another one for it to have any meaning. I stood twenty or more feet away from them and blasted at them with soft-nose 190-point shells in my lever-action Savage 303.

I always searched the house thoroughly, turning back the bed, poking into every conceivable hiding place with the barrel of the rifle, whenever we had been away from the house, if for no longer than to go shopping in Susanville.

My brother Joe and his wife stopped by to visit us on their way to Berkeley, where my brother was to lecture for a year at the University of California, and we drove down to Reno to pick them up.

At some time afterward the young postmistress at Janesville, the tiny hamlet six miles to the south of us where we received our mail, came to visit us. I let her read part of the first draft of my novel, and she said she knew it was going to be a good story because it gave her tremors of gooseflesh, which she said was a sure sign of the spiritual value of any book she read. Her body was deformed as the result of a polio attack when she was a child, but she had very beautiful eyes. She told us that Janesville and Susanville had been named after the two daughters of the pioneer who had founded them and that the region about Honey Lake had been known as the "never labor" land in the early days when there had been an abundance of water, because all the settlers had to do was sow their crops in the spring and go out once again in the fall and reap them. But times had changed and the large lake basin was dry, except for one small pond, and was overgrown with sagebrush that turned the landscape into a sea of purple in the fall. It had made me think of Zane Grey's western *Riders of the Purple Sage,* which had fascinated me in my youth.

Fertile Myrtle came over to help us entertain our visitor by showing her the network of veins growing out from her vagina caused by so many childbirths. I retired out of politeness during the exposition, despite my curiosity. We commented on her little red-haired daughter, who looked as transparent as Dresden china in the sun, and I remarked that she could do with more vitamins.

We drove the postmistress home and were invited by her parents to come the following week for dinner. We learned that they, like most of the settlers in that area, had originally come from Georgia, and I thought perhaps there was some truth in the story that the

Ku Klux Klan had been burning fiery crosses in the surrounding mountains. But they were very nice and she herself (I have forgotten her name) was one of the kindest, most obliging and understanding persons I have ever met of any race.

Near the end of our stay, when I had finished the first draft of my novel *Lonely Crusade* and we were preparing to return East, Hugo took two weeks' leave and we went to Oakland and picked him up. By then he had been transferred to Oakland as chief of the shore patrol on Seventh Street and the surrounding black ghetto.

Several things happened during those two weeks which always bring Hugo back to mind in sharp focus—a heavy-set man with the blunt brown face of a Filipino and a cauliflower ear from the time he had been middleweight champion of the Navy, in his neat blue chief's uniform with six gold hash stripes down the sleeve, which caused rear admirals to return his salute in the streets. Hugo was a strict disciplinarian, so much so that when we were living in Los Angeles and had tried to find him a nice wife from among Jean's friends, no woman would have him despite his ranch and assured pension. He commanded the respect of everyone, from brothel keepers to the proprietors on Oakland's famous Seventh Street, one of the gaudiest, most violent, treacherous, and dangerous main streets of any black ghetto nation.

Before leaving Oakland, he took us to lunch in a small home-cooking restaurant in a back room of one of the largest and rowdiest bars. There were no customers in the restaurant when we arrived. The proprietor, a big tough-looking man who presided over the bar, escorted us into the restaurant telling Jean what a straight shooter and real man was her brother, the "Chief," and how proud he was to reckon himself one of the Chief's friends, and what would we have to drink—it was on the house. I do not remember his name, but for the sake of this anecdote I will call him Mr. Jones.

When Mr. Jones went out to the bar to get our drinks, a buxom, light-complexioned woman came from the kitchen to take our order. There was a thin black woman standing behind the counter cutting thin slices of sandwich bread with a long thin knife. She had looked at Hugo expectantly, it seemed, but he hadn't noticed.

After the yellow woman had taken our orders, Hugo said to her, "Mrs. Jones, I want you to meet my sister and her husband, who's a writer."

I half stood to shake her hand but the woman tittered, flushing embarrassedly, and fled back into the kitchen. I sat down, feeling like an idiot. The black woman looked at Hugo and said, unsmiling, "Aw, Chief, you're always kidding." Hugo looked at her, bewildered. "Kidding?" he repeated stupidly. At that moment Mr. Jones returned with our tall cool drinks and served them with a flourish. The black woman said: "Chief introduced Florella to his sister as your wife." Mr. Jones looked at her, then back at the earnest face of Hugo. "Aw, Chief's just kidding." At first Hugo looked perplexed, but their insistence that he was just kidding seemed to anger him. He slid to the end of the seat and stood up, looking from the dark woman to Mr. Jones. "I wasn't kidding," he said gruffly. Mr. Jones looked as though he didn't know what to say. "I always thought she was your wife," Hugo persisted. At that moment the yellow woman came in from the kitchen with a plate in each hand. Jean tugged at Hugo's coat-tail and whispered tensely: "For God's sake, shut up and sit down." Hugo looked about stubbornly, a slow flush showing beneath his ruddy brown skin. "But I thought she was his wife," he insisted. The yellow woman turned quickly around and took her plates back into the kitchen. Mr. Jones went hurriedly back into the bar. Hugo was left standing in the middle of the floor, looking like an overgrown idiot. The black woman had stopped slicing bread and she stood perfectly still, the long thin knife in her hand, and asked quietly, "What made you think she was his wife?"

"Oh, Hugo!" Jean cried involuntarily. I thought at first she was going to say: "Don't answer that question!"

Hugo was a serious man and he didn't want them to think he was kidding when he wasn't kidding. But one look at the woman was enough to tell him she had reached the wrong conclusion and he didn't want that to happen. "It wasn't nothing," he said. "It was just one night I was passing on patrol and I saw a light in here so I looked through the glass door and ever since I been thinking she was Mr. Jones's wife."

The black woman said, "I'm Mrs. Jones."

Hugo could tell by her expression and the tone of her voice that he had put his foot in it.

"It wasn't nothing," he hastened to add. "It was just—" (Afterward Jean confessed she had the same thought as me, that Hugo was going to say: "It was just they were making love.") But instead, the red now glowing brightly through the brown of his skin: "It was just they were checking the money in the till."

Jean sighed with relief. The black woman didn't smile but her face muscles relaxed and her body became less rigid and she resumed slicing bread.

"That's Chief all over," she said to Jean. "Always kidding."

Of course we were introduced to Mrs. Jones formally and eventually the yellow woman tiptoed in furtively with our food, but we never did see Mr. Jones again. When we left, he was nowhere to be found.

On the way back I let Hugo drive. He had been used to driving the high-seated Navy command cars and he set my teeth on edge driving my Mercury. We stopped in Reno and bought four ten-gallon cans of paint, two of flat base, one of white lead for the big house, and one of green lead for our house; and for the next week all three of us painted steadily. We jacked up one corner of the big house and built a pier to make it level. It took the paint fairly well and glistened whitely in the sun. The old unpainted clapboards on our shack were so dry that the paint was soaked up as if by blotters, and the house turned out a sort of weathered-looking greenish brown; but it discouraged the lizards that lived in the walls, and probably the snakes too. At least the paint would help preserve his houses, we thought, pleased with ourselves for our good deed.

Unfortunately, less than a month after we had left we received a letter from Hugo saying it had burned to the ground.

On one of his periodic visits there during the war Hugo had met some people who worked at some type of highly guarded government plant about twenty miles away, across the Nevada line. It was to this plant that Joe Mello had moved when he left the farm. It was a small emergency village of prefabricated gray houses and a government store for the families of the workers, enclosed by a high wire fence which was guarded night and day. It might have been a power station, but it looked exactly like the pictures of concentration camps in Nazi Germany.

When the deer season opened in California I got a license to kill one deer with more than nine points. I drove Hugo over to that plant to pick up his friend, a young man with bright tan skin like polished shoe leather and large dumb eyes of the exact same color. He impressed me as being a Mongoloid, and I wondered how Hugo had ever come to know him. It seemed that Hugo had once promised to take him deer hunting, so we brought him back to the house for supper and then sat up and drank whiskey until eleven o'clock at night, at which time we set out to climb the dangerous rocky mountain in back of Hugo's ranch. We climbed all through the black dark night—the moon had already set when we started out and there was not a star in sight. Perhaps it was for the best. When I later saw the trail that we had climbed, I would have never ventured it in the daylight. Hugo was sick several times, vomiting over chasms he couldn't see, and several times his friend (who now reminds me of Carson McCullers' *Reflections in a Golden Eye*) lay down on a narrow ledge and said he couldn't go any farther. I was in the best physical condition and I kept on, forcing them to continue or become separated, chiefly because I couldn't tell at any time where we were. We were surprised to discover ourselves on the peak when the sun rose next morning. It was very cold, but the whole valley between the California and Nevada Sierras stretched out before us; we could see both the town of Susanville and the plant in the desert quite well. It was a wild and desolate landscape, but very beautiful. We lay there for a short time to get our breath, huddled together to keep warm; then we got up and looked around more leisurely for any sign of deer. We knew the mule deer abounded in the mountains, because I had seen their spoors everywhere and on several occasions I had seen them grazing in the deer bush quite near to the house.

In about fifteen minutes we saw a herd emerge from the shadows of a gully: a fine old buck with a magnificent spread of antlers, followed by three or four younger bucks, then a dozen or more does with their fawns. They paused, all standing rigid and motionless, sniffing the air and looking about. We were about a hundred yards above them and about three hundred yards distant. It was my gun and my license so I took the first shot. I aimed low and a little ahead of the second buck, although they were still motionless, and squeezed the trigger. I don't know whether it was considered a difficult or easy chance, or whether I aimed correctly—none of us had ever been deer hunting before —but I hit the buck and his hindquarters collapsed while he tried to leap with his front feet. All the other deer leaped into simultaneous motion, with the old stag leading. They seemed to be flying. I handed the rifle to Hugo's Mongoloid friend, but before he had jacked a cartridge into the chamber and had taken aim, the herd had headed into another gully and had disappeared. The deer I had shot was still trying to pull himself forward with his front legs.

We scrambled down the mountain like maniacs and discovered the bullet had hit the deer in the spine. I couldn't bear to see his eyes. I quickly shot him through the head. We counted his points; he had eleven. We were jubilant. We had killed a deer at our first try. But we didn't know a damn thing about the sport, if you call it a sport. Personally I felt more like a murderer.

Hugo said we should tie its feet together and suspend it over a pole and take turns in carrying it down the mountain. Our first problem was in finding a suitable pole. For all the poles I had seen lying about on my various walks, there was none nearby when it was needed. Hugo was the only one who had a knife:

it was a Boy Scout knife. While searching for it, he thought to look at his watch; the time was six thirty-seven. By seven o'clock he had cut down a pine sapling and stripped it. We tied the deer's hooves together and inserted the sapling between them. Hugo and I picked up the carcass and started to descend the steep slope. I had the lead. As I was picking my path down the slope, the deer slipped forward on the sapling and hit me in the back, knocking me down. I was panic-stricken for at first I thought it was an old stag that had slipped up behind me and was goring me. I turned loose the sapling, intending to roll free, but the carcass slipped off the end of the sapling and landed on top of me and we went rolling down the slope, one on top of the other at every turn. I was lying at the bottom of the slope, bruised all over and badly shaken, when Hugo and his idiot friend came scrambling down to my aid. The first thing Hugo said was, "We ought to bleed the deer." So he cut its throat and he and his friend held it up by the hind legs and let it bleed.

That was the beginning. All day long we carried the carcass down the mountainside; occasionally it slipped, and whoever was in front went rolling over and over with the carcass. Sometimes, when we had to ascend a slope to cross a ravine, it was the one behind. Finally we gave up on the pole and took the bloody carcass by the horns, one on each side, and dragged it down the slopes. The fur on its back wore off from being dragged across the rocky ground, and then the skin, and finally the flesh along the back part of the spine was becoming black and raw and was wearing away. It was pitch-dark when we dragged the frayed, scarred, bloody carcass into Janesville. We went there because after night had fallen we had lost our way and the lights of Janesville were the only lights we saw.

When we went to the garage to rent a car, a group of neighboring farmers came from the general store to look at our kill.

One of them said, "You should have gutted it when you first killed it. Now the meat's no good."

And on learning where and when we had shot it, another

said, "When you kill a deer in the mountains, you always have to know how you're going to get it out."

They tell me now, I thought bitterly.

We hired a truck and took our deer carcass home and the senile old Texan from next door hobbled over with Fertile Myrtle and their little girl, who so resembled Sparkle Plenty in the Dick Tracy comic strip—evidently Jean had told them we had gone deer hunting—to inspect our kill. He advised us to clean it and quarter it as soon as possible and coat the quarters heavily with a mixture of flour and salt and black pepper and hang them in the trees outside with a collar around the ropes so the rats couldn't get to them. We cleaned it and gave Jean the heart and liver to cook for supper, then quartered it and did as we were told; and wearily we sat down to eat. I didn't care so much for the heart—Hugo's friend relished it—but I enjoyed the liver. As tired and hungry as I was, I probably would have enjoyed anything.

Then wearily, I drove the young man back to his concentration camp in the Nevada desert. When we got back it was midnight.

When I got out to look at the hanging quarters next day at noon, they were covered with green flies, mosquitoes, and moths, and huge field rats were climbing down the ropes as far as the tin collars and trying to jump off onto the meat. I fetched my rifle and shot at one rat, which had caught hold of a front quarter, but all I succeeded in doing was to shoot a hole in the meat. There was also a definite smell. We decided that the meat was unfit to eat, so we took one quarter over to the old Texan and Fertile Myrtle, not without passing on our opinion. They said they would eat it. I wished them well. In fact, next day they said it was the best venison they'd ever eaten.

Then I put another quarter in the car and Hugo and I took it to our young friend who had gone hunting with us, saying it was the least we could do. I'm not sure he agreed with that.

The remainder we threw away. Actually, we burned it where we usually burned the snakes. It smelled better: in fact it smelled damn good. But we didn't regret it.

And then Hugo took the car out to see a neighboring farmer about getting a tenant for the next year. I cautioned him about the roads, but he maintained he was accustomed to them, and there is nothing you can say to someone who knows more about the subject than yourself. However, I should say here that the country roads leading off from the highway were mostly made by the natural sand and gravel that had been shaped and leveled by bulldozers. Whenever it rained, the water drained from the middle of the road to the edges in little rivulets which, when dried, left the surfaces of the road rutted like a washboard. A car traveling on these roads was subject to drift at any speed as if it were on slick ice, and driving slowly will not help unless one drives under five miles an hour. I found the best speed to be between twenty-five and thirty miles an hour, and trusted to luck.

I imagine Hugo was driving very slowly and very carefully; however, the car drifted slowly off the road and came to rest in a patch of the tiny boulders. The damage was done when he tried to get the car back onto the road. There was a boulder protruding between the cylinder block and the radiator, its point striking up exactly between two fan blades. When Hugo tried to back the car out, he must have heard the tearing sound of the fan blades on the rock and the subsequent sound of the bent and twisted fan blades tearing the radiator to bits, but evidently he believed that the powerful engine would overcome any obstacle and he had only to give it more gas. The fan and radiator were destroyed.

We went to see the Ford dealer in Susanville. But it was 1946. The American motor industry had not made any cars or parts since the beginning of the war, and the parts we needed were unavailable in California. Perhaps if we had the time to wait they might have been shipped from the factory at Dearborn in two or three months.

It was dark when we returned. Jean was not at home. We called her and then searched the house and outhouse and all about for fear she was snakebitten and helpless. But she was nowhere to be seen. We were not alarmed—after all, nothing could happen to her. We inquired whether they had seen her next door and then whether they had seen anyone call at the house, a car or someone on horseback, as there had been occasions in the past when horsemen roamed the hills. But they had seen no one. Then we became alarmed; we remembered the rumors about the Klan, we thought of the isolation. Anyone could have driven up from the highway and departed unseen.

I fetched my rifle and we searched the nearby hills, calling her name, then all the area about the house, both of us with torches. Then we crossed the street and searched the barns and dilapidated farm buildings. It was approaching midnight and we had found no sign of her. Now thoroughly alarmed, we set out for Janesville to try to enlist the postmistress's family to help us organize a posse.

About three miles down the highway we found her stumbling aimlessly along, sobbing to herself. We thought at first she had been attacked. My first emotion was a violent rage: if I discovered who attacked her, I would blow off his head, I wouldn't give a damn who it was.

But she threw herself into her brother's arms and denied that anyone had approached her, but begged him to take her away. We were both flabbergasted. She said she didn't want to live with me. Finally Hugo persuaded her to return to the house, chiefly perhaps by explaining that he couldn't take her away that night if he wanted to because the next bus to Reno wouldn't pass until nine-thirty the next morning and we didn't have any other means of transportation.

We eventually discovered the reason for her sudden animosity. She had been reading some of my manuscript, which I had advised her not to do. The black wife of the black protagonist in my book *Lonely Crusade* is named Ruth; and I think the relation between her and Lee (the protagonist) is one of the most beautiful love stories in American fiction; but both characters have pronounced race and color complexes. I did not intend to portray myself or anyone I knew. But Jean thought that I had patterned the character Ruth after herself, and she was chagrined and hurt to learn I had had this opinion of her after all the years of our marriage. I think it was chiefly the complex about color which I ascribed to Ruth. Jean was a very beautiful woman and she knew it and she was hurt to think I thought she had any kind of inferiority complex because of her color. As a point of fact I didn't. I had known many white women who were envious of Jean's color and figure; but then Lee Gordon had nothing in common with me, either. After all, I had been to prison; I didn't believe in the sublimity of people, black or white, any more than I believed in their depravity; I believed that people were capable of anything. But for the purpose of my story I had to give this couple a belief in the integrity of whites, and at the same time certain fears and complexes resulting from their race. Jean hated it.

Hugo dismissed it with a laugh, which I don't think she considered very brotherly. But I spent many hours then and for years afterward trying to convince her I had never thought of her as Ruth. But I'm afraid she never really believed me; and I often wondered if I had drawn a true picture of which I was not consciously aware.

We couldn't live on the ranch without a car. We sold it where it stood by the side of the road, and took the bus to Reno and the train to New York City.

We were reconciled and happily excited when we arrived in New York a few days later.

I remember that summer as one of the most pleasant of our life. Despite the rattlesnakes and other minor nuisances, it had been a calm and creative period, and we had enjoyed making love in complete isolation, at any hour of day or night, to the constant sound of the wind in the leaves of the huge overhanging oak. We had been completely dependent on one another, which was good, and I had assumed the position of the breadwinner, something we both recognized and accepted as just and right.

I finished the book during the winter of 1946 at Wading River, Long Island, in a tiny flat over a one-car clapboard garage on an estate owned by a New York doctor. The place had a history. It had long been owned by two elderly women, sisters I believe, who had employed it as a home for orphaned children.

It consisted of four or five rather picturesque cottages, all with names, and the big white house where the Saffords lived during the summer, on nine acres of land. Dr. Safford's wife had a sister who worked in some government office which had to do with auctioning property for back taxes; and when this property appeared on the lists to be auctioned she informed her married sister and Dr. Safford got it for a pittance. He had converted it into a summer colony, and during the summers it was occupied chiefly by writers who contributed to *The New Yorker* magazine. But the winter we stayed there the property was deserted save for the deaf caretaker, who, in addition to being deaf, was drunk most of the time.

Our flat consisted of four tiny rooms, but we lived almost entirely in the one large front room heated by a Franklin stove, except when Jean was using the kitchen. For company we had Dr. Safford's pregnant English setter bitch, Susie, who used to spend her nights and most of her days asleep before the open Franklin stove, her big belly fat with puppies whose birth seemed imminent, sleeping so soundly that she didn't stir even when sparks would fly from the dry red cedar wood I gathered and burn holes into her fur. We had promised Dr. Safford we would feed Susie and let him know when she dropped her litter. We seldom saw the caretaker, or anyone else. The property was on a hill adjoining the woods, off the beaten path, and no one came that way who didn't have business there. The rich and exclusive town of Wading River was northwest of us, toward the Sound.

I was getting to like isolation. One might think I'd have had enough for a lifetime, but prison is not isolated; in fact, the worst part about prison is the large number of prisoners always about you.

Susie delighted me. She was such a bitch. We would feed her an immense bowl of cornmeal gruel cooked in the consommé of boiled beef bones, which she would gobble up, bones and all, before leaving the house each morning. But later we learned that many residents of Wading River thought it was a disgrace the way we starved Dr. Safford's dog, because each morning when Susie left the house she made the rounds of the houses in the village, eating all she could beg. If the sun was shining when she returned, she would lie outside on the snow in the sunshine and sleep until it was time to come in and eat her afternoon meal and lie before the open fire.

I did good work—in fact too damn good, as I was later to learn.

The Saffords brought their family down and occupied the big house during the Christmas holidays. He had two children by a former marriage: a daughter who was a jazz buff, and caused her father a good deal of concern by sitting about small nightclubs until the early hours of the morning, mesmerized by black jazz musicians; and a big-framed, silent teenage son with corn-colored hair who spent most of his holiday chopping logs for their big fireplace. And from his second marriage he had a precocious girl-child of about four when we were there, who used to dance at her mother's instigation when they were entertaining grownups and would brook no distraction when she was performing her ballet. Once she banged me in the face with a sofa pillow for not paying attention. I left the house. I was not accustomed to children hitting me in the face. Her mother came over to see if I was angry. I wasn't angry, I explained to her, I was simply bored.

One weekend, Ralph Ellison and his wife Fanny came out to visit us. I borrowed a shotgun from our neighbor down the hill and Ralph and I went looking for cottontails. We didn't find any rabbits, but Ralph bagged a big male squirrel, and we all had to admire the size of its testicles before it was prepared for the pot. It was a special treat for me to have Ralph visit. I had met him when I first came to New York and lived in my cousin's apartment on St. Nicholas Avenue, and I had invited him and Fanny to a party I threw once when Henry and Molly were out of town. We had always got on well together, and I liked Fanny.

But mostly we were alone. We had an old car at our disposal, which we drove into the village sometimes when we went shopping or to the post office and occasionally when we went to Riverhead. But mostly we walked. We took long walks through the woods, gathering dead branches that had fallen from the red cedars that abounded in the woods. There was a cauliflower plot on the other side of the woods from which most of the edible cauliflowers had been picked. By January, when the sun shone, it smelled to high heaven. And farther on there was a section of the long pile of Long Island potatoes, reaching almost from one end of the island to the other, which had been sprayed with kerosene to render them unfit for human consumption as part of the federal price control program. In that year, 1947, with all the starving people in the world, we wondered why these millions of tons of potatoes couldn't be shipped abroad. But I read that the cost of shipping would be prohibitive. Just like America, I thought; lots of money for the war-ravaged governments of the world but nothing for the hungry people to eat.

Strangely enough, the white residents of Wading River were the least curious I had ever seen. I supposed they were too well-heeled and secure to worry about a black couple in the neighborhood. They were neither friendly nor unfriendly; they didn't see us and we did nothing to make ourselves conspicuous.

The last thing of any importance which happened before we left, besides finishing the last draft of *Lonely Crusade*, which I was to learn most critics didn't consider important at all, was Susie dropping her litter. We had been asked to watch for the event and telephone Dr. Safford in New York. But when the time came she disappeared. We searched high and low for two days, then telephoned our alarm to Dr. Safford. He advised us to look thoroughly underneath all the accessible cottages, especially those which had chimneys built up from the ground. And that was where I found her on the morning of the third day. She had crawled underneath one of the deserted cottages to the base of a cold brick chimney and had dug a hole to drop her litter. I had to crawl on hands and knees and then on my belly to reach her, and at my approach she bared her fangs as though to bite me, but she didn't have the strength to rise. I took her in my arms and crawled back into the daylight, and in just three days she had become nothing but bones; the back of her spine, the weakest point of all setters, had given away and she couldn't stand. We roused the deaf caretaker and had him open the basement to the big house so we could lay her by the furnace. I crawled back to the pit and brought out her litter, little blind animals that looked like the drowned bodies of white rats, one at a time. There were eleven of them but two were dead. We took the live ones to their mother in the furnace room of the big house, then telephoned Dr. Safford at Columbia University, where he lectured in neurology, and asked for instructions. He asked us to keep them warm and he would come as soon as possible.

Within three hours his car pulled up and his son began unloading cartons while he rushed to the basement and gave Susie and all her litter hypodermic injections. We left them to take charge; we were preparing to return to New York as soon as we found a temporary dwelling.

But a week passed before we could leave. A pen had been built for the dog and the puppies were strong and healthy, thriving on the diet of pap and condensed milk Dr. Safford had brought from New York. All nine had lived, and eight of them had the broad faces and definite markings of Dalmatians. In fact, the local vet had been willing to bet no one could tell them from pureblooded Dalmatians—and one, a female, much smaller and more delicate, had the definite markings of an English setter.

"That ought to tell us something," I said to Dr. Safford.

"Yes, it tells us they are dogs," he said.

We stayed temporarily at the Theresa Hotel in Harlem and Jean got a job as recreational director for Girls Camp, on Welfare Island, a part of the Youth House program where the delinquent girls were detained before trial in Youth Court, and afterward if they were committed for psychiatric therapy. Later we took a rented room somewhere in Harlem.

Blanche Knopf liked my book, but she suggested that I clear it with one of the editors to make certain it contained no libel. They were worried that my character Foster, the president of the aircraft company being organized by the union in my story, bore a resemblance to a National Steel vice-president who had resigned his job to become vice-president of a West Coast aircraft company during the war. But in fact I had patterned Foster after Louis Bromfield, who had no connection with any West Coast aircraft company. But the editor gave no thought to the Communist Party characters in my book whom I had patterned rather closely after real-life Communist Party members whom I had actually met when I first went to Los Angeles. However, I obtained a picture and a profile of the industrialist in question from the library of *Time* magazine, putting their fears to rest, and the book went to press.

Lurton Blassingame was my literary agent at the time and, taking advantage of Mrs. Knopf's enchantment with my book, he got me a contract and a two-thousand-dollar advance for my next book, which was to be drawn from my Hollywood experiences during the war and entitled *Immortal Mammy*. (It's probably just as well I never wrote that book, for my soul brothers hated *Lonely Crusade* enough as it was.) I settled down to await publication of *Lonely Crusade*, for which I had the highest hopes, and make notes for *Immortal Mammy*.

At last the day of publication arrived: October 8, 1947—I will never forget it. Jean's immediate supervisor, Alice Overton, had gone on a thirty-day vacation at the beginning of October and had given Jean the use of her flat on Welfare Island, a short distance from Girls Camp. It was a charming apartment with black furnishings on uneven red linoleum floors, in an old building at the northern tip of the island, and the north windows looked out on the garden surrounding the lighthouse. It extended the width of the building, and from the western windows we could see the shoreline of Manhattan and the tall, luxurious apartment buildings on Sutton Place, and from the eastern windows the refineries and wharves of Astoria, Long Island. My father had come from Cleveland and was staying with us to celebrate the great event, and I was scheduled to appear on the Mary Margaret McBride radio program, and on a CBS program for books, and on the day of publication I was to speak to Macy's booksellers; from there I was to go to speak to Bloomingdale's book department.

I got up early that morning to catch a Seventy-ninth Street Ferry, which would take me to Manhattan in time to get to Macy's at eight-thirty, the time for my appearance. I had left Jean and my father on the island and I was to return in time to take them to the studio for the Mary Margaret McBride program.

When I arrived at the Macy's employee's entrance on Thirty-fifth Street, the manager of the bookstore was standing in the door waiting for me. He said a number of the clerks hadn't arrived and we could have coffee in a nearby luncheonette while waiting for them. I'd had coffee but I thought perhaps he wanted coffee, but it turned out that he wanted to tell me they had reconsidered the idea of my talking to the booksellers and some of them thought it would be too much like showing favoritism. In the past it had provoked the anger of authors who'd been excluded, and they had finally decided to stop the practice. He was very sorry that it appeared as though I had been singled out, but it applied to all authors, and he was particularly sorry the decision had been reached at this time because he liked my book, and felt that I would have something important to say.

I had heard the exact phrases uttered by various editors so many times before that I understood. They had canceled my appearance. I shook hands warmly to show him there were no hard feelings—although if he believed that, he was an idiot—and hastened over to Bloomingdale's, on Fifty-ninth Street.

Bloomingdale's was open and I entered from the front, but I didn't get past the first bookseller. She said she hadn't heard of me and hadn't heard of my book, which was not on display, but she would ask the manager. One look at her face on her return told me the answer.

I couldn't imagine what was happening. I telephoned Jean to tell her to bring my father and meet me at the studio as I wouldn't have time to make the trip and return, and she said she had been trying to reach me at Macy's and Bloomingdale's to tell me

not to go to the studio; they had called and said my interview
had been canceled.

Dejectedly I went home. That was when my father made his
memorable statement: "Remember, son, New York is not the only
city that has skyscrapers. We have one on the new Union Station
in Cleveland."

That set the pattern. Everyone hated the book. The communist
review *The New Masses*, hit the stands with a vitriolic three-page
attack by a black communist, headed by a silhouette of a black
man carrying a white flag above a streamer saying "Himes Carries
the White Flag." The *Daily Worker* and the *People's Voice*
launched attacks, *Ebony* magazine ran an editorial entitled "It
Is Time to Count Your Blessings," in which it said: "The character Lee Gordon is psychotic, as is the author, Chester Himes."
The *Atlantic Monthly* said: "Hate runs through this book like a
streak of yellow bile." *Commentary*, a Jewish journal, ran a long
diatribe by a professor at Brooklyn College in which my book was
compared to the "graffito on the walls of public toilets." James
Baldwin wrote a review from the socialist newspaper the *New
Leader*, headlined "History As a Nightmare." After having promised Blanche Knopf in my hearing at a reception at Van Vechten's
that he would write a good review for the Marshall Field newspaper, the Chicago *Times*, Willard Motley wrote a vicious personal attack charging me personally with statements taken from
the dialogues of my characters . . . and so it went. Carl Van
Vechten said he thought it was a great book, but all the soul
brothers to whom he had talked had condemned it. Lurton Blassingame told me he had heard of attacks the Communist Party
had launched against bookstores that sold the book, by buying
copies, damaging them, and taking them back to the stores and
demanding their money back on the ground the book was trash.
I remember reading a review in some journal whose name I
have forgotten which complained about the expensive format and
the quality of paper on which the book was printed.

The left hated it, the right hated it, Jews hated it, blacks hated
it. I will say that Richard Wright wrote a laudatory preface for the

French translation, published by Editions Corrêa in 1952, but when it was published in the United States he had nothing to say, even though he had written the joint review for my first novel, *If He Hollers Let Him Go*, and Arthur Miller's book *Focus*, for *P.M.*

I had attempted to be completely fair. I had written what I thought was a story of the fear that inhabits the minds of all blacks who live in America, and the various impacts on this fear precipitated by communism, industrialism, unionism, the war, white women, and marriage within the race. It was not too big a scope; this was our daily life during the war. I did not record a single event that I hadn't known to happen; the characters were people who either had lived or could have lived; the situations were commonplace. The writing might well have been bad, but the writing was not criticized in one review which I read. What *Commentary*'s critic most disliked was the characterization of Abie, whom he called "a Christ-like Jew." The soul brothers disliked most the argument put forth by Lee Gordon that the Negro did not want equality, he wanted special consideration, and that it was logical that he should want it and necessary that he should have it.

I think that many of the critics on the big weekly reviews disliked most the characterization of the industrialist Foster, who in my book called President Roosevelt "a cripple bastard, with a cripple bastard's sense of spite." I had heard these words spoken in a Cleveland, Ohio, country club. Maybe the critics had heard them too—maybe that was what they most disliked, my audacity in repeating them. I thought it was obvious that I was not trying to be audacious, but what is obvious to me is not always obvious to others. I think that what the great body of Americans most disliked was the fact I came too close to the truth. Reactionaries hate the truth and the world's rulers fear it; but it embarrasses the liberals, perhaps because they can't do anything about it.

Of all the hurts which I had suffered before—my brother's accident, my own accident, being kicked out of college, my parents' divorce, my term in prison, and my racial hell on the West Coast—and which I have suffered since, the rejection of *Lonely Crusade* hurt me most. Because I had gone out on that limb, and I had been in prison for seven and a half years and should have known better. I had tried to be fair. It is the one single thing no one will forgive you for, neither the communists nor the fascists, the rightists nor the leftists, the white racists nor the black racists. Maybe it is impossible, anyway, as many believe. Certainly it is not very diplomatic. One will make more enemies by trying to be fair (marked by impartiality and honesty) than by trying to tell the truth—no one believes it possible to tell the truth anyway—but it is just possible that you might be fair.

I went to Blanche Knopf and asked her to support the book, to put all of the most vicious criticisms from opposing groups into one advertisement. But she thought it best to let it alone. She said every writer must expect a certain amount of adverse criticism. Perhaps she was thinking only of my own good. But just then I needed support badly.

3.

It was then that I decided to leave the United States forever if I got the chance. I could not be a communist because I am not a joiner. I could not be a reactionary, even if I had wanted to, because they wouldn't have me. The whites rejected me, the blacks didn't want me. I felt like a man without a country, which in fact I was.

For the next five years I couldn't write. I reworked my prison novel, *Black Sheep*, cutting it down to half its original size, and I tried to write a stage play from *If He Hollers Let Him Go*, but these were just reflex motions. Jean got a job as recreational director for the Federal Housing Projects for New York City, which necessitated her visiting all the various boroughs, and I worked at anything I could get—dishwasher, janitor's helper, snow shoveler, and similar jobs now forgotton. We lived in a rented room in the Bronx and did not see very much of each other. Jean wanted me to stay home and write. If I had been able to write I might have welcomed the opportunity, but I couldn't sit down at her expense and do nothing.

I was invited to Yaddo, the writers' colony in Saratoga Springs, for May and June of 1948. I had a room in the West House, across the hall from the girl, Patricia Highsmith, who was then writing her book *Strangers on a Train*, from which Hitchcock has made a movie classic. I was turning over an idea for a story about a halfwit preacher serving a term in prison, who becomes a stool pigeon and causes the death of several fellow inmates; and to get myself into a creative mood I was reading an English translation of Rimbaud's *A Season in Hell* and Faulkner's *Light in August* and Joyce's *Finnegans Wake*. But just as I began actually writing—I had written fifty-odd pages—I was invited to read a paper on "The Dilemma of the Negro Writer" at the University of Chicago under the auspices of the Chicago South Side Community Center and a university class in creative writing. I didn't know the woman who conducted this class, but I was happy to oblige my old friend Horace Cayton, the director of the South Side Community Center, who was co-sponsor. I went to Chicago and stood before a predominantly white audience in Mandel Hall, with an ice-cold clarity derived from two Benzedrine tablets and a half bottle of champagne, and told in explicit terms what I considered the dilemma of the Negro writer. My speech was followed by a dead silence. That time I didn't try to be fair. I sought to tell the truth. The reception was the same. But I didn't give a damn.

I stayed in Chicago for the following week and tried to submerge my revulsion in drunkenness and sex. But the old hurt had been reopened. I returned to Yaddo, and until the period of my visit expired, I was drunk every day.

At that time I was the only black at Yaddo. I don't really know if this had anything to do with what happened to me there. Perhaps I was sick when I went there and Yaddo just brought it out. I don't know. But I do know I was sick when I left. I think Jean felt truly sorry for me then; she used to go about with me to the crummy bars and dives and take me home when I became too drunk to walk. But that was all she could do; that and support me. I suppose that was all anyone could have done.

It was Jean's losing her job that saved our marriage and myself. Her job was simply abolished. The support of the family reverted to me, and I had to take my position as the man and the husband.

The first job I took was as caretaker for a summer resort in New Jersey owned by a Hoboken real estate promoter named Frank Bucino. Mrs. Bucino, a voluptuous blonde from the South who had been a hairdresser before her marriage, told us that her husband was Frank Sinatra's godfather. He was a small dark Italian with a bad eye, always accompanied by a tall, blond Swede who looked almost exactly like a fictional bodyguard and killer called Sure in one of my *Esquire* short stories, *Strictly Business*. Mrs. Bucino's chauffeur, who drove her out to the resort occasionally in her Town and Country Chrysler, was a good-looking muscular young Italian of middleweight size who, but for the lack of facial scars, looked as though he might have been a prizefighter. Once I saw him leap over the bar in the big barnlike dance hall and flatten a big loudmouthed yokel with one blow.

Mr. Bucino had bought the place several years before at a public government auction. At the beginning of the war it had served as a training camp and parade ground for the German-American Bund, and I had seen newsreels of it with the American Nazis marching. It contained the original dwellings and public buildings used by the Bund. There were incredibly neatly constructed one-room cottages and aluminum trailers scattered throughout the woods, which bordered on a large lake. On the opposite shore was a YWCA summer camp. Frank and his Swedish bodyguard had supervised the construction of a small beach on their end of the lake which had been marsh, by the simple expedient of placing layers of old railroad crossties, purchased for a song, over the marsh until it became solid enough to hold the yellow sand. Once a truck had slipped over the edge and sunk out of sight, and it took all the firefighting equipment in the area to haul it out.

At front, facing the road, was the old wooden building that had contained the original tavern there before the bund. It was flanked on one side by the driveway, which led to the public buildings and far beyond to the settlement in the woods, and on the other by the well-kept parade ground where the Nazis had marched.

Mr. Bucino had converted it into a summer resort for Italian-Americans. We lived upstairs in three rooms over the kitchen and bar in the old tavern, and for company we had a little cunning black-and-white mongrel we called Uncle Tom and a liver-spotted English springer spaniel named Brownie who went with the house although no one knew who his rightful owner was, and a beautiful Irish setter bitch with manicured toenails that Frank's Swedish bodyguard brought out one day and asked us to keep. We saw an advertisement in the personal column of the Sunday New York *Times* the following week, offering a reward for the return of or information concerning a two-and-a-half-year-old Irish setter bitch with a tiny white heart on her chest. That was the dog the Swede said he had found all right, but we figured we'd let well enough alone.

We stayed there all winter, until our job expired when the crew came out in the spring, and had a lovely time. Frank gave us a hundred and fifty dollars a month and all expenses except food. We had a coal-burning hot-air system, which I had to keep going; Jean cooked on the big kitchen range, and we ate at the big kitchen table, surrounded by our hungry dogs. For emergency transportation, we had the chassis of an ancient Mack firetruck with cabin, which we used to drive all about the countryside as though it were a modern Jaguar sports car.

There was a small lake in front of the property, Lake Islip, I believe, with a restaurant and roadhouse on the other side, which Jean and I never visited, but our little dog Uncle Tom was a great favorite with the hard-drinking weekend customers. And also in the woods bordering this lake there was a large natural spring with a large bed filled with watercress, which we gathered in quantity for salads.

At the end of November it turned cold and snowed heavily. We loved walking in snow-whitened woods with the dogs running madly ahead—at least the gun dogs. Uncle Tom stayed closely to heel. Brownie was a good dog, a good watchdog and a brave dog, and when the big dogs of the neighborhood gathered in the parade grounds, he was always the diplomat and the peacemaker. We used to watch him from the window, getting between two big dogs twice his size to keep them from fighting. The Irish setter bitch was a troublemaker, and we kept her indoors most of the time. We had built warm doghouses for both Brownie and Uncle Tom outside, and Brownie used to protect Uncle Tom from the other mongrels when he was at home. But he was away a great deal of the time; and the farmers complained that he was raiding their henhouses. Whenever Uncle Tom got mad with us he'd go out to his house and draw the curtain and sulk. During the winter, when the lake was frozen over, he used to slip across the ice to the kitchen of the roadhouse to beg, although we punished him when we caught him; and once, during a quick thaw, he broke through the rotten ice in the middle of the lake. He couldn't swim, and a group of villagers had watched his desperate effort to climb back atop the rotten ice and we were sent for. I grabbed up an extension ladder and roared down to the lake in the old Mack truck, but the puppy couldn't get onto the end of the ladder; a brave village youth crawled out on the ladder and dragged him from the water. We rushed him back to the house and wrapped him in warm blankets and spoon-fed him brandy eggnog. Two days later he was fawning on the white people and disagreeable toward us as ever.

We had a fine time that winter. Horace Cayton and his wife Ruby drove out to visit us. I discovered how to get into the coin box in the bar's jukebox, and we played the coins over and over and drank the strange drinks left over in the bar, potato whiskey among them, and ate all the prefabricated fruit-cakes in the deep freezer. Eleanor Bucino came out and gossiped with Jean and playfully aimed her big white titties at me as Southern white women will. I wrote the three-act stage adaptation of *If He Hollers Let Him Go*, and we didn't miss the world. We loved our isolation, but it came to an end.

That summer I worked for the first time in a Jewish summer resort in Sullivan County. It was like the Bronx set down in hot rural terrain, although there are some fabulous hotels in the area with some of the biggest names in show business entertaining there during the season. But as the bus driver who brought a load of us back to the Bronx at the end of the season said, "Bronx is Bronx."

We had taken a furnished room in the Bronx and I left Jean there doing part-time social-welfare work while I went up to the hotel to work as a bellhop. There was no time on that job to play at writing; we got up early and went to bed late. When I wasn't busy at bellhopping, which included cleaning the lobby, relieving at the switchboard, helping wash dishes in an emergency, and serving tea every afternoon, I helped the chambermaids clean the so-called cabanas scattered about, and swept the horse manure dropped by the hotel's team from the drives, which I would wrap up for any guests going home that day, or I would help Joe, the other black bellhop, vacuum-clean the swimming pool, repair the chains securing the terrace chairs, mop the dance floor of the casino. I made money by renting chairs and tables, which were supposedly free, to the guests to gamble at bridge and poker.

During the big week of July 4, seven of the staff, including me, had severe attacks of ptomaine poisoning, and were sick for three days. It was a strictly kosher hotel; we had meat days and dairy days with separate dishes. The staff ate at a big table in the kitchen in two shifts while the proprietor, a short, square, rugged-looking walleyed man with short-cropped stiff gray hair, stood over us to see that we observed the rules, or perhaps that we got enough to eat. I learned later that he was a good man, and always fair. Perhaps that's why he had merely eked a living from his hotel in twenty years.

I was there strictly for the most money I could earn, but he liked me for that and asked me to come back the next season. It had been a severe grind, what with having ptomaine poisoning

and not even having time to read, much less write, and I had
no intention of ever returning there.

However, I was becoming adapted to the manners and customs
of New York Jews and it seemed natural that that winter
found me working again for Jews, this time as caretaker for the
Copake Country Club on Lake Copake, owned jointly, I understood, by two brothers from Jersey City, Sam and Sidney
Zazuly.

Copake, as we called it, was the most luxurious place we had
so far worked. The Zazulys were interested in art and literature
and had seen some of the reviews of *Lonely Crusade*, but
neither had read it. They expected to find me temperamental,
but they preferred that to putting up with someone from the
neighborhood who would let his friends come and help themselves
to Copake property.

The main body of the country club was situated on an island
connected to the mainland by a short bridge, the guest bungalows
built along roads encircling the big main dining room, which rose
on an elevation in the center of the island. There were a
casino and dance hall with a terrace, children's camps and play-
grounds, and a big garage. The club had its own water system.
Across the lake on one side was an eighteen-hole golf course,
Sidney's pride and joy, and the larger guest bungalows; and
across the lake on the other side were the smaller, less elaborate,
less expensive bungalows. We were given a Town and Country
DeSoto for our private use, and rooms in the servants' quarters,
and Jean had to cook for Sam and Sidney and other people
who came out from time to time. I was supposed to make minor
repairs necessitated by the weather, but mostly I was to guard
all of the property both on the island and bordering the lake to
keep the natives from taking away the furnishings or what they
would. But not too much was expected of me other than to
keep the natives at their distance.

In case of any emergencies with the car, the pump, or other
equipment, I could call on the local mechanic, a big easygoing

young man named Ken who had a deputy sheriff's badge and always wore a ring-handled, long-barreled .45-caliber Colt revolver in a low-slung cartridge belt like the last of the gunslingers.

It was very cold that winter: the lake froze over in December and was invaded by the ice fishermen driving their cars onto the ice, drinking and singing at night around bonfires built on the ice. My job was to keep them off the Copake Country Club property and call Ken if the situation got to be more than I could handle. At first I had very little trouble. In January we had one of the worst hurricanes in the history of New York State and we fled to Sam Zazuly's bungalow built low along the lake for protection, and sat it out all the long howling, frightening night with a case of Irish whiskey shipped to me the week before from Macy's, expecting the bungalow to go any minute. That bungalow held, but a number of others were destroyed, and the wind blew down a line of ancient oak trees straight across the island and all the high-voltage power lines in the area. The lines short-circuited on both the island and the shore, and the basement of our bungalow was flooded, cutting off the central heating. We had built such a fire in the chimney that a fire broke out underneath the floor and the fire trucks had to come from Hillsdale, the post office address, roaring over those high-voltage power lines like gangbusters.

We moved off the island into Sidney's house across from the entrance and drove up to Montgomery-Ward and Company in Albany, New York, and picked up some sump pumps to drain the basement of Sam's bungalow. It was during this operation that we discovered a hogshead in the basement filled with a light golden homemade wine that tasted a little like Muscatel but was dry and very strong. It kept us in supply until we left.

When spring came and the summer came back, my job terminated. I bought a fifteen-year-old Plymouth sedan with part of the money I had saved, and we went to Bridgeport, Connecticut, and rented a room in the home of a widow who worked as a domestic. Why Bridgeport? Why not Yonkers? Or New Haven? Afterward, I never really knew. At the time I knew that Bridgeport had a Socialist mayor, and I vaguely remembered driving through it once, and it had seemed such a pleasant town.

Each morning I drove out to Barnum Park and found a quiet spot of shade beside the Sound in which to park. I sat on the back seat with my typewriter on my knees and wrote. The sounds of the lapping of the waves and the cries of the seagulls fishing in the rocky shoals were ineffably soothing, and I was at peace with my work.

Our money ran out about the middle of July, and we decided to go to New York City, where Jean would try to get a job in the Welfare Department. I advertised my car for sale in the classified section of the evening daily "First $100 gets sound bodied Plymouth sedan containing floating-power motor."

The day the advertisement ran, Jean took our last twelve dollars and went to New York City to put in her application. She intended to return that evening, so she left me only a half dollar for cigarettes.

At eleven-thirty that morning I contracted to sell the car to a young black worker at the G.E. factory who was to return with the money shortly after he got off work at four.

At three-thirty I drove down to the corner of Fairfield Boulevard to buy cigarettes. As I started back, when pulling from the curb, my front bumper caught in the fender of a new Buick Roadmaster that was passing on my left, and jerked it off. The Buick was driven by a white lady, dressed immaculately in a mauve-colored tweed suit that looked as though it might have cost more than I had earned from my second book. She must have been a very important person, for despite the fact she had been driving on the wrong side of a one-way street, and that her breath smelled pleasantly of excellent cocktails, she sent for a policeman and had me arrested for reckless driving. Not because she hated blacks or wished to humiliate or harm me in any manner, I learned afterward; simply because her husband, who was the chief staff doctor of the veteran's hospital, was continuously cautioning her to drive carefully, and she intended to prove by the record she had done so.

But I wasn't worried. I hadn't broken any laws. How could they arrest me?

I found out shortly that to arrest me required very little skill, only authority. The policeman said, "Follow me," and mounted his motorcycle. I followed in my battered jalopy.

The desk sergeant set my bail at twenty-five dollars. "But I'm a well-known American writer," I said. "You can release me on my recognizance."

The desk sergeant said the law didn't permit it.

I should have told him I was a porter, I thought. All white Americans trust black porters and black mammies—even with their children.

It was Tuesday and my landlady wasn't due home until Thursday and I knew no one to whom I could appeal. However, the desk sergeant gave me permission to telephone my wife at eight o'clock, when I expected her home from New York. But the guard shift changed at six and the night guard had no orders concerning my telephoning. I knew how much Jean would worry when I failed to come home, and as the night wore on, despair set in. "Don't let it throw you," I cautioned myself. "Despair is characteristic of the black race."

At eleven o'clock the next morning I was taken to the magistrate's court. But the driver of the Buick had suffered from such severe shock she was unable to appear, and the hearing was postponed for a week. However, I was permitted to telephone. First I called our house. Receiving no reply, I telephoned Jean's brother Andrew, in Baltimore. Andrew was a chaplain with the rank of major, stationed at the Pentagon but living in Baltimore. He promised to wire a hundred dollars to the city jail immediately.

Jean had had to stay overnight in New York and didn't get back to Bridgeport until eleven. The telephone had been ringing when she let herself into the house but it had stopped by the time she answered it. She noticed that the car was gone and thought I'd sold it, but when the young black called at eleven-thirty with the money to buy it, she began to worry. She noticed then that the bed hadn't been slept in, and she was afraid I'd been hurt. She began telephoning the hospitals. It wasn't until after one o'clock that it occurred to her I might have been arrested for some traffic violation. She called police headquarters and learned that I was being held on a charge of reckless driving.

At the same time Jean was talking to the desk officer, I was being hustled into a Black Maria along with other prisoners committed to the county prison. Since I hadn't made bail by then I could be held no longer in the municipal jail. At the county prison I was mugged, fingerprinted, given a uniform of blue denim with a number stenciled on the shirt, and locked in a cell on the third tier. I kept telling myself that the money for my bail would arrive any minute, and tried desperately not to think of Jean.

When Jean arrived at court she learned I'd been unable to raise bail and had been committed to the county prison. First, telegraphing her brother Andrew for twenty-five dollars, she rushed to the county prison, but was informed that prisoners were not permitted visitors unless they had a pass from the court, and then only during visiting hours on Tuesdays and Thursdays. It was Wednesday. She rushed home to see if the money had come and found a wire from her brother stating that he'd already wired a hundred dollars to the city jail.

So she rushed back to the city jail to learn that the money had already arrived but, the prisoner having been committed to the county prison, it had been returned to the telegraph office. After getting a pass to see me from the prosecutor, she hastened to the telegraph office to draw the money. But the telegram was addressed to me and they wouldn't give it to her. She explained that her husband was in the county prison, waiting for the money to make bail. They said she'd have to obtain a statement from me, countersigned by the warden, authorizing them to pay her the money. She rushed to the county prison and, luckily, got an audience with the warden. He said he was sorry, but prisoners were not permitted to receive money from the outside. And he could not permit her to visit her husband until visiting day. Then she began to cry.

By that time it was four o'clock in the afternoon and the telegraph office closed at five. In the meantime, I had been marched to the mess hall for my supper of stale bread, macaroni, and boiled cabbage, and marched back to my cell.

Luckily, the warden couldn't bear to see a woman cry. No doubt he thought she seemed to be a decent black woman and wondered how those decent black women always got mixed up with some no-good black man. He relented, impressing upon her that he was breaking the prison rules, but he would see what he could do. He had a statement typed, giving her the authority to draw the money, and sent it by a guard to my cell for me to sign. Then he countersigned it, and by then it was fifteen minutes to five.

Jean ran down the stairs and looked for a taxi. On the second street she found one and reached the telegraph office one minute before closing time. She drew the money, returned, and bailed me out. When I went into the waiting room, I saw at once that she'd been crying. Her body was trembling all over and her eyes looked huge and dark with anguish in her small heart-shaped face.

"Let's get out of here," I said.

We went back to police headquarters, where I had parked my car, and found a traffic violation ticket on it for parking overnight. I put the ticket into my pocket, started the motor, and drove back to the house.

The young brother who wanted to buy the car was waiting for me on the porch. I knocked twenty-five dollars off the price because of the bent bumper and crumpled fender, and the brother was satisfied.

Jean fixed a makeshift dinner and we ate silently. Afterward I said, "Let's pack."

We had two wardrobe trunks and three suitcases, but they wouldn't hold everything we owned, so we left some clothing and several paintings in the basement. We found a transfer man to take the trunks to the station, and at eight o'clock the next morning we caught the New Haven Limited to New York.

That incident shook me. It wasn't that it hurt so much. Nor was I surprised. I believed that the American white man—in fact all Americans, black or white—was capable of anything. It was just that it stirred up my anxiety, which had gradually settled down somewhat. It scrambled the continuity of my memories, probably of my thoughts also. That is practically the last thing I remember about the United States in such vivid detail. I wish it weren't so. It's a tragedy, but my own, however, just my own.

After that everything was a hodgepodge. I am not certain of the truth of what I do remember. What I think are memories of actual events might in reality be memories of bad dreams and nightmares. All the time following, until I went to Europe, seems like a period of recurring blackouts. I wonder what you call that? Shock, perhaps.

We roomed somewhere in Harlem, but I don't remember where. We lived, but I don't remember how; I don't remember working, except for a week or so as doorman for an expensive Jewish hotel on the boardwalk in Long Beach, Long Island, and again a few days sometime later in another Jewish hotel in Long Beach when the Jewish high holy days were being celebrated. But that wouldn't have kept us alive for a week.

I think it was about then that Lurton Blassingame, who was still my agent, sold my short story The Snake to Esquire. And I remember visiting Richard Wright in his house on Charles Street in Greenwich Village shortly after he returned from a year's stay in France. Dick had left his house in the hands of a rental agency, and they had rented the basement flat beneath their first-floor residence to two girls who were supposedly students. But while Dick was away, the agency did not keep a very strict watch over the house, and it seems the two girls became four and they opened the stairway into Dick's own apartment and a couple of young GIs, just demobilized, moved in with them. All of them were white, I must add. When the Wrights returned the girls disappeared, but the Communist Party's Daily Worker, which had it in for Dick, ran a front-page article about the prostitution being carried on in Richard Wright's house, beneath the banner: RICHARD WRIGHT'S HOUSE IS A PIG STY.

When we arrived, the two young men who had lived with the girls were there, voluntarily, abject in their apologies and filled with awed respect for "Mister Wright" and offering to make whatever amends they could.

And Ellen was stomping around, highly indignant, declaiming that she had never kept a dirty house, as if these two abject respectful boys would ever dare think so.

I was not as sympathetic as I might have been if Ellen hadn't taken Jean all over the Village in her search for an apartment just before they left for France and put their house in the hands of an agency. That basement flat would have suited us fine. But I did not remind them of that, for my mission there was to borrow some money. From the time I had met him after the publication of *If He Hollers Let Him Go*, until his death, Dick and I had a somewhat secret understanding that I wouldn't ask him for any favor he did not want to do, and he wouldn't do it. Evidently this was an emergency—perhaps I was writing *The Third Generation* then—but I don't remember. I wanted to borrow five hundred dollars.

Dick told me that he did not keep that much spending money on hand; that with the exception of an annuity he had made for his daughters, Ellen kept all of their money in her name. But he would try to get me a loan from the Authors' League Fund. He telephoned his literary agent, Paul Reynolds, and Reynolds telephoned the Authors' League Fund and then called Dick back to tell me to go by their offices on East Thirty-ninth Street and pick up my check.

It was on that same afternoon, perhaps while we were waiting for Reynolds to call back, that a package was delivered from Harper & Brothers, containing black leather-bound copies of Dick's three books *Uncle Tom's Children*, *Native Son*, and *Black Boy*, and a letter from Dick's editor and close friend, Edward Aswell, editor-in-chief at Harper's, to congratulate Dick on the sale of

239,000 copies to date of the trade edition of *Black Boy* (not counting, of course, the Book-of-the-Month Club distribution).

And it was that summer, I feel certain, that I submitted my prison story, which I had cut in half and changed to the first person, to a young editor at Rinehart whom I had met at a party given by Van Vechten's niece on Fifty-fourth Street. I had made the protagonist of my prison story a Mississippi white boy; that ought to tell me something, but I don't know what—but obviously it was the story of my own prison experiences. This young man, Bill Raney, I think his name was, impressed me by saying he had accepted a book for publication that his senior editors viewed with grave doubts, but he was gambling his job on it he believed in it so completely. The book was *The Naked and the Dead* by Norman Mailer. I thought he was the type of editor I needed.

The senior editors at Rinehart also viewed my prison book with grave doubts. Then Bill went to Henry Holt as executive editor, with a friend, Ted Amussen, as managing editor. At Bill's suggestion, I withdrew my book from Rinehart and submitted it to Holt—he said they hadn't anything of consequence for their next year's fiction list—and evidently I settled down to writing, even though now I have no memory of it.

No matter what I did, or where I was, or how I lived, I had considered myself a writer ever since I'd published my first story in *Esquire* when I was still in prison in 1934. Foremost a writer. Above all else a writer. It was my salvation, and is. The world can deny me all other employment, and stone me as an ex-convict, as a nigger, as a disagreeable and unpleasant person. But as long as I write, whether it is published or not, I'm a writer, and no one can take that away. "A fighter fights, a writer writes," so I must have done my writing.

My next lucid memory is of our going to a farm in Connecticut, beyond Stamford, somewhere off the Wilbur Cross Parkway, where the agricultural branch of the University of Connecticut is located. The farm was owned by a Madison Avenue attorney named Halperin, who had a number of movie people as clients.

It was a beautiful farm that had been used formerly to breed and train thoroughbred horses, and the neat wooden stables with wooden floors were still in existence and could well have been lived in by people who don't mind the scent of horses. There was a big white house well back from the road, secured by a locked gate and surrounded by acres of rolling lawns of the greenest grass I'd ever seen. Aside from the stables, there were a small barn for cattle and a pigsty where Mr. Halperin kept his big yellow rooster locked up, and a large red barn not far from the house with a hayloft at top and garage space for his maroon Buick limousine and Mrs. Halperin's Olds 88 below. Some distance out back there were a house for the servants, which we occupied, and a house and enclosed yard for fowl, which when we arrived was occupied by a flock of white ducks. Beyond were the corrals, in which Mr. Halperin had installed doghouses for his Shetland shepherds, male, female, and three offspring. A Shetland shepherd is only about one third of the size of the more familiar shepherds. The male, Jeff, was one of the bravest dogs I have ever known; whenever I heard a suspicious noise over at the main house, some five hundred yards distant, which was unoccupied most of the time we were there, I would get my shotgun and release Jeff, whom we let sleep in our house, and he would race across to the house like a streak of light and keep on encircling it at high speed until I arrived. Evidently he had been trained. Mr. Halperin told me once he was valued at fifteen hundred dollars. I believed him.

We had a jeep for our personal use and there was a lake in the woods on his property with a summer house on its shore. We would drive there and fish sometimes. It was well stocked with fish. Once I caught several small fish and left them on the line in the water while we ate a picnic lunch, and when I went for them I found only their skeletons.

The duties were light, consisting mostly of riding a tractor mower about the expanse of lawn and preparing and serving meals the weekends the Halperins came out. They always brought fabulous lamb chops from the top of the gigot, or filet mignons, which Mr. Halperin insisted on barbecuing himself over charcoal on his outdoor brazier. Life there was like something in a Holly-made film, from the time the Halperins arrived on Friday evening with their maid in his fishtail Cadillac, until they departed late Monday morning. In between we would feed them and serve them and clean up after them and Mr. Halperin and I would discuss farm problems, which neither of us knew a damn thing about, and in fact none existed. I alluded to this episode in my book *The Primitive*.

Besides the yellow rooster in the pigpen, there were a little bantam hen in one of the wagon sheds and seventeen fat white ducks in the wire-enclosed chicken yard. Mr. Halperin decided to put in some laying hens, so he came out one weekend and killed the ducks by standing outside the wire fence and shooting them with a shotgun. After which he drove off to order two dozen pullets and pick up a laborer in the city to pluck the ducks, which I had refused to do. The following week I cleaned and whitewashed the henhouse, forked the chicken yard, bought two one-hundred-pound sacks of chicken mash and scratch, drove over in the jeep and picked up the pullets and installed them in their new home. But I'd been feeding them from a sack of old mash, which happened to be pig mash, and the eggs were ill-formed and had soft shells. When Mr. Halperin came back the following weekend he examined the soft-shelled eggs and stated categorically that their deformity was due to the rooster fertilizing them. The man who had plucked the ducks stopped by for his pay after dinner, and the three of us sat around for two hours, drinking Canadian Club highballs, trying to decide what to do with the rooster. The laborer suggested that the rooster be castrated, but I said they'd first have to find the testicles, so Mr. Halperin went into his library and brought a book on poultry raising, but all he discovered about roosters was a section of the anatomy referred to as *primaries*. Being an attorney who was familiar with all manner of terms, he was able to state authoritatively that the primaries were the testicles, but there was no way to get to them. I couldn't understand how the rooster, who lived in the pigpen a half mile distant from the chicken coop, could have fertilized the eggs, but of course I didn't say so, and continued to respectfully drink Mr. Halperin's good whiskey. Finally the solution burst upon Mr. Halperin like a brainstorm. He banged dramatically on the table with his open palm and said in the voice of a general giving an order to charge: "Chester, kill the rooster!"

And that, I had thought at the time, is mankind's solution for every problem.

But as a rule when the Halperins left, we would take out Mrs. Halperin's Olds 88 and drive into New York City or just about the state of Connecticut, charging the gas to their account, and once we drove swiftly up to a town outside of Burlington, Vermont, to visit a couple we had known from Los Angeles, Bill Smith and his wife Helen, and their family. But we could never stay away more than a couple of days because of the dogs. I don't think I wrote much then, but we had a good time, and learned a lot about Connecticut, which I think is one of the most beautiful states in the country, and saw the shaded plots of Connecticut tobacco, which is used for the cover leaves of expensive cigars.

In June, my brother Joseph had arranged for me to come down to North Carolina College, the state college for blacks in Durham, to conduct a two-week seminar in creative writing. When we told Mr. Halperin we were leaving, there was a bit of unpleasantness, for he had expected us to stay on as cook and butler for them all summer. It was the first unpleasantness I'd ever had about quitting a domestic job, because I'd always let it be known that I was first a writer, and I was somewhat surprised to find that Mr. Halperin held such a low opinion of black writers.

However, the following week he returned with a white butler and cook, and we were taken by the butler with our luggage to the railroad station.

Joe had been a professor of sociology at North Carolina

THE QUALITY OF HURT

College ever since he left the Columbus, Ohio, branch of the Urban League some time during the 1940s. I hadn't been in the Deep South since I was twelve or thirteen, when our father had taught at Branch Normal College in Pine Bluff, the year of Joe's accident. Joe had graduated magna cum laude from the Fine Arts College of Oberlin and also took his masters there. While I had been in prison he had attended Ohio State University where he took his Ph.D and earned a Phi Beta Kappa key. He had worked on his thesis during the years of the depression, and some thirty-odd WPA research assistants in the undergraduate school had been assigned to help him, in addition to the readers provided by the Ohio State Society for the Blind. Mother had kept house for him and read to him and studied with him so diligently that she often said she could have taken a doctorate in sociology herself.

He had married Estelle Jones when he was working for the Urban League, and mother continued to live with them, but she felt she had a vested interest in his life which she didn't wish to share with his wife. So there was always tension in the house, which I'm sure kept Joe pretty upset.

It was then, having nothing else to occupy her compulsive drive, that Mother began tracing the history of her half-white family, the Bomars, out of slavery. It was from her notes I got the idea for my semi-autobiographical novel, *The Third Generation*, but I didn't actually use any of her material—she was so closely related to the white planters, the Bomars and the Clevelands, I didn't think the American public would accept it. But I wish I had now. Americans have learned they cannot reject our history.

She died in Columbus while living with Joe and Estelle after *If He Hollers Let Him Go* had been accepted for publication but before it had been published. Despite the fact she had opposed my marriage to Jean, I loved her intensely, and her death upset me very much. I thought it so rotten unfair that she didn't live to see my book published having spent so much of her dreams and her love on me.

So I didn't know how it was going to go for Jean and me in
the South with Joe and Estelle that June, 1950. But it went
exceedingly well. Joe lived in a pleasant six-room one-storied house
on Formosa Street, which had been owned and occupied by the
president of the college before he had moved to the president's
"mansion," and it had a big back lawn laid out for croquet. And
Estelle was very pleasant.

I was a celebrity on the campus. It seemed as though all the
faculty had read reviews of my latest book, *Lonely Crusade*, and
it didn't matter to them that the reviews were adverse, for most
of them hadn't read the book anyway; and the few who had, had
liked it, and anyway the white people's bad criticism of a good
book by a black writer was to be expected.

The United States was engaged in the Korean War, and the
NAACP's legal branch was suing the city of Durham for equal
school facilities in accordance with North Carolina state law. My
appearance at the university gave the white dailies a subject,
ostensibly pro-black, to avoid the issues of the war and the
NAACP suit. Every day, the two white papers devoted considerable space to my seminar, all out of proportion to its importance. I attended the hearings in the federal district court.
That was the first time I saw Thurgood Marshall, who was not
actually pleading the case but had stopped by to give advice and
moral support to the two young Negro attorneys from Virginia
under his supervision. His appearance alone in the court seemed
to rattle the white defense, and the newspapers reported on his
visit as though Khrushchev had come to town.

The summer courses given at North Carolina College are mostly
for black teachers from the elementary black schools throughout
the state, who are adult, with their own big automobiles and
material possessions and ways of life. They look upon the professors as contemporaries. Joe seemed to be well liked and respected,
perhaps because of his scholastic attainments but I have a sneaking suspicion it was also because he was blind. As a race we have
a great sympathy for other people's misfortunes and handicaps.
Sometimes I think it is our failing. But because of this great

sympathy and respect for Joe, they showed respect for me, too, and that was quite surprising in view of the fact that all of them knew I had been to prison. Most blacks in the United States of the same age or generation as myself know I have been to prison if they know me at all, but most refer to it as "the trouble he was in when he was young." Going to prison for a crime is not considered such a disgrace by blacks as it is by whites; and in European countries, where there have been so many political prisoners, it doesn't matter at all.

Estelle had the same old Dodge I remembered from ten years before, when they lived in Columbus, and she always asked me to drive. I wasn't particularly happy about driving in the South: I had a bad temper and I wanted to avoid trouble. But it was like driving anywhere else—priorities were controlled by the traffic laws. They don't discriminate against cars, just people. One day we went down to visit a distant relative who was minister of the Negro Presbyterian church in Greensboro, and were served roast ham and potato salad, and before we returned home late that night we had visited a number of people in outlying towns and on the campus, and all of them had served roast ham and potato salad. On our last visit, late at night, to a colleague of Joe's, when we were served a cold buffet of roast ham and potato salad we became hysterical. I started to ask if it had any biblical connotation—Ham, son of Noah—but I was afraid they wouldn't get it.

We visited the Duke tobacco plant and walked down Chesterfield Avenue and visited Duke University, and were impressed by the beautiful gothic structures made of native granite, and by the lovely green campus with its magnolia trees in bloom. Strangely enough, the black citizens of Durham were just as proud of the architecture of Duke University as the whites.

And we visited the offices of the North Carolina Mutual Insurance Company, owned by blacks and employing only blacks, housed in its own building in the center of the white business district in Durham. It had its own bank, also, where most blacks in Durham did business. There were many rich blacks in Durham, those connected with North Carolina Mutual and those speculating in real estate, and in construction, and in the undertaking business, and in the professions, those who ran building aid societies, and those with other business ventures, and even some who worked in the Chesterfield factory were well off. We were taken around and shown well-kept black neighborhoods with big brick houses which were said to have cost from thirty-five thousand to seventy-five thousand dollars to build. Joe was working on a sociological study of the Negro family of North Carolina, with numerous black elementary teachers doing his research, and one day I drove him over to the State University for whites at Chapel Hill, where he was having the cards processed by a computer. He was treated efficiently and with respect, the way I suppose any other professor of any race on the same mission would be treated. That ought to prove that education is the answer, but then there was always the fact of his blindness.

Jean and I did not have any unpleasantness of any kind. Once we drove to the offices of a milk company to get some ice cream and Jean drank from the public fountain, much to Estelle's alarm, but nothing happened; perhaps no one saw her.

I received a letter from Bill Raney at Holt which I interpreted to mean Holt had accepted *Black Sheep*. I became anxious to get back.

Joe and I got on well but we weren't intimate. Too much had passed. We had each suffered our lonely crises, which we could not share. We handled each other as though we were made of fragile glass. And Estelle went around with a forced smile as though determined to be pleasant under any circumstances, but perhaps her smile was genuine and her behavior natural. Jean seemed the most relaxed.

We had had a wonderful visit, but I was relieved when we left.

We got tickets on a through train from Miami to New York in advance and we arrived at the station just in time to board the train so we would not have to wait in the Jim Crow lounge. It was a lovely train, the *Silver Streak* or something like that; it was not Jim Crowed in the Southern states it passed through, and

we spent most of our time in deep armchairs in the bar and arrived in New York on Saturday night.

It had been a successful trip. And now it was having a successful ending—the acceptance of my book. We were happy. We put
up at the Theresa Hotel and just had time to buy a dozen bottles
of Irish whiskey before the liquor stores closed. Then we telephoned all the people we knew and invited them to the hotel for
a party the next day. We felt like celebrating; we had had so
damn few things to celebrate. Numbers of people showed up the
next day and we had a celebration memorable even in the Hotel
Theresa.

I had wired Bill that I would come in and see him Monday.
Early Monday morning, I got up with a hundred-degree hangover
and went down to Holt's on Fourth Avenue downtown, to sign
my contract and pick up the check for the advance. When I
entered Bill's office and saw the neatly wrapped manuscript on his
desk, I knew that something had happened. He was as straightforward as could be expected under the circumstances. He said
he had accepted the book; in fact way back in the spring before
we had gone out to the Halperins', he had introduced me to the
publicity director and had said then that they would publish the
book; but his superior, Ted Amussen, managing editor, had flatly
turned it down and the directors of Henry Holt, whoever they
were, had supported him. He went on to say he and Ted had
almost come to blows, but at that moment that didn't interest me
—a rejection is a rejection regardless of the slings and arrows.
I would have liked to talk to Ted—I had never met him—but he
was staying in Washington, D.C., where he was ghost-writing
General Omar Bradley's reminiscences.

We had been extravagant, thinking the book had been accepted
and we would have a sufficient advance to begin housekeeping in
a rented room somewhere. After our hotel bill was paid we had
only twelve dollars left. Our trunks were still in the checkroom
in Grand Central Station, where we had left them when we went
to Durham.

I wired my old friend Bill Smith in Vermont that we would

arrive in Burlington at ten o'clock Tuesday morning to stay with him until times got better.

Bill was one of those eighty-percent-white blacks on the borderline of the races who generally originate in the borderline states. He was from Kansas City, where his black father in name had been an important doctor and chief of staff of the black hospital, but his real father, according to him, was a wealthy white man. He had been brought up between the two races and two fathers by an adoring mother, herself damn near white, and as a consequence had lived a wild, adventuresome, insecure, aimless life. He looked like a white man with a clipped mustache, and he was in good physical condition for his age, for he was in his fifties at the time, with something of the build of a middleweight prizefighter, which, among other things, he claimed he had been in his youth. He had also worked at the same time as Roy Wilkins, executive secretary of the NAACP, for the Kansas City *Call*, a local black newspaper, which gave him the claim to being a journalist.

Bill had gone to Los Angeles at about the same time as we had, and had married Helen, the vivacious brownskin society editor of the L.A. black weekly, the *Sentinel*, and they had bought a little house with a falling porch for nine hundred dollars. Bill didn't mind manual work, as long as it was for himself, and he personally repaired the little house, built a new porch, and painted it during Helen's first pregnancy. Helen was in the public hospital when she gave birth to a white, blue-eyed, towheaded baby girl, which amused the members of the staff so much, to Helen's great annoyance, that Bill went over to the hospital with his pistol and threatened to shoot the next person who made a snide crack about the baby's parentage. I suppose that was the beginning of Bill's race consciousness; it had never troubled him before, but in Los Angeles he became highly sensitive, as it happens to all blacks who go there sooner or later, and as it had happened to me.

The Second World War had begun and the migration to the West Coast was increasing daily, with the resulting housing shortage, and the price of real estate had begun the rapid escalation which was to become legendary. Bill sold his house, for which he had paid nine hundred dollars, for fifteen hundred dollars, bought another for that and sold it for thirty-six hundred, bought another for that and after repairing it and improving it sold it for nine thousand dollars; then he bought a big house out in a white neighborhood off Western with a large lot containing a small rental bungalow. Helen had kept her newspaper job and in the meantime Bill had worked at anything interesting, including a stint at the farmers' market in Beverly Hills, and buying up several bushels of sheepskin scraps from a coatmaker and cutting them up for powder puffs, buying an old thirty-six-foot cabin cruiser with a fine old Chrysler marine engine but a tremendous hole in its aluminum hull, which he repaired and floated in San Pedro Harbor. He would have become a fisherman except for the fact that the Navy didn't permit any boats to leave the harbor unless they had a license dating from before the war. Bill rented his bungalow to an interracial couple who gave wild parties— the black husband was a piano player in a club out on the Strip—and built another one at the back of his lot for his in-laws.

At the time Bill was writing dialogue for various Hollywood screenwriters and made a fair income, and with Helen's salary from the *Sentinel* and the income from their property, they were doing quite well except for the fact the white residents of the neighborhood resented them living there. From what I gathered, most of the resentment was toward the interracial couple, but Bill's house faced the street and he was the one most often seen, and he took it as a personal attack. I think that was when he began collecting pistols. He knocked down a couple of white men on the street and the police came around to give him a warning. Some neighbors threw some milk bottles and trash onto his front porch one night, and if it hadn't been for Helen's pleas he would have shot up the neighborhood. He was that type of mulatto black who will shoot a white man on sight.

By then they had a little boy playmate for their oldest daughter, Anne, and another was on the way, and Helen wanted them to pull up and move East. My father was living with us in L.A. at the time Bill was having all this trouble, and strangely enough he exerted a little influence with him. With all our combined efforts we were able to restrain him from killing anyone, but he kept beating up the white neighbors one after another.

By the time the second boy was born, *If He Hollers Let Him Go* had been published and we had moved to New York. Bill was getting along on his first novel, too, and I think he was influenced by our move, for suddenly he sold his property, bought an old Fleetwood Cadillac, and drove across the country to Vermont. Bill got twenty-three thousand dollars in cash for his property, and there was some unpleasantness about the check given in payment. Bill wanted it cashed and the cashier of his bank said they didn't have that much cash on hand on Friday afternoon. Bill got the cashier of the bank on which it was drawn to intercede and his bank grudgingly paid him the twenty-three thousand dollars in old five-dollar bills, taking until eleven o'clock that night to count it, and he had to take it home in a Campbell's Soup carton. He kept it in that carton in the boot of his car all the way across the U.S.A.

In a village called Westlake, Vermont, he bought a little house facing the square and immediately became the subject of controversy; some of the residents disliked him on sight, but he made friends with others. Bill was like that. Everyone liked Helen and the children. They had chosen Vermont because of an article Dorothy Canfield Fisher had written about the Vermonters liberal attitude toward blacks.

We had visited them in Westlake a couple of times before; we went with him the day he first inspected the farm ten or twelve miles distant which he had since bought and to which we were then going.

Bill had finished and published a book under the pseudonym Will Thomas. It was one of those antebellum stories about the mixtures of races in the South and the passions of, and aroused by, the octoroon; the story was somewhat autobiographical, I suspected. It did poorly but brought them to the attention of the

Fishers, who had invited them to dinner and initiated one of those white-black relationships that are so highly prized in the United States. Also it influenced *Ebony* magazine to do a photographic story about the Smith family and their farm in Vermont.

The children had grown since we had last seen them and the daughter and the older boy attended the school where Helen had begun to teach as their money ran out. Bill was as busy as a beaver, but he wasn't earning much money. He was in the midst of writing his Vermont story, at the suggestion of Dorothy Canfield, and he was hoping to get a Book-of-the-Month Club award for it on the strength of the Canfields' connections; but Dorothy Canfield had meant for Helen to write the book. He was also conducting a biweekly discussion of news topics on the Burlington radio.

However, it was summer when we arrived and no one was doing much of anything. The children had a goat for a pet, and a big brown-and-white hound had attached himself to the house. Bill was keeping him as a watchdog, against Helen's wishes, but that dog was so timid it wouldn't have whimpered at sight of a burglar. We went around with Bill and visited some of their neighbors, among whom were some English people on the next farm who had something to do with the United Nations. Using the recipe of a neighbor, Bill had made and bottled several cases of beer from white potatoes, which he advised me against drinking because of its high fusel oil content. We used to sit up in the dining room at night and hear the bottles exploding in the basement like an artillery barrage. And Bill was also raising white Leghorn chickens for sale to an A & P supermarket in Burlington, at the manager's suggestion.

The first time Bill took some chickens in to sell, the manager told him to put them on the scale. Bill asked sarcastically how could he get live chickens to stay on the scales. The manager told him to put it to sleep, and when Bill asked how? the manager said, "Oh, come off it, you know how to put chickens to sleep." Bill immediately sensed a racial connotation and bristled up: "What do you mean I know how to put chickens to sleep?"

The manager saw he was angry and the people in Burlington gave Bill a wide berth when he was angry. The manager said apologetically, "Hell, you're the most sensitive man I ever knew. I didn't mean to hurt your feelings: I thought all colored people knew how to put chickens to sleep." Bill gave the manager a vicious look and said, "I don't know, you show me." "All right," the manager agreed, and tucked the chicken's head beneath its wing and laid it on the scale. The chicken lay without moving while he weighed it. He did the same with the others. He paid Bill silently and looked at him quizzically as Bill left fuming, and drove furiously the eighteen miles back to his farm.

He drove the car up on the drive without announcing his arrival and ran around to the chicken yard in back and grabbed all twenty-eight of his remaining chickens, one by one, and tucked their heads beneath their wings and left them lying on their backs.

Jean and Helen had been gossiping inside, and hearing the chickens squawking, Helen came to the back door to see what was alarming them. By then Bill and I had returned to the car to take the groceries inside and Helen didn't see us. But she saw all of their chickens lying in the yard on their backs with their feet in the air as though stone-cold dead. She let out a shriek and ran back into the house and said to Jean, "I've got to reach Bill in Burlington, something's happened to the chickens and they're all dead."

Despite Bill's temper, we had a fine time, and sometime before winter, I must have received some money from somewhere because I remember paying Bill for board and lodging, in fact having to force the payment on him, and kissing Helen goodbye when we left and wondering why she looked so alarmed. Later Jean told me that at their wedding Bill had knocked down everyone who tried to kiss the bride.

It must have been sometime during that period that I changed literary agents, because the next thing I remember is Margot Johnson being my agent and telling me her favorite story of the Hollywood studio offering sixty-five thousand dollars for the mo-

tion picture rights to Willard Motley's *Knock on Any Door* and
how she "took the money and ran."

Margot was trying to place my prison story, *Black Sheep*, and
I think she must have had a version of my novel *The Third
Generation*, but no publisher was willing to invest in me at the
time, and shortly we were faced with our major problem of all
the years of our marriage: *How to live?* On the basis of her past
experience at Girls Camp, Jean got a job as recreational director
of the New York State Women's Reformatory at Mt. Kisco. She
was given a room in the building that housed the other women
warders, and two days a week off. I took a furnished room in the
house of the spinster daughter of a former A.M.E. bishop in a
small neighborhood on the edge of White Plains, inhabited exclusively by well-to-do middle-class blacks. The *Life* photographer
Gordon Parks had his home there at the time.

Although the house I lived in was the oldest in the community,
and had the most charm, I thought, it was the smallest and perhaps the coldest. Jean would arrive about noon of her first day
off and catch the last train back at about 11:30 P.M. on her second day to report for work next morning, giving us about thirty-
four hours together, which was the only time I was ever warm in
that house. Our landlady was of the poor but proud variety and
considered us her inferiors. She was so much like my own mother
had been in that respect that I forgave her.

As I lived within commuting distance of Pleasantville, New
York, I tried to get some sort of editorial job in the offices of
the *Reader's Digest*. I figured they owed me something for re-
printing the *Ebony* editorial "Time to Count Your Blessings,"
censuring my novel *Lonely Crusade*; but they had eliminated the
reference to me as being psychotic, perhaps aware of the fact I
could win a suit against a white publication. Of course they had
no suitable opening for a person of my capabilities, so I left the
editorial offices and walked around to the mailing room, where I
got a job typing metal stencils for the addressograph machines, at
piece rates. I must confess I ruined more of the metal plates than
I got right and after I worked overtime on my first day the super-

visor felt they could save money by keeping me away, and I was fired. It was the week before Christmas, and at least I had earned enough to buy Jean a cheap Christmas present.

Our landlady took another roomer, a buxom young dark-complexioned black woman who sported a fur coat made from some animal unknown to me and a luxurious jet-black ponytail of unidentifiable hair. The landlady invited our new neighbor, her boy friend, and Jean and me to Christmas dinner.

Jean had to work most of the holidays, and I had no word from anyone in the publishing field, not even a Christmas card from my agent, and I slowly began to lose confidence in myself. The White Plains YMCA, a strictly Jim Crow institution at that time, desperately needed a day porter to clean and wax the linoleum tile in the lounges and television rooms, clean and service the showers in the men's locker rooms, clean and wax the floors of the two gymnasiums, and clean the tile terrace about the swimming pool; and I got the job. When I quit at the last of March, three months later, the director said I had been one of the best porters they had ever had and he hated to see me leave, but he would give me a good recommendation. I told him I was going to devote my time to writing. "But how will you live?" he wanted to know. That was the question.

I had saved a little money and I went back to Harlem and took a room on Convent Avenue. Jean came in and spent one night out of the week with me, but I remember being very lonely at that time. I had not got over my shock from the reception of *Lonely Crusade* and I did not look up any of the people I had formerly known. I had not been on speaking terms for some years with my cousins Henry and Molly Moon, and I did not wish to see any of the people I had met through them. The Richard Wrights had long since returned to France, and I was ashamed to contact the Ralph Ellisons, or even Langston Hughes, whom I had met in Cleveland the first year I came out of prison. There was no ill will between us; it's simply that I'm like an animal—when I'm hurt and lonely I want to go off alone in my hole and lick my wounds. I hate exhibiting my wounds and scars and I don't know

why I'm doing it now. I suppose I just want to get it on the
record before it's too late.

✓ I visited my eldest brother, Eddie, during that time. We had
first seen Eddie shortly after the publication of *If He Hollers Let
Him Go*, and discovered he was living in Harlem. Before then I
hadn't seen him for more than twenty years. I had always heard
Mother refer to him as having wasted his opportunities and squandered his chances for a better position in life by marrying an
uneducated black woman and working as a dining-car waiter; and
despite the fact that I had been to prison and worked at almost
every conceivable menial occupation, I rather looked down on
him and considered myself a higher class of being because I was a
writer and was married to a social worker. I had always been
something of a snob, and a snob I have remained, despite the
record of my life. I suppose that simple contradiction has caused
many people to dislike me. It has little to do with race. I adopt
the same attitudes toward white people. But most of the feeling
of superiority was knocked out of me during that lonely period
in Harlem, rooming in a household of perverts and being supported by my wife working as a common guard in a women's
prison regardless of her title. I was grateful to Eddie for inviting
me to visit him and his wife and play stud poker with his friends
and eat his wife's Southern fried chicken and biscuits and watch
wrestling matches on their television set, which I had always considered the prime pastime of morons.

The manuscripts of both *The Third Generation* and *Black
Sheep* were making the rounds of the publishing houses at that
time, but I had almost lost interest. That summer I had convinced myself I was a failure as a writer, and poverty and loneliness and our enforced separation had convinced me I was a
failure as a husband. After fourteen years of love and marriage we
had lost each other. It was no one's fault, really. We had been
together longer than anyone expected. One might say my sins
had caught up with me—the sins of pride and arrogance. And I
was beginning to pay. Jean stopped coming to visit me and to
support me, and I was faced with the necessity of having to support myself.

4.

The purely animal need of food and shelter sent me back to work again as a bellhop at the New Prospect Hotel in Sullivan County, where I'd suffered from ptomaine poisoning and to which, despite the fact that the proprietors had liked me, I'd sworn never to return. I was vulnerable and defeated, and I hated all the people whom I dared not insult for fear of losing my job. I hadn't learned then how to survive without my wife, and should I fail at writing, which I felt that I had, I was afraid I might go quickly down to skid row. Crime was no longer open to me—in fact it never had been. I had been an amateur. As my French translator was to say to me years later: "Himes, you are a puritan." I had always been a puritan; I was repelled by petty crime and any form of obscenity (I taught myself how to say the word "mother-fucker," which shocked and repelled me when I first heard it), and I abhorred lasciviousness and exploratory sex, even though Jean and I had indulged ourselves in every desire. I wouldn't have been able to pull off any sort of crime for gain, and the only occupation I could have gotten would have been the lowest of the menial. At the time that job at the New Prospect Hotel was the best I could get.

I was relieving the switchboard girl in the lobby of the hotel when the telegram came from William Targ, vice president and editor-in-chief of the World Publishing Company, that he had accepted *The Third Generation* for publication and would pay an advance of two thousand dollars. I had been saving my tips and had enough money for the fare back to New York. I went out into the kitchen and told the co-proprietor I was leaving, and went across the yard to my room and packed my bag. As I was standing by the gate trying to thumb a ride into town, he came out of the hotel and paid me what was due and had Joe, the other bellhop, drive me to the station in the old pickup.

Margot Johnson was still my agent, and it was to her I went to pick up my check for eighteen hundred dollars. I still had my room on Convent Avenue, but the first thing I desired now that I had money was to sleep with a white woman, and the only white woman in the city I knew at the time who was likely to sleep with me was Vandi Haygood. I had spent a weekend with her in Chicago many years before, when Jean and I had been living in Los Angeles. Vandi had been acting director of fellowships for the Rosenwald Foundation during the war while her husband, the director William C. Haygood, had been in the Army; and I had been given a Rosenwald Fellowship to complete my first novel, *If He Hollers Let Him Go.* I had been to New York, for some reason which I have forgotten, and on the way back to the coast I had stopped in Chicago and spent a wild, drunken week of sexual extravagance with Vandi, and for a time afterward she had genuinely loved me.

But for the past five or six years, since the ending of the Rosenwald Foundation, she had been working as an executive for the International Institute of Education in its offices at Fifth Avenue and Sixty-seventh Street. Her job was to write summaries of all applications containing a prospectus, to be presented to the State Department for screening and afterward to all U.S. foundations to be considered for grants. But she also worked closely with the Ford Foundation, doing what, I never knew.

Vandi was glad to see me. She was coming to the end of an affair with a young Jew whom she had tried to get to marry her, and she always needed a man. She couldn't go to sleep without a man beside her, any man. I knew this, of course, but nevertheless I began living with her and we had a rather ardent affair steeped in sex and alcohol. My book *The Primitive* was about our affair, and although it doesn't tell the whole tedious story of my eighteen months with her, it gives the essence of the affair; in fact it is rather exact except that I didn't kill her. I left that for her own race to do; they had already mortally hurt her before I began to live with her, and it was no more than right that they should be the ones to finish her.

But I came near to doing it. By the Christmas holidays of the following year, 1952, I had spent the last of my eighteen-hundred-dollar advance and Vandi was getting bored. When she went to Chicago to visit some old lover after telling me she was going to Washington, D.C., on business, I hurt her seriously. Physically, I mean. I began slapping her when she admitted the truth and all the hurts of all my life seemed to come up into me and I went into a trance and kept on slapping her compulsively until suddenly the sight of her swollen face jarred me back to sanity. We had been in bed at the time and it was the Saturday night following Christmas. For an instant I thought that she was dead.

She couldn't go to work; she had lost her sense of balance. She reeled about with her blackened face like a drunken woman. She was ashamed for her own doctor to see her. I had to telephone to a doctor in Harlem to ask what to do; he didn't want to prescribe treatment over the telephone, but I was as ashamed for him to see her as she was for her own doctor to see her.

She didn't leave the house for two weeks. I stayed there with her, wallowing in guilt, and nursed her, bathed her, treated her, fed her, bought the food and cooked it, and kept her maid out, while I cleaned the house.

With my knowledge and consent (she would have done it without my consent), Vandi had been sleeping with a man in his sixties who was either a West Coast industrialist or a Democratic politician in the Roosevelt administration, or both, and ofttimes I had left the house when he arrived in town and returned only after he had gone, usually to find Vandi lying fully dressed in bed, staring dismally at the ceiling, and a neat stack of hundred-dollar bills lying on the bed table. I had never thought that what Vandi had to give was worth so much, but the old codger must have liked it.

At the end of her convalescence, her elderly lover came to town and wanted to see her for an afternoon. I dutifully left the house and went to a movie on Forty-second Street. When I returned, the stack of bills was there and Vandi was lying on the bed, with a very faint bluish shadow beneath her smooth white skin, looking depressed as ever. But it freed me of my guilt. I picked up a bill, tempted for a moment to stay and play the pimp, then left and went to my room on Convent Avenue in Harlem and telephoned my friend Bill Smith in Vermont, to tell him I was coming. When Vandi went to work the next day I hadn't learned then what I was to learn later. The final answer of any black to a white woman with whom he lives in a white society is violence. She knows as well as he, that no one, neither white nor black, will support his contentions. There may be many who will plead his cause, but if she is adamant, there are none who will take his side. Of course, like me, he might not give a damn if anyone takes his side or not as long as he thinks he's right. And the only way to make a white woman listen is to pop her in the eye, or any woman for that matter. But it is presumed only right and justifiable for a black man to beat his own black women when they need it. But how much more does a black man's white woman need it; maybe she needed it when she became his woman.

At least I had got some clothes while living with her. At that time, Kaskel's was a big pawnbroker on Columbus Circle with an outlet store on Fifty-seventh Street which sold new suits of good quality and seconds or those slightly damaged by window display, and I had bought two new suits from them at about half the customary retail price; a beautiful three-button suit in Oxford blue flannel the likes of which I've never seen since, and a two-button suit in beige wool gabardine. In addition I had bought a good suit of dark-gray herringbone tweed from Rogers Peet at Forty-second Street and Fifth Avenue and a gray burberry overcoat from a shop on Fifth Avenue called Nica Rattner, as I remember. And some shirts and ties and good English-made shoes from Brooks Brothers, and some odds and ends, summer suits, shirts, pajamas and such, all seconds, from Klein's and Gimbel's.

I still had the trunk that I had bought secondhand and the horsehide suitcase given to me as a going-away present by Jean's nephew when we went to Los Angeles before the war. The suit-case was as good as new, and I had painted the trunk and the one which I had bought for Jean with several coats of transparent plastic paint when I had been working as caretaker for Frank Bucino. It was a green wardrobe trunk with brass corners and studs and a lock as strong as a safe's. And it was big. I had taken it everywhere with me, on my jobs when I went caretaking, out to the Coast, all around New York, with the greatest of ease; I don't know how I did it. But the taxicabs were bigger then, and my trunk would fit on the floor in back of a DeSoto taxi.

I gave up my room and took my suitcase, typewriter, wardrobe, and another steamer trunk with me to the Smiths' in Vermont. Bill and Helen were sorry about my separation from Jean but Helen was happy in a sour sort of way that I had left my white paramour.

It was very cold in Vermont that winter. As a rule the tempera-ture dropped to about thirty-five degrees below zero at night and rose to about ten below zero at noon; but I had lived in such cold weather during my winters of caretaking that I was prepared for it. They heated their farmhouse with a two-burner fuel-oil stove beneath the staircase in the central room off the kitchen which served as a combined sitting-and-dining room, and it was quite warm. Bill had his study off this room where he had his type-writers and desks and reference books and boxes of manuscripts, and where he smoked his pot when Helen and the kids were off to school, and contemplated on the injustices of racism.

He was rewriting his Vermont story of that time; he had fin-ished it and the publisher had rejected it and he was trying to revise it as suggested, but he didn't agree with the editors. I settled down to help him, typing and proofreading simultaneously a couple of hours each morning before taking my hour's walk along the frozen country roads.

I had acquired the habit of taking Dexamyl from Vandi; they were a combination of dexedrine and amylobarbitone which sharpened the mind incredibly and gave one a sealed-in concentration, but on the other hand slowed the physical reflexes and decreased the appetite. These are called "Purple Hearts" in London. Vandi and I had always drunk ourselves blind at night in order to get to sleep; and she took barbiturate sleeping tablets on top of that. I suppose that was what eventually killed her. But at the Smiths' there was never that much to drink, so I tried to walk off the effect.

My father died out in Cleveland while I was there, and I telephoned Vandi to borrow money to attend his funeral. She did not like it at all. She felt that I was taking advantage of her, knowing that under the circumstances she couldn't refuse, and of course I was. I flew to my father's funeral, and the homosexual undertaker made a pass at me. Jean hadn't come and I was miserable, but I had been prepared for my father's death; he had been seriously ill ten years before and had had several major operations removing parts of his intestines and liver. And then earlier that winter he had fallen down the stairs in the house where he roomed and had broken his hip and had never got over it. All the same it was a depressing funeral. Afterward I ate with my brothers and their wives and caught a plane back to Vermont.

I realized there was nothing to keep me any longer in the United States; both my father and my mother were dead, my wife was gone, the only friend I had in all the publishing world was my editor, William Targ, and I knew he was going to do what he could for *The Third Generation* whether I was there or not.

All that held me there was the lack of money. And then Margot Johnson sold my prison story, which I had retitled *Cast the First Stone*, to Coward McCann, for a twelve-hundred-dollar advance and I decided to leave on that and take my chances. I was not unknown in Europe; *If He Hollers Let Him Go* had been published in England and France and the Scandinavian countries, and *Lonely Crusade* had been published in England and the previous year, 1952, in France, where it had been chosen by Paris critics as one of the five best books from America published in France that year—along with books by Herman Wouk, William Faulkner, Ernest Hemingway, and Scott Fitzgerald. I had corresponded with the translator, Yves Malartic, during the translation in 1951, and he had urged me then to come to Paris.

I went down to New York City and applied at the consulate for a passport and made a tourist class reservation on the French Line S.S. *Ile de France* for the sailing on April 3. It was only the last of February, but it was necessary to book passage far in advance for an April sailing; and of course my sailing was dependent on my getting my passport in time, but I had been assured that the passport would be mailed to me in Vermont in a week or ten days.

Then I bought a rather expensive Linguaphone course in French and returned to Vermont with the records and the text and a determination to learn the French language before I sailed. Bill studied with me but our hearing was not the same and quite often we sought the French Canadians in the neighborhood, especially the storekeeper, to settle a dispute concerning pronunciation. There were two things I did not know at that time which greatly complicated the issue: French Canadians do not speak Parisian French, nor even provincial French; and I am tone-deaf and could not distinguish the French vowel sounds. Ignorant of those small but important factors, I studied diligently, and rattled off senseless phrases, which I would never be called upon to use, with a parrotlike inaccuracy.

Assuring myself that on my arrival I would speak French like a Frenchman, I wrote to Richard Wright and Yves Malartic, and an old friend, Dan Levin, living in Paris at the time, that I was sailing on April 3 and would arrive in Paris the night of April 10, and asked for the names and addresses of hotels where I might put up temporarily.

I had known Dan back in Cleveland during my WPA days, when he had been editing one of those little literary magazines to be found all over the country; and I had seen him again in New York after the war when he had been working as an instantaneous translator for the United Nations. Dan had served in the Pacific and had written one of the first war novels, which in a way was a forerunner of the Jewish writers' treatment of the war theme which had its culmination in Norman Mailer's *The Naked and the Dead*. Jewish writers never glorified war like the Hemingway school. Thinking of it, I remember that Dan fought in the Spanish Civil War before that and had written a short story from that experience which I will never forget. It was about a young poet in the line of prisoners to be shot by the soldiers of Franco. He wanted to write a poem to tell his story to the world, which he would pass back to the end of the line because the soldiers of Franco, being Catholic, always showed their mercy by sparing a certain number, or perhaps only one, out of those to be executed. When he had gotten his scrap of paper and stub of pencil and had written his poem and passed it back, the question was raised, "Suppose we are all shot?" He shrugged and said: "But if we are all shot, there is no hope for the world anyway."

I received a deluge of letters from Dick in response to my inquiry. First he wrote of how pleasant and stimulating life was in Paris; then of how cheaply one could live. That was my first experience with black expatriates who have become self-appointed civic boosters for their favorite European capital. All this I took with a grain of salt; I didn't expect any utopia and I had always found white people much the same wherever I had been in the United States. I didn't expect the Europeans to be greatly different. After all, Americans were their descendants. I just wanted out from the United States, that was all. I had had it.

Dick informed me that he had written the preface for the French edition of *Lonely Crusade*, entitled *La Croisade de Lee*

Gordon, which was the first I had heard of it. Next he listed the various items necessary for cheap and comfortable living on the Rive Gauche, where one could prepare meals in one's hotel room; such items as American toilet articles and medicines which were unobtainable in France, Kleenex, drip-dry nylon shirts, pajamas and underwear, an American can opener, and above all an alcohol stove. He advised me to bring my money in twenty-dollar travelers checks, which were best for the black market. He warned me against expecting rooms with baths, which was more or less an American indulgence, as the French didn't think excessive bathing was healthy, and furthermore, baths cost. And as a favor which he would greatly appreciate, he asked me to go to Harper & Brothers and see John Fischer, who was then editor-in-chief, and get the complimentary copies of his latest novel, *The Outsider,* which was being published that month, and also bring him two reams of twenty-pound bond typewriting paper. And lastly, for me to get a second-class ticket on the first boat train leaving Le Havre and he and my translator, Yves Malartic, would meet the train in Paris.

About that time I received word from Bill Targ that they had sold the reprint rights for *The Third Generation* to New American Library for a ten-thousand-dollar advance and that I could draw my half of the initial payment of five thousand. Suddenly I felt confident. I don't know what effect money has on other people, but it has always given me a confidence that nothing else has. I have noticed that Europeans condemn this as a fault, especially as applied to the American black; but even now I still derive more confidence from money than from all Europe has to offer me.

Then a long chatty letter came from Dan Levin, repeating some of the advice given by Dick, and informing me especially of the Hotel de la Vigne, on the street of the same name in the Latin Quarter a stone's throw from the Café Monaco, run by a retired Army officer and his wife, where I could perhaps always get a room in an emergency.

Then a letter arrived from Malartic saying he had been in

touch with Wright, as he always called him, and he would join him at the Gare Saint Lazare to meet my train. I would know him, he added, by my book *La Croisade de Lee Gordon*, which he would be carrying face forward in his right hand.

But I had not yet received my passport. Three weeks had passed since I had filed my application and I had been told I would receive it in ten days or less. Time was getting short. I telephoned the consulate in New York City and was informed my application had been forwarded to the State Department in Washington for screening. At that time anyone with a Communist affiliation was denied a passport, but the first thought that struck me was the consulate had discovered my prison record, which I had not mentioned in my application. I had written that I was a citizen of the United States and I had thought that was enough. But I was seized with the fear that I might be denied a passport because of it. I dug up my certificate of restoration of citizenship signed by Governor Burton of Ohio, who was then a justice of the Supreme Court, along with the reviews clipped from the Communist press, and sent them to the Passport Division of the State Department.

I never learned what turned the trick, but I suspect it was those reviews of *Lonely Crusade* from the Communist press, particularly the one from the *New Masses*, which compared my book to the "foul words that drooled from the cancer-rotted mouth of Bilbo"; but my passport, signed by Secretary of State John Foster Dulles, arrived a week afterward, and I left bag and baggage for the Albert Hotel in New York, which from that time on I have given as my United States address.

Only one week remained before the date of sailing, and I had many things to do. First I went to the offices of the French Line on South Street, confirmed my reservation, paid for my ticket, and returned to the hotel with my luggage tags and stickers. That made it real. Before then it had been a dream; but by that act I had turned them "loose in the big corral," as the crap-shooters say. Then I went up to the A. & S. Shubert Agency, with which Margot Johnson was affiliated at that time, and picked up my check for $2025 and continued up to the American Express Company and changed it into travelers checks. That night I took Vandi to dinner and we made up. She was happy and excited because she was coming to Europe two weeks later and it pleased her to know there would be a lover on hand when she arrived. Then I drew in my thoughts and concentrated only on the details of my journey. It is no small thing to leave the United States at the age of forty-three—especially if you are a black man and have never been farther than Montreal.

I went shopping for the things Dick suggested that I bring. To Gimbels for drip-dry nylons, among which were some white nylon shirts, airless and uncomfortable, made in Japan, evidently for coolies judging by the way they were cut. To Wanamaker's for a pair of tan wing-tip Oxfords to take turns with my cordovan crepe sole walkers. To a stationery store on Fourteenth Street for Dick's twenty-pound bond typewriter paper. I went by Harper & Brothers, where Dick's book *The Outsider* was on display in the entrance showcase, and picked up his six complimentary copies from John Fischer. Then I went to a hardware store on Broadway to get the alcohol stove. I was to learn, after trudging and subwaying for the next two days all over Manhattan and Brooklyn that Americans didn't use them. Finally someone suggested that I try Abercrombie & Fitch, the sporting-goods store on Madison Avenue where Hemingway bought his overcoats. They had them, but theirs were for camping, not for cooking in your hotel room. I bought a two-burner Primus pressure alcohol stove, which could be converted to kerosene, for fifty dollars; it was to become a legend in the Latin Quarter, where alcohol stoves cost only a few francs.

By the time I had packed my wardrobe trunk it weighed just under the 250 pounds' allowance on my ticket for "hold" luggage. We were to sail Monday and it was then Saturday. I sent it to the French Line dock.

That night I visited Vandi, intending to stay over until Sunday night, but the usual altercation developed—I don't remember what it was about—and while kicking at her with my bare foot I broke my big toe on the step leading down into her sitting room. The ball of my foot swelled so I could not get into a shoe, and I knew of no private doctors who were available at that time of night for broken toes. I didn't think of a hospital. I sat up in the kitchen all night with my foot in a basin of ice water and contracted a cold. Sunday morning, before Vandi got out of bed, I went to a white doctor I knew in Harlem who lived above his clinic on St. Nicholas Avenue—and derived most of his income, I suspect, from treating venereal diseases—and had my toe X-rayed. He said my foot should be put into a cast to keep from developing a bunion but I said I was sailing the next day. He gave me a shot of cortisone and some tablets to take at intervals and told me to see a doctor the first thing in Paris.

I taxied back to the Albert Hotel with my foot in a felt slipper and spent my last night in the United States, sitting alone in my room, nursing my broken toe, and hating Vandi.

Book II

1.

I arrived on board that cold overcast Monday morning on April 3, 1953, wearing a felt slipper and my gray burberry coat, following a porter with my three pieces of cabin luggage: my black horsehide suitcase dating from 1941, my Remington portable typewriter dating from 1931, and a brand-new tape recorder. When I think about it now, I don't remember how I felt. It was the first time I had been on an ocean liner and it was all very strange. I don't think I was either happy or sad; I didn't have time for trifling emotions, I was totally occupied with the newness. A little frightened, not of anything in particular, just afraid of the unknown. I don't know how the astronauts feel the first time they venture out into space, but I know I would feel the same as I felt that morning on the *Ile de France.* My thoughts were most preoccupied with the fact that there I was on board and I didn't know what to do.

Most of the passengers were milling around on the upper decks, waving goodbye to the thousands of people lining the docks. But no one had come to see me off. I hadn't been in contact with Jean for more than a year and I didn't think she knew that I was leaving. The last time I had seen her had been on Christmas Eve of 1952, when I had taken a bottle of King's Ran-

som scotch to the flat on West Twenty-third Street where she lived
with her white girl friend and had blacked out and broken her
girl friend's nose; and the only thing I remember about it is
wrestling with a cop and falling down a flight of stairs and waking
up the next morning lying on my bed in my room on Convent
Avenue, fully dressed, with a wound over my left temple and
blood all over my suit. I hadn't seen her since. And I didn't expect
Vandi to be there after our altercation of Saturday night. I
hadn't told my brother Edward that I was leaving. And Joe was
in North Carolina. And there was no one else.

I went down to look for my cabin. The *Ile de France* was an
old luxury ship with three classes. First class was elaborate, with
its gilt and mirrors and tapestries and inheritance of splendor from
one of the most extravagant monarchies in the history of the
world; and second class was a faithful replica of café society
adornments then prevalent in Paris; but third class was for the
meek and the poor and the Americans. My cabin was in third
class on the bottom deck, between the turbines and the deep blue
sea, I was later to learn. None of my three cabinmates were
present, and I sat down on the upper berth, where my luggage
had been placed.

While I was sitting there alone the steward entered and looked
at me in surprise, then presented me with a bottle of champagne
that had been sent by my editor, Bill Targ. He will never know
what that did for me. Suddenly it brought me back into the community of people. At least there was someone in the world who
knew I was alive. As I started to go back up on deck, James
Putnam, whom I had known as the secretary of the United States
chapter of the Pen Club, brought in a stylish, nice-looking, gray-
haired woman and introduced her as his divorced wife. She had a
cabin on the same deck and she knew none of the passengers, he
said (and I thought, damn right), and he had seen my name on
the passenger list and wanted us to be acquainted. I don't know
how she felt, but I was grateful for an acquaintance. The siren
blew for the visitors to go ashore and Mrs. Putnam suggested that

I go up on C deck and get assigned to a table in the dining room because soon lunch would be served.

The table to which I was assigned was occupied mostly by young white women. The young woman on my left was a full-blown English chorus girl with long curly blond hair and an accent I was later to learn was Cockney who said she had been on a singing tour in the United States and Canada. She was lush, slightly coarse, and overwhelmingly feminine. I had very little to say to her; she was nice, but not particularly interested in me. On my right was a young woman from Wellesley College, one of a group of four at our table who were making a European tour. They were all coolly cordial and seemed at first to be waiting for an opportunity to help me overcome the hazards of sailing, by helpful suggestions no doubt, but after a time they gave me up. They probably discovered I wasn't the kind of black to welcome helpful suggestions from young white American women from Ivy League colleages. There were others at the table, no doubt some males, whom I don't remember at all.

I noticed one other black at my setting, a tall, athletic-looking, well-groomed young man who was a professional basketball player, but we never spoke to one another as many white persons think blacks do automatically.

I don't remember too much about the first days at sea, other than that I was always on the verge of seasickness and drank a lot of wine to keep the rich food down. We had the typical French breakfast of coffee and bread but lunches and dinners were excellent and at each of these meals several bottles of wine were served. Only a few of us at the table drank wine, and the English chorus girl and I generally consumed two bottles together at each meal, of which I drank by far the most. I think that was what put me out with the girls from Wellesley, but it made a favorable impression on the French waiter, a virile-looking black-haired man of about thirty-five, for he always served me the best portions. I remember having my bottle of champagne chilled and offering it about the table, but in the end the English girl and I had to drink it.

I remember the first time I tried out my newly learned French on the French waiter.

"*Avez-vous fini?*" he asked to try me out.

"*Oui, merci, je suis fini,*" I replied complacently.

He threw up his hands. "*Ah non, monsieur! Vous n'êtes pas fini. Vous avez fini,*" he corrected.

The young women tittered, but not maliciously; nevertheless I was embarrassed. Seeing that I was lost, the waiter explained sympathetically, "It is not that you *are* finished, m'sieur, you look far from *being* finished, but you *have* finished dining."

That was the first I realized how little I had actually learned of the language.

I met my cabinmates, but for the life of me I only remember one. He was a young Austrian concert violinist with large dark eyes behind rimless glasses and thick long black curly hair. He had his violin in its case in the cabin. Mrs. Putnam told me she had read of him and he was quite famous for his age. Sometimes I came upon him practicing in the cabin when no one was about and we became more acquainted with each other than with our other cabinmates.

I joined Mrs. Putnam whenever I found her alone in the public rooms and bought her drinks and chatted with her. She was very pleasant and liked me and was always careful to do nothing to emphasize my ignorance of traveling.

About the third morning out, as I was staggering down my corridor feeling seasick as hell, on the way to my cabin to go to bed, I saw a woman frozen to the wall like a person struck with vertigo. I had seen her before in the dining room but she hadn't seemed particularly attractive and I hadn't paid her any attention. But now I looked at her as sharply as a queasy stomach will permit. She looked about forty, rather thin and not very tall, with a mop of short brown hair which looked rather unkempt; she wore a longish, rather tight dress that seemed old-fashioned to me, but it showed her flat stomach and a figure that wasn't bad at all. She had a face that you might call pert and had probably been considered pretty in her youth, I thought, but she had become rather scrawny about the throat and neck like a sex-starved American female. She wasn't the type who would normally have interested me, but upon seeing her there, obviously in distress, I went quickly to her aid. She watched me approach through widened brown eyes in which the black pupils were distended as though she were panic-stricken at sight of me or else was carrying an overload of drugs; and her eyes stared directly into mine with such intensity I felt a tremor of shock. I touched her arm, my mouth opening to say, "Let me help you," but before I could speak, she threw herself against my body, her fingers digging into my arms, and cried, "Don't leave me! Please don't leave me!"

I drew up sharply and jerked my hand away from her. This woman is crazy, I thought.

And immediately she pulled herself away from me and seemed to regain her composure. Her voice became sane and apologetic: "Oh, I'm so sorry, but I was suddenly terrified of all these closed doors. I do have these attacks of claustrophobia. Please forgive me."

" 'S all right," I muttered ungraciously, irritated beyond reason. Why do these frightened white women pick on me? I thought. But I did glance down the corridor. And it was true, the rows of blank closed doors flanking the shabby strip of carpet did look eerie. The sea was rough and everyone was staying in that morning. And those rows of blank gray doors looked more cheerless than a prison range. I smiled at her understandingly.

But either she didn't want to be understood or she misinterpreted the meaning of my smile. She blushed scarlet and seemed overcome with embarrassment. I had the feeling she would have liked to sink beneath the deck. What the hell? I thought.

"I'm quite all right now," she said, averting her face. "Thank you so very much."

She would have rushed away but I clutched her firmly by the arm and said, "Let me help you to your cabin." I was damned if I was going to be put off like that, having been stopped and had my queasy stomach churned up. Like a cop I escorted her grimly to her cabin.

Then I fled up to the third-class deck and clung to the railing in the bitter cold and was as seasick as I have ever been.

I was watching for her when she came into the dining room for lunch, but she did not look in my direction. After lunch I staggered through all the third-class public rooms looking for her to ask if she was all right. Eventually I found her bundled up like a cocoon in a deck chair, and I dropped down into the vacant chair beside her. I don't remember all we talked about that first time. I learned that her name was Mrs. Alva Trent Van Olden Barneveldt and that she was returning from her aunt's in Philadelphia to see her husband and four daughters in Kerkrade, Holland, to try to arrange for a divorce. I can't say I was terribly interested. Her married name had sounded so pretentious I was instantly unsympathetic. She said the black basketball player who sat at her table had told her my name and the title of *If He Hollers Let Him Go,* which he had read. I started to comment about my second novel, *Lonely Crusade,* but just the thought of it brought on another attack of seasickness and I jumped up in the middle of a sentence and staggered out of sight.

We looked for each other and smiled when she came in for dinner. I drank a substantial quantity of wine to stave off another attack of seasickness.

As a consequence I was already lightheaded when I first found her in the third-class lounge. She asked had I been seasick that afternoon or just bored, and I looked at her suddenly in a different light. Outside of her body, of course, the most appealing thing about a woman is a sense of humor. I admitted I'd been seasick and she offered to show me to the third-class pharmacy where I could get some tablets for seasickness, and if I liked, she knew how we could get into the cabin-class quarters. I kidded her about being such an experienced traveler and she said yes, she had made fourteen crossings, and I shut up. Mrs. Putnam came into the lounge before we left and I asked her if she would like to come along to cabin class. As a rule the classes were kept strictly separated and the necessary passageways between them either locked or guarded, but it was early in the season and the liberal French officers had no objection to third-class passengers enjoying the second-class conveniences if they were venturesome enough. There were more unattached young women in third class than in the other two classes combined, and those gay young officers favored sharing the wealth. And of course they couldn't make an issue of our going there, too. The pharmacy was a cubbyhole near the door that led into cabin class, and when I stopped to get some seasickness tablets Mrs. Putnam went ahead, thinking we would follow. Evidently she had been there before also. But when I started to follow, Alva held back, pretending to fix a stocking, and when we finally went ahead, Mrs. Putnam had disappeared.

The lounge we entered was a huge two-storied affair, with the bar and dance hall on the first floor, and tables which afforded more privacy about the horseshoe balcony. The murals and the décor were supposedly adapted after a famous Paris café before the First World War. There was a gay crowd on hand, an orchestra was playing, couples were dancing, and the young white coated stewards were dashing about between the tables, serving drinks. Alva wanted to dance but I pleaded off because of my injured toe, although by then I had begun wearing a shoe again, so we took a table on the balcony and watched the others dance while we drank whiskey and sodas.

"Why did you come to Europe?" she asked.

"Why?" I must have looked startled because she elaborated, "I mean what do you want to do?"

"I want to be rich and famous," I replied.

And that was when I first heard her laugh. It exploded, loud, mannish, raucous; her face went pink and her eyes watered. Couples from all over the balcony turned to look at her. Evidently I must have looked put out, for she reached out with spontaneous gesture and touched me lightly on the cheek.

We sat up talking until morning. She told me that she had married a young, over-sexed Dutch student of dentistry in 1938 when she had been an exchange student from Bryn Mawr to the University of Bonn. His name was Jan Van Olden Barneveldt.

She had been a naïve eighteen-year-old virgin and very pretty, people had said, and he had courted her with a jealous zeal which had frightened her as much as anything. As long as she remained with her sister she had felt protected, but that summer when he had invited her to visit his family in Kerkrade, her sister had gone to the South of France to visit friends. Taking advantage of her ignorance, her suitor had posted the banns. And she, not knowing their significance, received the first inkling that she was to be married when his mother offered to go with her to buy her wedding dress.

In a panic Alva wired her aunt in Philadelphia, asking what to do.

I gathered that her father had been rather prominent in the field of public education. Her mother had come from a very wealthy and socially prominent family but they had lived on their father's salary until his death. There had been three sisters, rather close together in age, known as the Trent girls. Her mother had died shortly after her father's death, before either of the younger girls entered college. Their aunt, on their father's side, had been appointed their guardian. Her maternal aunt, however, was quite wealthy and after her parents' death set up seventy-five-thousand-dollar trust funds for each of the three girls, and by European standards she was considered wealthy.

Her eldest sister had married a motion-picture actor and was living in Hollywood.

The aunt had been out of the city when the telegram arrived and by the time she had returned and cabled the terse answer: CATCH FIRST PLANE AND COME HOME, Alva had already married her passionate suitor. She had been in a strange country surrounded by strange people who were all friends or relatives of Jan and greatly desired his marriage to the pretty American heiress, and she hadn't known how to get out of it.

By then it was rather late and Alva and I were both in a trancelike state, either from the whiskey or from looking into one another's eyes. The conversation, or rather her confession, assumed a shocking fidelity to sexual detail I have encountered since only in Mary McCarthy's book *The Group*. I suppose, basing my judgment on these two sources, that this is exclusively symptomatic of women educated in the Ivy League women's colleges.

At any event Alva confessed all of the harrowing sexual details of their marriage, looking younger and prettier by the moment. And I, an old ex-convict and tuft-hunter, who had consorted with pimps and whores and Harlem society matrons in my time, was shocked to the core.

Her husband had taken her by train to Paris for their honeymoon.

Upon arrival he engaged a room in a small hotel on the Left Bank and sought eagerly to consummate their marriage but found it impossible. An operation was needed. He left her there, frightened and bewildered, and took separate quarters for himself while friends of his, young student doctors, performed the necessary operation. She was made a virtual prisoner. He had her meals sent in and only came himself to make love then left immediately afterward. "Jan has an enormous penis," she added. "But he's very good-looking." I couldn't quite understand why she found that objectionable; all the same I was too mesmerized to interrupt.

Jan took her back to his home where she became pregnant and too late for an annulment, her aunt requested she come to see the family doctor in Philadelphia.

Jan joined her there before the child was born and demanded that she be given her inheritance, which wasn't due legally until she became twenty-one. Her aunt was at first opposed, but the family attorney advised to let her have it; whatever might happen, the newlyweds should start their married life with every asset available.

They went to visit the sister in Hollywood while she was in confinement, and Jan enrolled in the College of Dentistry at the University of California at Berkeley.

Their first daughter was born in the United States. They returned to Kerkrade where her husband took over his father's practice. From the very first, her husband had gone out with other women. It seemed to her that he made a point of seducing all of her good-looking women friends. However, they stayed together and before the war she had given birth to another daughter and one during the war.

When the Germans overran Kerkrade he collaborated with them and became the dental surgeon for the headquarters staff in Maastricht. She spoke German fluently and because of her husband's collaboration she was not interned. But as he spent most of his time in Maastricht, she suffered the hardships of the others.

Her first serious nervous breakdown occurred during the war. Her marital life was rocky and she expressed a general abhorrence for the sexual act; nevertheless, she had already given birth to three healthy and beautiful daughters when she went into the hospital in Maastricht for her fourth. As a result of lack of food and other physical hardships she was in poor health and the baby was stillborn. She had wanted this baby. In fact, she had wanted all of her children; they were her life. But on being told that it had been born dead she appeared to have adjusted to the hurt and disappointment and settled down to weep—something she did quite often during that time, I gathered. Then, the day before she was to leave the hospital, following the evening feeding, a nurse brought a baby into her room and said it was hers. It was the hospital custom to let mothers hold their babies for a time before bedtime. When the mistake was discovered and the supervisor returned to take the baby, she wouldn't give it up. She had become convinced that it was her own and she screamed and cried and fought for it and finally had to be put into a straitjacket. For a long time afterward she had believed that it was her own baby and that the mistake had been made in taking it away from her. Her husband had come from Maastricht and had tried to quiet her, saying she would get him into trouble with the Wehrmacht because she was not acting like a Hollander and it would be discovered she was an American. The secret of her nationality had been well kept, mostly because she had suffered like the others without protest, but if she continued to accuse the hospital of stealing her baby for a German mother, someone was certain to inform on her. Finally, for her safety, he took her and her three daughters, all of whom spoke German fluently and had developed many German characteristics, across the border into a small village in Germany and passed them off as dislocated Germans.

She swore that numerous persons within the Axis—both government and army officials—knew the exact time of the Allied invasion of Normandy weeks in advance, and I was to hear this again from the lips of many Parisians, but I refused to believe it. But she hadn't expected me to believe it; she had just come from the United States where she hadn't found anyone willing to believe it. She contended it was the reason she crossed back into Holland, which, like listening to the BBC, carried the penalty of death.

She contacted the advance units of Patton's army and supplied valuable information about Wehrmacht troop concentrations and military installations, for which she was cited by the U. S. Army and was proclaimed a heroine in the headlines of the Philadelphia daily papers. But her husband was tried for collaborating with the Nazis and sentenced to a year in prison.

In my mind, what happened to her and her daughters during the year he was in prison has always remained obscure. I have always suspected that there was an element she left untold. She was ostracized by the people of Holland because of Jan's imprisonment.

When he was released from the army prison, he returned to

Maastricht, where she was then living since their house in Kerkrade had been bombed, resolved to take his daughters. Legally they were Hollanders and he was entitled to them. She escaped with the elder two in a command car with two American Army officers. Jan pursued them with his old prewar American car loaded with Dutch police. After a wild ride through the night, they crossed the border into Germany, and she and her daughters were put aboard a U.S. bomber returning to the States that took off just as his car came into view with an addition of U. S. Army M.P.s.

The Philadelphia papers carried the headline: HEROINE DIVORCES NAZI HUSBAND.

But the American divorce was not recognized in Holland, where she had been married to a native husband, and he kept their youngest daughter.

He bombarded her with letters, telling her how much he loved her, how much her daughter missed her, how wicked it was to keep the three daughters apart and out of school, and how very sorry he was for everything. It had been that way from the beginning; from the time he'd had his first jealous rages and begged back after all his infidelities.

And she went back to him. His daughters adored him; he was a handsome and charming man. She applied for and received enough money from the War Restoration fund to rebuild their bombed house and re-equip his dental office in Kerkrade. They wound up with a modern and luxurious house and dental clinic. Again he courted her passionately. She became his wife again; and to guard him from other women, and herself from other humiliating experiences, she worked as his receptionist, assistant, and technician.

She became pregnant again, her fifth pregnancy. And he seduced her best friend while she was in confinement. She had a nervous breakdown. He could have had her sent to a mental institution. But her sister's husband, who was a friend of Jan's, prevailed on him to send her on vacation after the baby was born, her fourth daughter.

Jan sent her on a skiing vacation to Switzerland. There she had a third nervous breakdown following a ski injury and returned to the United States to prevent her husband from putting her into a sanitarium.

Her sister's marriage had broken up and her former brother-in-law had emigrated to the United States and set up practice in Atlantic City. When she became well again, and was looking for employment to escape complete dependence on her aunt, he had visited her and offered her a job as his assistant. She had worked for him for two years and now she was returning to Holland to divorce her husband and see her children.

Looking across the table in the almost deserted cabin-class café on the *Ile de France* that April morning in 1953, I knew that she was an innocent woman. She did not have to tell me, as she did later, that her aunt had taught her that the greatest sin one could commit was to hurt another person without cause. The innocence emanated from her. I had never known an innocent woman before. I suppose my mother had been innocent, but I had never thought of her in that way. I had always thought of her as a woman of iron will and ruthless determination and burning ambition; and that doesn't leave much space for innocence. My wife had never been innocent despite the fact that she had loved me fiercely, and had satisfied me completely. Nor were any of the other women whom I had known before.

She had begun crying by then. She had a small face with a high forehead and a wide thin-lipped mouth and small bright brown eyes. And when she cried, ignoring it, striving to indicate that she was not employing it one way or another, that it was just happening uncontrollably and that was all, it was as though her heart was sweating from too much emotional exertion. But she did not wish for it to incite pity; and it didn't.

"You know, my husband made me pregnant five times but never made me an orgasm. Why was that, do you suppose?"

Hell, I didn't know. I wasn't accustomed to women not having orgasms.

In my own way I was as innocent as she was. The difference was that she was a good woman, and I have never been a good man. She was a good woman, and a gentle woman. She impressed me that morning, in particular, as being good. I have never known why. Or how. I no longer remember. But I know the impression formed that morning never changed.

But I thought then and now that she was a little crazy, too. She had been so very hurt by life. Hurt by her husband, by her children, and hurt by the people in the strange, cruel country where she had gone to live. Perhaps she had first been hurt by her parents' deaths and later by the death of her eldest sister, married to the Hollywood actor, who had been found drowned under suspicious circumstances in six iches of water. But she was bound irrevocably to her husband by this pain, in which he had participated in giving and taking. He had hurt her so much that she belonged to him forever. And no doubt she had hurt him very much, too. But no matter how much she despised him and wanted to be free of him, she would never belong entirely to another man. But I didn't know that then. I was just beginning my life away from America, and there were a lot of things I didn't know then, not the least of which was the very land from which I was fleeing.

She was dreadfully afraid to go back. Just the thought of it set her whole body to trembling. He would want her back. He would woo her and use every appeal to have her live with him again. He had all four children, whom he would never give up; he might not permit her to see them. He needed her. Perhaps he belonged to her as much as she to him. And she was so terribly afraid that he would win her.

"Tell me what to do," she begged. "You're a writer. You should know."

I have always felt that there are some things I do know, perhaps very few. I think I know the American blacks better than any European will ever know them and I resent all white chauvinist Europeans who pretend to be authorities on the American race problem.

But at that moment I felt like a damn fool. What should I know that she hadn't already learned the hard way?

But I remember saying, seriously, pompously no doubt, and now I'm certain it was amusing: "The communists have a technique of rejection that always works. Just keep repeating 'no' over and over and over again; but change the manner of saying it each time. Sometimes forcefully; sometimes angrily; sometimes regretfully; sometimes hopefully; sometimes encouragingly; but in the end, it always amounts to 'no.'"

The sun was coming up when we went down to our cabins. I took her in my arms and held her for a moment, but I did not kiss her, as though kissing her would have been wrong. I wanted only to comfort her. How strange we blacks are. I did not want to make the slightest gesture that might disturb her, as though she were my patient and I were her nurse.

My cabinmates were asleep. I took a big drink of whiskey from my private bottle, undressed in the semidark, and climbed into my upper bunk. I thought of her for a long time. I wondered what it was I felt for the hurt women I had known. Not only the hurt white women, but for my wife too when she'd been hurt. But with her it had been different. I had hurt my wife myself, and all the hurt white women I had ever met had been hurt before I had met them.

The next time I saw her was when she came in to lunch. She gave a little wave and I waved back and smiled. All the women at my table facing in that direction became suddenly engrossed in each other and the others seemed alerted by mental telepathy. What the hell? I thought. None of them had shown interest in me, so why should they make such a point of not seeing Alva?

I caught up with Alva before she left the dining room and asked would she come with me to the cabin-class bar and have a drink. She seemed somewhat withdrawn, as though she felt she had talked too much the previous night, but promised to join me in a couple of hours. All of the copies of my books that I had brought, with the exception of *Lonely Crusade* in the French translation, *La Croisade de Lee Gordon*, were packed away in my trunk, but I went down to my cabin and fetched that and Dick's *The Outsider*, for her to read, although God knows when I expected her to have time to read them.

While I was sitting alone at a table on "our" balcony, waiting for her, Mrs. Putnam joined me. It seemed that she had lived for some time in France and she was interested in *La Croisade de Lee Gordon*. She mentioned my long tête-à-tête with Alva the night before with sly amusement. A couple of South American men sitting at an adjoining table asked if I was a writer and she said yes, I was a great American writer, and they looked dutifully impressed, with their tongues in their cheeks. We chatted about this and that, just passing the time, until several hours later when Alva arrived. She had been to the coiffeur and changed her dress but was obviously constrained by Mrs. Putnam's presence.

Mrs. Putnam left shortly, claiming pressing chores, and Alva instantly relaxed and became strangely animated. The two South Americans, who had been alone all this time, seemed to think I was a great man with the ladies and kidded me slyly, calling me Mickey Spillane. One of them danced with Alva, but shortly afterward they had two women of their own and left us to ourselves.

Alva was impressed by my book—I learned later she was trying to write one herself—and we talked about my career until dinner. By that time everything to be said about my career had been said, and I had got in a few words of praise about my famous friend, Richard Wright. I pressed *The Outsider* on her when she went to her cabin to freshen up, telling her it was a great book.

That evening was much the same as the previous evening, except that we got to bed earlier. She apologized for not having heard of Richard Wright, but I must remember she was behind the German lines and they did not get American books. But she promised to read it. Then we talked of her again, her life, her children, her husband, her future, which she confessed was the sixty-four-dollar question. Even if she was successful in divorcing her husband she would not receive any alimony, for he had discovered she had been living with his dentist friend in the United States and had filed a countersuit.

After two days I just wanted to lay her and have it done with. I had said all I had to say about her husband and I was sick and tired of hearing about him.

Emotions between black men and white women are erratic, like a brush fire in a high wind. For a time they burn brightly, burning everything in their path; but they are subject to skip over green patches or turn abruptly about and flicker out on the ashes of what they have previously burned. So it was with me late that second night. I had reached the green patch of sexual necessity. Not so much that I desired her, I just wanted to shut her up.

I could see in her eyes she realized what was happening. She said she was tired and wanted to go to bed. I walked her down the dimly lit corridors to her cabin and stood passively while she kissed me and said good night.

I had several stiff drinks before retiring to my cabin. The young Austrian violinist was still up and he watched me silently, declining a drink. Then he informed me that the ship's captain had invited him to play in the last night's program the following night to be held for all classes in the cabin-class café (where Alva and I had spent most of our time) and he could invite whom he wished to sit at the entertainers' table. He said he would like for me to come as his guest and bring my friend whom he had seen me with.

Alva and I talked but little the next day before the program. She chose her subjects cautiously, but I was inclined to discount most of what she said. She talked of the village life under German occupation. She told of how the villagers stole the pigs the Germans had requisitioned and brought them to her house and slaughtered and cooked them behind sealed blackout curtains, using some device, which I have now forgotten, to dispel the odor of cooking pork, for they all could be executed for the act.

Of how the villagers put blankets and mattresses up to the doors and windows to gather about an illicit radio in the black dark to listen to the BBC and the voice of Churchill, the words she had to translate in whispers, because listening to the BBC was punishable by death. In fact it was so much easier and cheaper to shoot people than imprison them. But when she started again talking about her husband I became bored; and when she claimed he had driven his American car a hundred and twenty miles an hour along the road bordering the river Maas, I became irritated and told her she didn't know what she was talking about—that she meant kilometers per hour, which was only about seventy miles an hour, furthermore, damn few American cars would go that fast before the war.

"Don't be annoyed with me," she said. "I love you."

I became so angry I couldn't see. I think that was the first and only time I ever consciously thought of her as being white. It was such a white remark. But I don't think she meant it like that.

I waited for her at the bar that night, wearing my Oxford blue suit and black shoes, glumly drinking scotches. The band was playing and couples were dancing. The place was rapidly filling up, third-class males in tweed and sport jackets, cabin-class in blue and black, and first-class in dinner jackets and black tie. Most of the women wore evening gowns, but you could easily tell the first-class women by their jewels and degree of exposure. It was more difficult to distinguish between tourist and cabin-class women because many of the young women in tourist class were American students from affluent families and the wives of American teachers and journalists and government officials and businessmen stationed in Europe who were saving money on their fare for more essential things. But all were gripped in a state of high excitement. All except me, it seemed. My broken toe hurt, barring me from dancing, and I felt stuck with Alva when I could have found prettier and more amenable women from the throngs I noticed who seemed bent on giving their bodies away before the night was over.

Then Alva arrived in a mink-dyed muskrat draped over a black evening gown, looking slightly anxious in a delectable sort of way. I felt immensely better. I like my women to look anxious.

We were rather subdued as we walked through the glittering couples on the dance floor to the long table adjacent to the band stand, reserved for the entertainers, but I was very proud of her. She looked self-possessed and elegant. Our host, the young Austrian violinist, had saved places for us next to him. Among the other entertainers, I noticed my tablemate the English girl chatting gaily with a dark European. I nodded to her and her companion subjected me to a moment's scrutiny until he saw that I was accompanied by a woman. I smiled inwardly, realizing he had suspected me of being a jazz musician.

Each of the artists to perform that night was given a bottle of iced champagne, and the steward, making the same mistake of thinking I was a jazz musician, assumed it was for me and opened it when the violinist was absent. We waited for a while for him to return; then Alva suggested that we drink it and get him another bottle. There was no lack of help in consuming it and on top of the scotch I had drunk beforehand it made me rather gay. When our host returned after his wildly applauded performance, the waiter came over to serve his champagne, and finding it gone, became rather abusive. I tried to order another bottle, but he understood me to demand they give him another free bottle and stormed away in disgust. The violinist said it didn't matter, but I got hot under the collar and I followed the waiter back into the pantry. We began shouting at each other in different languages—an occurrence I was to experience all the years I lived in France—until a steward with a good command of both languages understood that I wanted to *buy* another bottle. I took out a twenty-dollar bill and the atmosphere became immediately jovial and the waiter patted me chauvinistically on the back and a steward showed me the label of another bottle and someone else produced a silver bucket and ice and we returned with the champagne like conquerors. As I remember, it had cost about five dollars, and I had thought, What a hell of a performance for five dollars. I had attracted so much attention that the celebration was spoiled for Alva.

I persuaded her to come down to my cabin with me while I got my coat and we would walk around in the moonlight on the deck. I can't imagine that she didn't divine my purpose, for my cabin was at the bottom of the ship and the deck was just outside, but she came along and we found the cabin as deserted as I had known it would be.

I closed and locked the door and took off her coat and began kissing her. She returned my kisses silently and pressed her body against mine. And suddenly I was caught up in an overwhelming desire that surprised me.

"Oh no!" she cried, and burst into tears, snatched up her coat and fled from the room.

I stood there, trying to get the meaning of the scene. Then I went out and found her lying alone in her cabin, crying as though her heart would break. I knelt beside her berth and kissed her eyes and her mouth and her throat and when I kissed her hands she lifted my face and looked at me.

"I love you," I said.

"Oh, my darling, I will come to you as soon as I'm divorced," she sobbed.

"Yes, yes," I said.

I doubt now if I knew what I was saying at the time, or if at that moment I really wanted her to come to me, or in fact realized that was what she was saying. I must confess here that where women are concerned I have always been an ass. But I have never felt more of an ass than when her elderly cabinmate came in a few minutes later and caught me in that position. It had nothing to do with the panic of a black man caught in a white woman's room; strangely enough, the question of race never occurred to me. It was simply that I've always had a tendency to view all situations from a writer's point of view; and I could see myself through what I imagined were her eyes, a grown, forty-odd-year-old half-drunk black man kneeling in his best blue suit on the dirty cabin floor raining kisses on a hysterical wife and mother already embroiled in a messy domestic situation—for I had no doubt that her cabinmates knew all about her affairs. I left quickly and apologetically, promising to see her next morning, but minutes later, she came into my cabin having obliterated all signs of hysteria, and suggested taking a walk on deck.

We went up and walked around the deck in the cold moonlight and swore undying love until it got too cold for kissing; then we went inside and found a vacant table on the balcony above the dancers and feverishly planned the future. By then I was cut completely loose from reality; but I don't think it showed. I have quite often found myself in similar situations, which may be described succinctly as "rescuing damsels in distress." It's a hold-over from the dreams of my childhood. I am completely blinded to my own welfare if there is a damsel in distress—and she doesn't really have to be a damsel, or even in real distress for that matter, just as long as I believe it.

She said that her husband would meet the ship in Le Havre when it docked next day and drive her back to Kerkrade and he would use all his charm and influence and everything in his power—the custody of their daughters, of their house and clinic, the threat to her reputation, the refusal to give her any money, to make her come back to him, and she was deathly afraid. I repeated my advice about saying no, and promised to give her some of my Dexamyls, which would render her immune to any of his blandishments. She promised to return to me by May 1, whatever happened. I gave her Richard Wright's address and told her to contact me there to let me know the exact date and time she would arrive. It was then that I might have tried to determine whether her intention was to leave her husband or to come to me, had I not been so intent on rescuing her.

But the ship had set the scene for extravagant emotions and I don't suppose ours were any more extravagant than those of many others on board that night.

I think I can truthfully say that I was in a state bordering on shock all the next day. We had remained awake until far past daybreak and I did not attempt to get any sleep with all that was to be done. In addition to an emotional hangover and a physical hangover, which had left me feeling punch-drunk, I suffered all the panic and anxieties and instinctive fear of the unknown I had suffered on embarking. I worried about Alva, about whether she would have the strength to meet her ordeal, whether I had given her anything to support her when we parted. She scarcely knew anything at all about my past; she hadn't asked me if I was married and I hadn't told her. I wondered what she had seen in me that made her trust me and love me enough to want to return to me; and I wondered if I really wanted her to return to me, if I would feel the same after a month in Paris, and most of all what I would do with her when she did return.

I had thought that I was leaving the United States partly to escape American white women, but I had only kept an appointment with one in France.

And there were the chores, which had been made more difficult by my emotional hangover and physical debilitation. I had to pack and have my luggage sent up on A deck for transportation to the train. I had to tip the stewards; I didn't know how much to give them. I sought Alva for lunch but her cabinmates said she was ill and having a tray brought to her. I had to line up in the lounge and pass through customs—that took hours. Free again, I had only time for a last goodbye with Alva before the steward let her up on deck to disembark with the others not taking the train. I stood on deck, to which we had free access by then, and the last I saw of her was a tiny figure in a fur coat, going down the gangway, head up and shoulders back, bravely, I thought, to her risky and indeterminable future, until she met a big man in a black hat and a gray ulster on the wharf and they disappeared. No one will ever know how much that hurt me. I'm a sucker for the sentimental.

2.

I was late getting my boat train ticket and all those for the first boat train had been sold out, and that was the cause of all the trouble. Since I had to take the second boat train I decided I may as well take first class and ride in comfort because I was very tired and my broken toe ached. Being ignorant of Continental trains, I assumed that first class would be roomy and luxurious and provide an opportunity for me to stretch out and have a nap during the ride. My first altercation was with the porter. He wanted five hundred old francs to take my suitcase and tape recorder—I carried my typewriter—from the ship to the nearby train. The franc was then 348 to the dollar, and I thought that was damn exorbitant for what I had heard of the poor starving French. I hadn't come over to France to be an ambassador of good will; I was as argumentative, bad-tempered, and unsympathetic as I had been in the United States. I didn't want any sympathy from the French, but I didn't want to be overcharged by them. However, the porter had his way, chiefly because I would have either had to pay what he charged or carry them myself.

Secondly, the first-class compartment to which I had been assigned didn't give any hope of a nap. Eight of us, myself and seven strangers, most of them either oversized or bundled up so voluminously as to appear so, sat across from each other in a small compartment on faded purple plush seats, so close to those we faced that we had to maneuver sharply for foot space. And all of our hand luggage was packed tightly to the ceiling in overhead racks that didn't inspire any confidence. A fat, talkative South American couple, sat next to me, in the center on my side, squashing me into the ice-cold window, and these, I must confess, were the only occupants of that compartment whom I remembered, because they had so much trouble with the douaniers, I suppose. She was wearing a fur coat and had three others of unrecognizable furs stuffed atop their two immense leather suitcases on the rack over their heads. Once the man had to take down both cases and lug them into the passage and open them for inspection, and the woman had to try on each of the fur coats to establish herself as the owner. And then the husband disappeared in the company of two douaniers for a long time and it was assumed he had to open some luggage in the baggage room.

It was about 9 P.M. on April 11 when we left Le Havre. The train plodded through a cold black dark night and I looked out the window at the vague passing silhouettes, with here and there a dimly lit cluster of huddled gray-stone buildings springing from the gloom, and thought of all the wars that had been fought on French soil and the bodies of all the dead that fertilized the darkness and wondered what I had let myself in for. Once a flaming-red neon sign appeared in the black sky reading FORD, and I felt vaguely reassured, although back in the United States there had been nothing in the name to afford me any assurance. After what seemed hours the train pulled into a gloomy cavernous structure that was a smaller, older, grimier likeness of New York City's old Thirty-fifth Street Pennsylvania Railroad Station. According to the French course I had studied in Vermont, a railway porter was called *facteur*. A few porters rushed toward the first-class coaches and passengers began handing them luggage through the windows. While the other passengers in my compartment were taking down their luggage and squeezing into the passage, I pushed down the window and leaned out and shouted, *"Facteur!"* No one paid me the slightest attention. I craned my neck, looking for Richard Wright or a Frenchman carrying a copy of *La Croisade de Lee Gordon* in his arms, but there was no sign of either. Finally, when my coach had cleared out a little, I took down my luggage and carried it out onto the platform in two trips. Still no sign of Dick or Yves Malartic.

My coach was the first coach on the train next to the exit; the train had backed into the station. Crowds waited outside the ticket booths beyond the railing, greeting friends and relatives. I gathered up my luggage, carrying my suitcase and tape recorder in each hand and my portable typewriter under my arm, and followed the others out into the big gloomy station. I didn't see any sign of a waiting room, and I wouldn't have recognized one if I had seen it, so I stood in what I thought was a conspicuous place in the big cavernous lobby, thinking surely that one of my friends would see me. But after a considerable time, in which the train seemed to have completely emptied, I concluded they had met the first train as they had promised and had returned to their respective homes, no doubt expecting me to telephone. I had their telephone numbers but I didn't know how to use the telephone, and I decided it would be simpler if I took a taxi out to Dick's. There was a big neon sign over the side exit reading TAXI. I picked up my luggage and staggered in that direction. There were no taxis. I put my luggage on the sidewalk and waited. It was cold. I buttoned my coat about my neck and turned up the collar. Finally one of the huge old-fashioned box-shaped Renault taxis pulled to the curb beside me and the driver looked in my direction. I walked over and gave him the number in French, *"Quatorze rue Monsieur le Prince."*

He shrugged. *"Pas compris."*

I unbuttoned my coat and took out the two letters from Dick and Dan Levin I had placed in my inside pocket for just such an emergency and pointed to the letterhead of Dick's letter. His face lit up. *"Ah, m'suh luh Prance."* He waited patiently while I loaded my luggage into the back seat, which seemed about the size of the railway compartment I had just quit.

By then it must have been midnight. The lighting seemed abnormally dim for a big city and there was scarcely a sign of life on the streets. My taxi was the only car moving. When we passed through the Louvre in the black dark, I thought we were entering a walled city.

"*Louvre*," the driver threw over his shoulder as the big hearselike taxi curved perilously on cobblestones. I saw the vague silhouette of what seemed like an ancient fortress.

"*Ah oui*," I said.

After traversing a succession of dark narrow streets that could have been taken from the Hollywood film of *The Hunchback of Notre Dame*, we passed the first lighted and inhabited café I had seen and a short distance further drew up before the huge green carriage doors of a low brick building with a single lighted window on the fourth floor. I gave the driver a thousand-franc note and he gave me two dirty one hundreds in return, of which I gave him one hundred for a tip and he sat patiently and watched me struggle with my luggage. When I had dragged it before the doors across the wet sidewalk, I looked about for a pedestrian entrance. Fortunately the driver had remained on hand for a moment to see what I would do next, for with a great performance he condescended to get from his cab and cross the sidewalk to press the button that released the lock on the carriage doors, which, it became suddenly apparent, were the only doors. Through the crack I had a glimpse of a black dark cavern beyond. With an air of strained patience the driver reached inside and pressed the light switch and a cobblestone carriageway, flanked by a paved sidewalk leading back to wide curved stairs on one side, sprang into view. I saluted the driver and dragged my luggage inside. While looking about for a directory of tenants, I heard the door click locked behind me. I felt locked in a prison and suffered a brief moment of panic, but I had taken a number of my tranquilizers and the panic vanished almost instantly. I realized that I must climb the stairs until I found a door bearing

Dick's nameplate. The wall opposite the staircase contained only dark, curtained glass windows of what might have been a café closed for the night.

I picked up my luggage as best I could and started up the stairs. I hadn't progressed more than a few steps before the lights went out. I cursed and lowered my luggage onto the stairs and searched for my lighter. I was groping my way back toward the switch beside the entrance, holding the lighter before me like a torch, when a light appeared suddenly behind the curtained windows and a monster charged forth, the likes of which I had never seen. She looked like some prehistoric species of the human race; obviously female, judging from the huge drooping breasts topping a squarish big-hipped body beneath a flagging purple robe and the things in her hair, and she seemed in a rage. My first impulse was to run, but the door was closed and locked and I couldn't find out how to open it before she was upon me. I began reaching desperately for my letter from Dick, hoping she wouldn't mistake the gesture, and held it before her face.

"*Allez!*" she screamed. "*Allez! Allez! Vite! Vite! Vite!*"

I gathered the general meaning but I had then begun to get angry myself and I shouted at her in English that Mister Wright was expecting me. She pressed the button that unlocked the door and attempted to push me onto the sidewalk. I resisted and for a moment we tussled in the carriageway and the sour rancid smell of a sweaty body and unwashed hair nauseated me. "*Mes bagages!*" I had the presence of mind to shout. "*Mes bagages!*"

I noticed another vague shape behind the curtained door as she rushed back to the stairway, swept up my three pieces of luggage as though they had no weight, and rushed back to the entrance and flung them onto the sidewalk. As I heard my tape recorder and typewriter hitting the pavement, I suffered a moment of fury. She didn't know what she was doing. If she had been in Harlem, throwing a soul brother's fine possessions around like that, she'd have gotten her head cut off. But I didn't resist when she pushed me out behind them and slammed and locked the door. I felt as though I had inadvertently entered the cage of a raving lunatic.

Disconsolately I gathered up my luggage once again and headed down the street in the direction of the one lighted café. I discovered it was crammed full of drunken Americans. I had a distinct and sudden conviction that I was having a nightmare.

Someone told me in a southern United States accent that I might find a taxi around the corner a half block away. I carried my luggage to a sign that read TAXIS, and after standing in the dark and the cold for another half hour one of those huge hearselike taxis pulled up and I told him to take me back to the Gare Saint-Lazare.

I discovered the waiting room that time. It was called *salle d'attente, première classe.* But it looked so dark, gloomy, and unattended that I didn't care to use it, and in fact I wasn't certain it was open for use, so I stood in the now almost deserted lobby, surrounded by my luggage, hoping against hope that some English-speaking station official might notice my predicament and offer assistance. But the few uniformed personnel who passed didn't even look about at my tentative "Pardon me, sir," but hurried on as though the open arms of Danielle Darrieux awaited them, and if any gendarmes were about they watched over me unseen. But shortly a number of prostitutes gathered, buzzing about me like green flies. They came and went in a silent spectacle which might have been entitled *The Night the Whores of Saint-Lazare Came Out to Tempt le Nègre de New York*, but there was one in bare legs and a belted coat who stood her ground, waiting for the others to clear off perhaps, and might have even won me by her persistence until I remembered the letter from Dan Levin giving me the name of Hôtel de la Vigne, which was run by a retired American Army officer, where I could apply for a room in an emergency. I had spent all of my French money and only had a few American dollar bills, but somehow I managed to reach an agreement with the last taxi driver left, an old man in the smallest car that I had ever seen—I later learned it was the smallest Citroën ever made—with a dog huddled up beside him, to take me for a dollar, giving him the letter to read the address. He took me there and left me in the taxi while he went in to ask if they had a room. After a moment he returned, beaming, and helped me in with my luggage. The housekeeper, who had been awakened, said in fluent English that the taxi fare was five hundred francs. I told her I didn't have any French money but I was a friend of Mr. Richard Wright and she could trust me, pulling Dick's letter from my pocket to substantiate my claim. "Oh, you're Mr. Chester Himes," she said. "Mr. Wright has reserved a room for tonight for you."

It was all I could do to keep down the hysterics. She paid the taxi driver and took me to my room. As it didn't have a telephone, I decided to postpone calling Dick until morning. After drinking the half pint of whiskey I had left, I climbed into the big cold double bed and went to sleep.

In the meantime Dick and Malartic had met the first train, and, positively ascertaining I was not aboard, had retired to a café across the street on rue Saint-Lazare and had awaited the second. Stationing themselves at either end of the second-class coaches on the second train so as not to miss me, they waited. But as I was in the first-class section, in the first coach, I had alighted unseen by them, while they had still been looking for me at the other end of the train. I had grown impatient in a perfectly natural American fashion and had taken a taxi to his house. Dick's youngest daughter, Rachel, had been ill, and not being aware that I would appear alone, Dick had left instructions with the concierge not to let anyone up to his apartment. Dick was alarmed by my disappearance, and Yves Malartic was not the kind of Frenchman to spoil any American's good alarm, and had filled him with gruesome accounts of persons who had been known to disappear in the Paris gares and had not been found until months, even years, afterward, destitute and penniless if they were men, or sold into white slavery somewhere in North Africa if they were women.

As all his friends knew, Dick had an excitable temperament and was given to such self-indulgent exaggeration that the buzzing of a blowfly could range like a typhoon in his imagination. He rushed back to Ellen in a state of extreme concern and declared that something dreadful must have happened to me for I had completely disappeared and he must notify the police at once. Ellen took the more mundane view that some woman lay at the center of the mystery and cautioned him against undue haste lest the unraveling cause great embarrassment. At just about that time Alva telephoned from some place in Belgium, instantly justifying Ellen's suspicions, to ask if I had arrived. Ellen said accusingly that I seemed to have disappeared and asked if she could shed any light on the mystery. No doubt if Ellen could have read Alva's mind, she would have discovered they shared the same suspicions, but Alva expressed a concern equal to Dick's. Then Ellen asked the question for which Alva never forgave her, "Was Chester drunk?"

Early next morning I was awakened by a hammering on the door. Dick had stopped by on his way to the police to cancel the reservation until further notice, and the proprietor had informed him that I was upstairs in the room he had reserved for me sleeping. I could see he was alive with curiosity; he had always been extremely curious about me. He knew of my prison record and he had known Jean, and he suspected I had lived a life of wild and raging fury. I think I am one of the tamest men he ever knew, but he never came to know me well enough to know this. After we had sorted out the mixup, he invited me to lunch, saying Ollie Harrington would be there, and for some reason seemed called upon to apologize for Ollie's not coming down to the station the night before to pick me up in his car. But I saw no reason why Ollie should have felt obligated, or that Dick should have felt he thought so, for I didn't know Ollie that well. I had seen him in officer's uniform around Harlem at the end of the war, always in the company of high-society blacks whom I had met during the short time I lived with my cousin Henry Moon and his wife Molly. Most of the time Ollie had been escorting his blond wife, who I thought was Norwegian, and whom I remember best for her thick ankles and unshapely legs.

I dressed and went with Dick down the street to the Café Monaco for a French breakfast (*petit-déjeuner*) of chicory-tasting

coffee and a croissant; it was the café I had seen the night before
filled with drunken Americans, but in the morning it was filled
only with hung-over Americans. Dick greeted everyone with boisterous condescension; it was obvious he was the king thereabouts.
His apartment was only half a block up the street, which was
adjacent to the street of my hotel, and at that time the Café
Monaco was the most notorious hangout for Americans in the
Latin Quarter, and naturally that entire section between the
Odéon and Place de l'Odéon was a honeycomb of brothels,
bistros, caves, and the favorite cafés of homosexuals, male and
female. Later I learned that it was the custom of my fellow
countrymen to sleep with a French prostitute the first night of
their arrival and spend the following week or two trying to get
cured of VD. I seemed to have been one of the few exceptions;
but I noticed that all the girls, both amateur and professional,
having their morning coffee, were giving me the once-over, trying
to assess whether I was a man worthy of their attention or a fairy
trying to latch onto Dick.

Dick expected a gathering of our soul brother compatriots, all
of whom knew I was to arrive the night before, but not one of
them appeared, an eccentricity which I was later to learn was
the natural reaction of the envious and jealous American blacks
who lived in Paris—or anywhere else in Europe, for that matter.
They did not want any arriving brother to get the idea they
thought he was important.

So we spent the remainder of the morning looking for a permanent hotel room for me—a chore for which Dick had expected
help from the other brothers. Dick was very anxious for me to
get my trunk from customs so he could get his copies of *The
Outsider*. Before noon we had found a front room on the second
floor of the Hôtel Scandinavie, on the rue de Tournon, across
from the Café Tournon, a favorite hangout for Jewish war ref-
ugees, which was also patronized by some of the brothers.

Ollie had arrived by the time we got back to his house for lunch,
and explanations were in order. I was surprised to find Ellen had
become thin and blond with lots of make-up and a harried, dissatis-

fied look. One of the first things she said to me was that she and
Dick had gone completely French. I noticed Dick look sort of
sheepish but he offered no comment, and Ollie looked wise and
indulgent and his eyes twinkled knowingly. I didn't know what
to say, so I said nothing.

The lunch consisted of spaghetti and meatballs, which didn't
seem very French to me, and Ellen told me of Alva's call and
asked me who she was and I said I would call her back without
answering her question. I scarcely recognized Ollie—he had grown
stout, and looked more like a Balkan character out of an Eric
Ambler spy story in his neat salt-and-pepper tweed than a black
refugee from the United States. In a conversational lull, I told
Dick I had seen the film of *Native Son*, for which he had written
the screenplay, co-produced, and acted the role of Bigger Thomas;
and that when I had left it was showing in a chain of twenty or
more neighborhood theaters. He immediately brightened up and
rubbed his hands jubilantly, and said maybe he would get his
money back. He confessed he had spent more than a year in its
making and had initially lost a great deal of money in the pro-
duction. Then his agent called and I could hear him talking
about an advance from Gallimard for one of his books, which
they were publishing. At the same time Ellen was talking away
about the great expense of having her hair dyed weekly and she
had learned to do it with a rinse of Clorox, which served just as
well. I could believe the Clorox part, anyway. Then when Dick
returned, they both asked if I would like to go to a writers' colony
in La Ciotat, on the Mediterranean sea, run by a friend of theirs
named Daniel Guerin; he was quite interested in having me as
one of their guests. I said I'd have to think it over.

Julia and Rachel came in to say hello. I remembered Julia as a
tiny tot in New York, but she had grown to be the spit and
image of her father. But I had never seen Rachel before; she was
like a dark-blond doll and spoiled, and it was immediately apparent that she was her father's pet.

When Ollie left, Ellen asked me if I wanted to call Alva from there—she had the number—but I thanked her and said I would call later. I have always abhorred being overheard in my love talk.

Dick helped me move my luggage to the Hôtel Scandinavie and he was so impatient for me to get my trunk that I went with him to get his car from the garage where it was being repaired. He had taken a big American Oldsmobile with him to France and found it terribly difficult to drive through the old narrow streets of the Latin Quarter. But what made him give it up was a typical traffic incident. The Parisian police were impatient with big American cars blocking traffic in the congested centers, and once when circling on the Place de la Concorde, Dick had stopped to let the traffic open up ahead of him. However, there was a narrow space in the congested cars, and the traffic cop was impatient for him to move his car to make room for traffic flowing in another direction. He waved Dick forward into the narrow space ahead. Dick hesitated; it did not seem there was space for his wide Olds. The cop bore down on him gesturing to him to proceed, shouting, "Vite! Vite! Allez-y!"

Dick stepped on the accelerator and the big car with its hydromatic drive leaped forward into the narrow opening and crushed the fenders on both sides and on each side of the adjoining cars.

The traffic cop shook his head sadly and said, "Tch! Tch! Tch!"

So Dick had sold his Olds and bought a reconditioned Citroën traction avant. But late one night, several days before I had arrived, turning a corner into a dark narrow street he had hit a man on a bicycle and had knocked him a number of yards through the air and run over his bicycle. His insurance was paying all the costs; fortunately the man had not been killed, but at that time he was still in the hospital, and Dick's car had been in the garage.

But it had been repaired and as it was getting late in the day and nearing the time customs would close, we drove straight from the garage to the customs shed in the Gare Saint-Lazare. It was not until we were standing at the counter and I had presented my baggage check that I discovered that I had left my trunk keys in my suitcase at the hotel. There was insufficient time for us to return for them and get back before customs closed, and the douanier was approaching from the shed with my big green wardrobe trunk with its impregnable lock on a handcart.

Dick explained that I had lost my key but I would swear there was nothing in the trunk for me to declare. One could see the douanier was sympathetic, but it was such a big trunk and weighed more than a hundred kilos, which is a lot of trunk for France, and he wasn't much more than a porter himself, so he couldn't permit it to pass. Dick said that he would send for a locksmith to open the trunk and that I would gladly pay for it; and in desperation he said they could pry the trunk open with a crowbar. I wasn't having my good trunk pried open with a crowbar, or even opened by a locksmith, for all Dick's books, and he knew damn well I wasn't, but I didn't say anything. The douanier said he'd have to ask his superior and went and fetched him from his office in the rear. Then Dick began putting on his act. Beside us on the counter were several big cartons of Kleenex and one of toilet issue, still in the factory packing, being collected by a uniformed chauffeur apparently from the United States Embassy. Dick pointed to the cartons and said to the chief douanier in his bad French, "They can't even wipe their ass on French paper." There was a great animosity against the remnants of the United States occupation forces still stationed in and about Paris at the time, and signs were scribbled on every wall in the Latin Quarter reading: "U.S. GO HOME."

The chief douanier laughed at Dick's crack and passed my trunk unopened. For which I was damn grateful, for I had my own share of American toiletries, which Dick himself had suggested I bring, including Kleenex, American soap, toothpaste, toilet paper, etc.

The trunk fitted on the back seat in Dick's car, which was an *onze chevaux*, much to my surprise, for the Citroën, although one of the biggest and fastest cars of France, looked very small in comparison to the American land cruisers of that year. Together, blowing and panting, we got it up to my second-floor hotel room. Before we could get our breath, Dick insisted on my opening it so he could get his books, and without stopping for another thing, he took me through the dark narrow streets (it was already black dark by that time) to the English Book Store, run by a young blond Frenchwoman named Gaite, for her to put on display in her window. I noticed at the time that she paid far more attention to me as a male than to Dick's valued copies of *The Outsider*, but nevertheless the three of us stood outside the shop on the sidewalk for the next half hour listening to Dick discuss how the books could be displayed to their best advantage. Gaite spoke English, and was reputed to have had an immoderate curiosity about black writers, although I was never able to verify this; at first I was unable to find my way back to her store and later I didn't have time.

I ate alone that first night, not having yet met any of the other brothers, and later Dick took me to a nightclub down the street from him called La Romance, run by a Frenchwoman in her fifties with dyed red hair who was acquainted with him, as was everyone in the Latin Quarter, and perhaps in all of Paris, and who dominated the conversation, declaring loudly in broken English how much more destructive and uncouth and undisciplined and bestial the United States Army had been than the Nazis. "If the war had lasted, the Americans would have burned Paris to the ground!" she exclaimed.

I soon tired of her bullshit and said good night to Dick and went wandering off alone and was soon lost among the myriad of bistros and students on the boulevard Saint Michel and day was breaking before I found my way home.

Thereafter I found my first week in Paris exceedingly dull. I had dinner with Yves Malartic and his wife Yvonne and about a dozen of his acquaintances, including a couple of editors, an opera singer and her lover, and several others whose chief aim in life seemed to belittle Americans. I met them by appointment at the Deux Magots on Saint-Germain-des-Prés, looking elegant, I thought, in my Oxford blue suit, black shoes, and gray burberry (for it was cold), and greeted Yves, "Je suis très content de vous avoir," trying out my French. Yves was a little man, slightly over five feet, but we had corresponded a great deal while he had been translating *Lonely Crusade* and he was very friendly, but upon hearing my carefully rehearsed speech he looked puzzled and said, "Himes, you must forgive an uncultured Frenchman such as myself, but I do not understand English so well." I didn't try my French any more that night.

We all went to a restaurant nearby and I was presented with a menu written in French script, of which I did not understand a single thing, so I let Yves order for me. A young American white man sitting across the aisle from us said, "It's written in English on the back," but I didn't turn it over for fear of spoiling the obvious joke.

For a time they made fun of the existentialists, including *le roi* Sartre and *le dauphin* Camus; and then they started making fun of me in a sly fashion. First they started on my cigarette lighter, a nine-dollar stainless-steel Dunhill I had bought in New York. I told them it was English. Then they said I had greeted them in such strange English; did all *américains noires* speak such English? I said I had thought I was speaking French. At that they thawed and began on the food. They said the steak we had eaten had been horseflesh; had I ever eaten horseflesh before? I said in Harlem we not only ate horseflesh but ate hamburgers made of cat and stews made of dog, and that I had read that during the French Revolution the Parisians had eaten ragout made of rat. It was all in good fun and we parted on good terms and I promised to visit Yves soon. He lived on the seventh and top floor of a walkup on rue Montparnasse, near the corner of Boulevard Montparnasse, and advised that if I should call, it would be best to stand on the sidewalk across the street and shout up to him before attempting to climb nine flights of stairs.

I spent some afternoons at the Café Monaco outside on the terrace, which caught the sun when it shone, but it was mostly cold and rainy that April. I saw Ollie there and some of the other soul brothers, but I had little to say to them for somehow we didn't speak the same language and we weren't interested in the same women; I never visited any of them in their hotels or wherever they lived, and the most I knew of any of them except Dick was from chatting a few moments about nonsense in cafés. One day Dick asked me if I knew William Gardner Smith. I knew of William Gardner Smith—his book *The Last of the Conquerors* had been advertised across the front cover of the Signet edition of *If He Hollers Let Him Go*, much to my displeasure—and I said I would like to meet him. Dick took me over to the Café Tournon, across the street from my hotel, and introduced me to a moderately tall, pleasant looking brown-skinned young man who talked very rapidly in choppy, broken sentences, and said how glad he was to meet me, but it was very obvious that he and Dick did not like each other at all. *The Last of the Conquerors* had not been published in France, and I don't think it ever was, I don't know why; I think it is a fine book and compares favorably with Hemingway's *A Farewell to Arms*, to which it is very similar, both being intense love stories about very young people under conditions of war, and both giving the impression of being written by very young people with strong and subtle talents. But Bill had written another book of which I had not heard, *Anger at Innocence*, which had been selected by a book club in France, and since none of Dick's books had ever received that doubtful distinction, I think Bill felt a little superior about the matter, which was very normal for one so young, and he was young. Youth was the most outstanding characteristic of William Gardner Smith—youth and a naïveté.

One day, very much to my surprise, I received a note at my hotel from a French journalist named Annie Brierre, asking if I would care to come to her house to be interviewed for the newspaper *France-U.S.A.*, giving an address in Square du Roule. It was a private square not far from the Etoile, and Mme. Brierre's apartment was what I had always thought the apartments of the French minor aristocracy would be like. She was a big-boned woman in her fifties with the imposingly strong face and big nose of the old French, but somehow, looking even more masculine than many men, and with a straightforward, unaffected manner, she gave the impression of being entirely feminine.

She asked me what I thought of the marvelous "black opera" which was then showing in a theater on Avenue Mac-Mahon around the corner from her, and I said I had never liked the story of *Porgy and Bess*, but the music was superb. I gathered the impression she didn't agree, that she liked both music and story, but she didn't say so. She opened a pint bottle of a brand of scotch I had never heard of, and asked me what I thought of William Styron, whom she had interviewed for the previous issue of *France-U.S.A.*, and I answered truthfully that I had never heard of him. Then she asked my opinion of Hemingway, whom she had interviewed some time previous, and I burst out laughing. I apologized for my apparent rudeness and explained that her question had reminded me of an incident in a restaurant in New York called Cyrano's, where I was having a drink at the bar with my first editor, Bucklin Moon, while awaiting a table for supper. There was an elegantly dressed drunk occupying the stool next to me who was saying: "I don't really like *A Farewell to Arms*. After I had read it for the fifth time I really decided I didn't like it." After a time she decided that she liked me and asked me to phone her again when I was free, and then, shortly before I left, out of a clear blue sky, she remarked conversationally that it was such a pity that so many very nice American writers came to Paris and got entangled with such cheap and impossible women. I left, feeling duly warned, but at that particular moment I wouldn't have given a damn how cheap and impossible a woman was as long as she was young, healthy, and available.

Then a couple of nights later Mrs. Putnam called me at my hotel and asked if I would like to go with her to a rather special restaurant in Montmartre, run by a retired clown named Coco, if my memory is correct, and his wife. I said I would be delighted and she came by the hotel in her little bug of a Renault and drove through the streets of the Rive Droite, which were quite unfamiliar to me and up the steep mountainous hills to Montmartre. We were lucky to get the last table before the doors were closed and locked. All the tables were placed about the four walls in a continuous row, facing inward. There were not more than twenty, and all were filled with fashionable people of middle age, the men in dark suits and the women with bare shoulders and low décolletage, highly made up and glittering with jewelry.

We enjoyed a superb dinner in an atmosphere of laughing gaiety, after which Coco brought out his chef-d'oeuvre. It was a giant phallus, complete with testicles, of a beige meringue, mounted on a silver tray, which, starting at the pantry entrance, he proceeded to circle the dining room and present it to each woman for her to kiss. And each woman, in her turn, demurely took a suck from the tasty head, and it was passed on like children sharing a lollipop. Neither the women nor their escorts seemed the least embarrassed, and the women took on an alluring high color and were obviously aphrodisiacally amused without losing their dignity, as only Frenchwomen can be. Mrs. Putnam, though not at all embarrassed by the proceedings, observed them with amused clinical interest.

Upon returning to my hotel, I felt obliged to ask her to come up to my room, but she demurred with appropriate tactfulness. I kissed her good night and went up to bed, wondering why I was suddenly finding middle-aged women sexually attractive—first Alva, then Annie Brierre, and now Mrs. Putnam. I must be getting old, I thought.

Every morning either Dick or Ellen came by the hotel between seven and eight and got me out of bed so we could go across to the Café Tournon and have coffee. I had always been attracted to Ellen, ever since I had first met her in 1944, when she had been a plump, pleasant, brown-haired young woman with a very sweet disposition. I often imagined she felt some vague attraction for me also. But I couldn't understand why Dick felt called upon to come around so early, unless he wanted to beat Ellen there, which of course was silly, for I respected Dick more than anyone else I knew and would certainly never have done anything to embarrass him. At that time the Scandinavie was filled with homosexuals and a large number of young American girls who wished to cram a lifetime of sexual escapades into the short time they would have before they had to return home and marry. Dick once said,

"Chester, when it gets warm these American girls go down the street, flinging open their arms, and cry, 'Take me! Take me! I'm young and good in bed.'" As I have said before, Dick always exaggerated. But anyway, the residents in the hotel began to wonder what sort of arrangement we had—were Dick and I lovers, or Ellen and me, or did they take turns with me?

But generally I wouldn't see them again for the rest of the day. Ellen had the supervising of the household chores—they had a maid, of course—and tending to Rachel, and taking Julia back and forth to school, as is required of French mothers. So I spent most of my days at the Café Monaco and my nights at the Café Tournon. I met the black painter Walter Coleman at the Monaco. He was living with a short, hefty, redheaded, loud-mouthed Texan girl at that time; and they would have knock-down drag-out fights on occasion. She would stand up to him and fight like a man, and when they started cursing each other, "motherfucking" each other, you couldn't tell the white woman from Texas from the black man from Baltimore. But Walter had a highly volatile and rather likable personality and he and his girl began coming around to my room selling me bottles of gin and whiskey at half the price they cost in the stores: I never learned what they paid for them or how they got them.

I met other soul brothers: Ish Kelly, whom Dick wrote about in his book The Long Dream, calling him Fish Belly; Mercer Cook's son, who was attending the Sorbonne; Dr. E. Franklin Frazier, who was living in Paris at the time as head of the Mutual Security Agency and I visited him and his wife Marie, whom I had known from the period I lived with Henry and Molly Moon in Harlem. I had always liked Dr. Frazier and Marie; he was an extraordinary raconteur, and Marie also had a sharp sense of humor. She was a large, formidable-looking woman, with a face like an eagle's, and people who didn't know her thought she had a fierce temper. She told me that she always rode in the first-class coaches of the Paris subway on second-class tickets, and when the conductors asked her to move back into second class she would look at them fiercely and say in English,

"I don't speak French." They would shrug and move off. This worked excellently until one day when she had said to the conductor, "I don't speak French," a kindly white American woman sitting next to her volunteered, "Oh, I'll translate for you. I speak English." Marie glared at the woman and said, "I don't speak English either."

I met a young black couple named Hines at their house who had worked for some United States government agency in Monrovia, Liberia, and another single girl, Ruth, who had worked for the embassy in Monrovia. Ruth had been transferred to the Paris embassy as a secretary while the Hineses were on their way home. She was very kind to me, she took me to Leroy and Gaby Haynes' barbecue restaurant on rue Manuel for the first time, and bought whiskey from the embassy commissary for me at $1.65 per bottle for the finest scotch and $1.75 per bottle for the famous American bourbons, and cartons of my favorite cigarettes, Lucky Strikes, for nine cents a pack. She had a studio on the rez-de-chaussée of a nice apartment house up the hill from Place du Trocadero, equipped with all the modern conveniences—bath, built-in closets, etc. The proprietor had had it built for his daughter, who had gone off to live in Mexico. I used to visit her to pick up the whiskey and cigarettes and take baths, but she never let me make love to her. Black women can say no and mean it with such good humor that you aren't offended and will remain friends.

And then one night at the Café Tournon, in his abrupt jerky way, Bill Smith asked me if I wanted to take a walk down to the Seine with him. I said all right, and a big-busted redheaded girl named Rory Calhoun said she'd come along with us. I got to looking at Rory's breasts, aimed at me like howitzers, and suggested to Bill that he could leave us. Bill said he couldn't do that, she was married to a Dutch boy who was a good friend of his. Rory looked from one to the other of us and grinned like an idiot.

All Bill wanted was to borrow twenty-five hundred francs to go to Ringside, the jazz joint in fashion at that time which had become famous from the singing of Eartha Kitt and the visits of

Ava Gardner. I went along with Bill, but nothing interesting happened that night and I got cornered by a middle-aged black couple who wanted to discuss the race problem and I left. The joint is called the Blue Note now, famous for Bud Powell and Kenny Clarke.

I didn't know about the American Hospital at the time, and Dick had recommended a doctor in the quarter—J. Schiller, I think his name was—to treat my broken toe. Dr. Schiller had several spayed Siamese cats in his dreary dark apartment where his office was located, and I held them responsible for the nauseating odor of his office until I learned he was the VD specialist of the quarter. He injected my toe with cortisone and gave me a shot of penicillin, after which I could scarcely walk at all.

I had only been in Paris for one week when Vandi arrived. She had booked into the Hôtel Saints-Pères on rue des Saints-Pères, off the boulevard Saint-Germain, and I returned to my hotel to find her telegram from the ship just about the time she arrived, "COME QUICKLY: FOR YOU KNOW WHAT . . ." She was in her bath when I got to the hotel and I waited for her in the garden, which had by then been opened. She was just the same; she demanded that we first go to my hotel and go to bed. It was afternoon, but I had learned by then that that was the correct time for extracurricular assignations in Paris. Afterward she said my body was just like the statues in the Tuileries, and I wondered suddenly what had happened to the men in New York during the short time since I had left.

She was there for a week and spent most of her leisure time with me—chiefly, I think, because she didn't feel like breaking in a new lover. We were more affectionate than we had been at any time. I found it amusing the way American women instantly dropped all their sexual inhibitions on arriving in Paris. I took her by Dick and Ellen's—she had known them both from her days with the Rosenwald Foundation—and we found Dick typing industriously on his novel, which was later published as *Savage Holiday*, on the paper he had asked me to bring. Dick told us that the plot for the story had come to him suddenly several months previously when he had been in bed with a high fever. Later, when he had let me read the finished manuscript, I believed him. One morning I went and climbed the nine flights of stairs to Yves Malartic's penthouse to fetch him and Yvonne to join Vandi and me for petit-déjeuner. It was a lovely little place with huge French windows letting out on small terraces back and front, offering a breathtaking view of practically all of Paris; but, as is customary with these pleasant little top-floor rooms constructed primarily for the maids, it had no bath, and the "water closet" was in the corridor shared by the adjoining apartment.

It was chilly so we went to the closed terrace of the Dôme, at the corner of the boulevards Raspail and Montparnasse and sat near the oil heater and Vandi and I had two huge Cognacs to their amused consternation while they had their usual café-crème and croissant. They always remembered Vandi as the American woman who drank Cognac for breakfast. We sat around and talked until lunch, then went to a crêperie on the ground floor of the house in which they lived. Yvonne didn't speak English at the time, and Yves' speaking English was limited, although he had translated books by Dos Passos, Upton Sinclair, Sinclair Lewis, and many other well-known American writers; and Vandi didn't speak French any better than I did, so you can imagine how the conversation went. But they were fascinated by Vandi. In fact, all Frenchmen were charmed by her fair complexion and magnificent shoulders and firm breasts which had always been unimpeded by bras, her light curly hair, but most of all perhaps by her knowing sensual grin. Vandi was a big hit.

Ollie Harrington gave a party for her in his top-floor apartment in the Raymond Duncan building on rue Seine, but when we arrived the entrance and staircase were black-dark—Duncan turned off the electricity at nine o'clock to discourage visitors— and his tenants had placed stubs of candles on the floor beside the entrance for guests to light their way upstairs. But we didn't know that and I had left my flashlight, which all knowledgeable people always carried about at night in the Latin Quarter, in my room.

We could hear the noise of the party from the courtyard and I stood there and shouted at the top of my voice; but no one heard but Duncan himself, who came from his ground-floor residence and scolded us. Vandi told him to go to hell, and we left; but for years Ollie resented the fact I hadn't brought her to his party. We went searching for a cave in Saint-Germain-des-Prés, but they turned us back at Club Saint-Germain—I hadn't begun writing my *Série Noire* stories at that time and my name wasn't known to all the nightclub proprietors, as it was later—so we sat on the closed terrace of the Deux Magots, huddled up in our winter coats, until it was time to retire.

In her own way, having been associated with the Rosenwald Foundation, the International Institute of Education, and the New York and Chicago society of writers and publishers and blacks, Vandi was as famous as Richard Wright among the American group on the Left Bank; but she had no great desire to go anywhere but to good restaurants and to bed, and that was most of what we did that week. The American group in the Latin Quarter usually ate in a little restaurant on the ground floor next to my hotel or in the Acropole, a Greek restaurant off the boulevard Saint-Michel, but I had never been to either of these restaurants, and I took Vandi to such places as La Méditerranée, Tour d'Argent, Maxim's, and Chope Danton, much to the envy and resentment of the soul brothers, who thought I was keeping her away from them on purpose. Dick and Ellen took us to dinner one night to a famous cous-cous restaurant on rue de la Huchette, near Place Saint-Michel, and we met a young Jewish couple with whom Vandi was also acquainted, also with Mutual Security Agency, who invited us all out to their home in the suburb of Saint-Germain some Sunday, and afterward drove us home in their American car. For appearances sake Vandi and I got out at the Hotel des Saint-Pères and then walked back to the Scandinavie to go to bed, as it was fashionable at that time for the proprietors of the one-star hotels to affect an attitude of racism along with their anti-Americanism. Of course, that didn't make a bit of goddamn sense, but one learns that in certain areas the French are not sensible anyway, merely fashionable.

The highlight of Vandi's visit came one night when we were making love in my hotel room. A young French girl, who claimed to be a student, occupied the room adjoining mine, and the dividing wall was so thin one could hear one's neighbor turning the leaves of a book. When her boy friend (I never learned whether he was her lover) visited her, I could hear them conversing by the hour in passionate sibilant whispers, which always reminded me of the joke of the newcomer to hell listening at the closed doors of the various rooms to ascertain what one he would choose for the remainder of eternity. The newcomer listened at the closed door of the first room to the sound of grunting and panting and the clashing of flesh, but couldn't determine whether the occupants were fighting or making passionate love; at the closed door of the second room, heated voices were discussing the defects of all religions; at the third room there was the constant sound of bare feet treading the floor, etc., until he came to a room where he could only hear the sound of intense sibilant whispers, but try as he would he could not make out what was being said in such passionate intensity. He imagined the room filled with nude women whom passionate men were trying to seduce, and as he had always had such great success on earth, he decided that that was the place for him to spend eternity. He flung open the door and entered, certain to find a desirable nude to whom he could apply his infallible technique. Instead he found a body of men and women standing in a sea of baby shit up to their bottom lips, urgently cautioning one another in careful whispers: "Don't make waves."

But on this particular night the young man had been there and had left, and for a moment I imagined I could hear the young girl sobbing softly. But in the passion of our lovemaking we forgot her. Vandi was always noisier in bed than is called for, but the fact of being in Paris seemed to have released some inner compulsion to carry on in the act of consummation as though she wanted all the world to know.

Afterward, while we were lying nude in bed, there came a peremptory knocking at the door. Here I must explain the nature of the proprietor. She was a mean old crone with unkempt scraggling hair, a long pointed nose hiding her lips that seemed to meet her equally pointed chin, and an ancient deformed and twisted body which she covered with long dirty black shrouds that seemed to me a bit exaggerated; I always thought of her as the last of the broomstick witches. Her meanness was legendary; everyone on the street hated her. It was said she had collaborated with the Nazis during the occupation, but that was said about everyone who was disliked by his neighbors. On the wall of the office in front of the dirty room in which she slept was a large board that contained numbered fuses for each of the rooms of the hotel. The fuses consisted of tiny bulbs of the size used in flashlights, which permitted each room sixty watts of electricity free. If you used any more—say, a hundred-watt light for reading—it would blow out the fuse, and you would have to pay extra to have the fuse replaced and for the additional forty-watts of electricity. I first blew out my fuse when I tried to play my tape recorder. I dutifully paid for another and for the additional wattage required. Then I bought a reading lamp so I could read in bed, and with its wattage added to that required by my tape recorder, blew that one out. I went down to the desk; she shrugged to indicate she did not have any others. It was nine o'clock; I telephoned Dick and found where I could buy one before the shop closed if I hurried. When I returned with it, the old crone indicated that she couldn't install it until morning. She had already informed Dick she didn't know a single word of English and that I would have to provide someone to translate for me if I wished to ask her for something. I was so infuriated by the prospect of being in the dark until the next day that I went behind the counter and said roughly in English, "Give me the goddamn thing, I'll put it in." She gave me a vicious look and said, "I'll do it myself." When I told Dick what she had said the next morning when he came around to awaken me, he stopped at the desk to chide her about it. She denied vehemently that she had ever spoken a word of English in her life. As a consequence we weren't on the best of terms.

So when I cracked the door that night, peeping about the edge, and saw her standing there threateningly saying something about the gendarmes and my timid little neighbor standing behind her, staring at me from great big brown eyes (I had never seen her before), I asked in English what the hell did she mean. The French girl said, "Mademoiselle was screaming so I could not sleep." Vandi jumped out of the bed nude, and in a flaming fury, and flung the door wide open as though she were going out and slap the young girl's face. Vandi was a big, strong-looking girl, and at the sight of us both standing there in the nude (or mother-naked, as we say in my part of the world), the young French girl fled toward the stairs and even the old crone turned away with false modesty after she had taken a good long look at us. Both, however, retreated down the stairs. But our passion had gone and we dressed and I took Vandi home. On our way out we didn't see a soul, although we saw the curtain of the proprietor's front window pulled slightly aside as we walked down the street.

Next morning when Dick came around, the old crone was waiting for him and told him I would have to move as I was disturbing the young girl next to me, who was very nervous and high-strung and the only daughter of a good family in the provinces who had been sent to Paris and entrusted in her care while she studied in the Sorbonne.

When Dick came to tell me he was more filled with gleeful curiosity than I had ever seen him. "What were you doing to that girl, Chester? The girl next door said she couldn't hear you at all but Vandi was screaming at the top of her voice."

I said, "Hell, Dick, the girl's just frustrated is all. If she'd sleep with her friend sometimes such perfectly normal sounds wouldn't disturb her."

"That wasn't the way she told it; she said she'd never

heard anything like that and she was frightened. What were you using, Chester, your secret weapon?"

It didn't take an awful lot of Dick to get on my nerves and he saw that I'd had enough of his bullshit and dropped it for the moment. The proprietor came up as soon as she thought it was safe and said I could have a big room on the back court, which was vacant at the time, and it would be safer for my camp stove, she added, looking at it disapprovingly as though she had seen it for the first time. I was paying five hundred francs for my front room, but she said the back room would cost seven hundred francs, as she usually let it to three girls. We went and looked at it. It was a big T-shaped room on two levels with three single beds, a kitchen table for cooking, and a cupboard. When I thought of having to go through the trouble of looking for a room in another hotel and moving all my things, I took the room and paid the old crone for a week in advance as demanded, but I despised her for forcing me to it. I packed my trunk and cases and Dick stayed and helped me move. The story had already circulated through the hotel and when Dick and I were leaving, the two lesbians who had the room beneath me came out to the landing to look at me and grin sympathetically. Dick had noticed them before and was delighted with the opportunity to speak to them. He had a sharp curiosity about the sexual behavior of odd couples, lesbians, and prostitutes; in fact, if he had lived I think that sooner or later he would have made a serious study of the subjects. He stopped to talk to them and after a few moments I noticed they had become embarrassed and returned to their room. But he followed them and peered about inside their room as though it were a cage at the zoo, and I suspect he began to ask pointed questions about their love life, for shortly the masculine-looking girl slammed the door in his face. He was greatly stimulated by these encounters, and after a moment rushed away to write or to indulge in whatever else he had in mind.

By night the story was all over the American community in the

Latin Quarter; no one had ever heard of a paying guest being put out of a hotel room in Paris for making love. In time it became something of a legend—there were a number of Americans who knew me only as the man who got thrown out of his hotel room for making love—but fortunately I had left Paris by then.

Vandi left for Madrid that night and missed the brunt of the kidding, but my stock went up exceedingly. Every time I looked up from my drink in any of the cafés on the Left Bank, I would catch some girl staring at me appraisingly; or late at night, when I returned home, I would find some strange girl waiting for me on the sidewalk outside the entrance, and I didn't even have to speak—all I had to do was nod and they would follow me up to my room. But I am sure those who came were disappointed.

What really browned me off about the episode was that some of these strange girls were noisier than Vandi—noisy just for the sake of it—and besides, the lesbians in the room below me would often maintain an incredible chorus of love cries until daybreak. And the hypocritical old witch didn't say a thing.

To fill the gap left by Vandi, I took Mme. Annie Brierre to dinner one night. We stopped at the Deux Magots for apéritifs. Mme. Brierre was such a striking type of aristocratic Frenchwoman, obviously being kind to a clean-looking *american noire*, that the management sent us complimentary drinks— whiskeys—after our first. Afterward I took her to Beulemans a couple of blocks down the boulevard Saint-Germain, which turned out to be a famous restaurant, but I didn't know it at the time.

I never ceased to regard Dick's apartment with envy and amazement. It occupied the entire fourth floor of the building, and to me it appeared sumptuously furnished. The first room to the right of the entrance foyer was his book-lined study, with two large modernistic paintings, dozens of copies of his own books, several typewriters, his desk, a tape recorder, and overstuffed leather armchairs—all the paraphernalia of a working writer. It was the inner sanctum to which only selected visitors were ever invited. Beyond it were the dining room, the living room, the master bedroom, and at the back the bath, all overlooking the street. On the other side were a storeroom, pantry, kitchen, and the children's bedroom and nursery—eight rooms, exclusive of the bath and water closets. For this he was paying about thirty-five dollars a month for taxes and upkeep on an arrangement whereby he had put up a down payment against the price of the apartment which would become his in the course of time. But he had made many expensive improvements, including central heating and a hot water system, which was then considered a luxury in Paris houses.

Among the paintings he had acquired were a number by an artist who was then becoming fashionable in art circles. One day when Dick and I were sitting on the terrace of the Deux Magots, Mrs. Putnam came over to invite us to a cocktail party at the atelier of this artist the following Sunday afternoon. Dick phoned me right after lunch that Sunday, saying he was alone, and asked me to come over and pass the time until the cocktail party. While we were sitting in his study, the doorbell rang and he ushered in a surprise visitor, a tall, slender, blond man, whom he introduced as Mr. Schine. At that time David Schine and Roy Cohn were the investigators for the Senate committe on un-American activities, headed by Senator Joe McCarthy. Schine was gathering information about a man named Jarrel, who had been appointed to a position in the State Department, and he wanted Dick to give a statement that Jarrel had been a member of the John Walter Reed Club in Chicago at the same time as himself. Dick said that he himself had never been a member of the club, that he did not know any of the members, and that he did not remember ever meeting anyone named Jarrel. Schine seemed infuriated by Dick's reply, and he told Dick how he and Cohn pressured Langston Hughes into stating before the committee that he regretted some of his un-American political activities and writings.

Suddenly Dick asked Schine if he had read my novel, *Lonely Crusade*. Schine said he had never heard of me or my book. Dick advised him to read it. After advising Dick to refresh his memory about Jarrel, Schine left. Afterward Dick said, "That stupid son of a bitch thinks he can threaten me; I'll never testify. I've written everything I have to say about my communist affiliations." I had nothing to say.

Later, as we were preparing to leave for the party, the telephone rang. When Dick returned from answering it, he wore that look of malicious satisfaction which his close friends had come to know so well. He asked if I knew James Baldwin. I said no, but I had heard a great deal about him from an old college friend named Jesse Jackson who some years ago had left his wife and daughter in Columbus, Ohio, and had gone to live in Greenwich Village, as the protégé of a German Jewish refugee couple, to write children's books. Jesse had praised Baldwin as a genius. And I had read a review of *Lonely Crusade* that Baldwin had published in the Socialist Party's newspaper, the *New Leader*, but I had never met him.

Dick said that he had been instrumental in getting Baldwin an award for eighteen hundred dollars and a renewal for nine hundred from Harper & Brothers to enable him to write his first novel, which was eventually rejected by Harper's editor-in-chief, Edward Aswell, Dick's editor. The book had finally been published by Beacon Press as *Go Tell It on the Mountain*. He said Baldwin had "repaid his generosity" by "attacking him" in a number of published articles, the most recent of which had appeared in a new Ford Foundation quarterly called *New Directions*, if memory serves me right. I admitted having read the article, which had been published back to back with an article by a young Negro writer named Richard Gibson, in which I was mentioned derogatorily. "Now Baldwin has the nerve to call me to borrow five thousand francs (ten dollars)," he said gleefully.

He had made an appointment to meet him at the Deux Magots, and insisted that I go with him. I remember thinking at the time that he sounded as though he wanted a witness. I reminded him of our invitation to the cocktail party, but he had no intention of missing this confrontation with Baldwin. He persuaded me to call Mrs. Putnam and tell her we were held up by some changes he was making in his new manuscript, which had to be in the mail in the morning, and wouldn't be able to leave the house.

Then we hurried to the Deux Magots and found Baldwin waiting for us at a table on the terrace across from the Église Saint-Germain. I was somewhat surprised to find Baldwin a small, intense young man of great excitability. Dick sat down in lordly fashion and started right off needling Baldwin, who defended himself with such intensity that he stammered, his body trembled, and his face quivered. I sat and looked from one to the other, Dick playing the fat cat and forcing Baldwin into the role of the quivering mouse. It wasn't particularly funny, but then Dick wasn't a funny man. I never found it easy to laugh with Dick; it was far easier to laugh at him on occasion. Dick accused Baldwin of showing his gratitude for all he had done for him by his scurrilous attacks. Baldwin defended himself by saying that Dick had written his story and hadn't left him, or any other American black writer, anything to write about. I confess at this point they lost me. Then suddenly a large group of people approached us. I looked up and was startled to find Mrs. Putnam among them. They turned out to be the artist and his wife who had given the cocktail party and several of their guests. I started off saying we had just that moment finished work, but Dick and Baldwin kept on going at one another and no one paid me any attention. It wasn't long before Mrs. Putnam and all of her friends had gotten to the heart of the argument and taken sides. All of the women and the majority of the men, including the artist, took Baldwin's side—chiefly, I think, because he looked so small and intense and vulnerable and Dick appeared so secure and condescending and cruel. But in the course of time they left us to go to dinner, and still Baldwin and Dick carried on while I sat and watched the people come and go. Later we went down the boulevard to a Martiniquan café. It had grown late, close to midnight, and we had not eaten, but still the discussion went on. It seemed that Baldwin was wearing Dick down and I was getting quite drunk. The last I remember before I left them at it was Baldwin saying, "The sons must slay their fathers." At the time I thought he had taken leave of his senses, but in recent years I've come to better understand what he meant. Much later, while traveling in Crete, I read Mary Renault's book *The King Must Die*, and I was reminded of Baldwin's remark that night, "The sons must slay their fathers." And I realized suddenly that he was right. On the American literary scene, the powers that be have never admitted but one black at a time into the arena of fame, and to gain this coveted admission, the young writer must unseat the reigning deity. It's a pity but a reality as well.

In time I came to realize that Dick had been correct in accusing so many various people of attacking him: they *were* attacking him. American blacks must always get ahead in American society by walking over each other.

But afterward I used to tease Dick by referring to Baldwin as his son.

A few days later Ben Zevin, the president of World Publishing Company, and his wife Lillian arrived in Paris and put up at the Hôtel Meurice on rue de Rivoli, overlooking the Tuileries. World was to publish my autobiographical novel *The Third Generation* that fall, and Zevin had written to me that he would like to meet Dick. During the last of 1944, when Dick's best-selling autobiography, *Black Boy*, was at the height of its success, Harper & Brothers had run out of paper, which was rationed during the war. As a consequence they had farmed the book out to World to publish until they got their new consignment of paper the following year. But Zevin had never met Dick.

I telephoned him at the Meurice and arranged for him and Lillian and Dick and Ellen and myself to meet for dinner that evening. Dick and I went by the hotel about seven o'clock to pick them up. I remember their amazement at the size and comfort of the interior of the front-wheel-drive Citroën. We took them out to the Deux Magots, where Ellen was waiting.

Zevin said he would be our host if Dick would select the restaurant, and Dick chose the seafood restaurant, La Méditerranée on Place de l'Odéon where I had taken Vandi several times. The reason for his choice was soon obvious, for the proprietor knew him and treated him with great respect. We were given the best table on the glass-enclosed terrace, and except for Zevin we all followed Dick's suggestion and ordered bouillabaisse. Zevin had his customary meal when traveling abroad—filet mignon. Dick had tucked his napkin into his collar in the French manner and was holding forth in a loud voice, attracting a great deal of attention. A party of Americans at the other end of the terrace called the proprietor and asked who he was. Smiling affably, as only a Frenchman can do when handing out a subtle insult, the proprietor informed them that the gentleman was the President of the United States.

After a lively dinner, which for the five of us cost Zevin a hundred dollars, we all shook hands with the proprietor and prepared to leave. Dick's car was parked across the place in front of what was then the Luxembourg Salon of the Comédie Française, and the proprietor had sent all of his staff—chefs, waiters, doormen, everyone who wore a uniform—out into the street to form two long rows to Dick's car through which we passed like royalty. I think Zevin was a little miffed by this extraordinary attention given to Dick, for when we finally retired to Dick's house, after stopping by at La Romance nightclub, a controversy developed between the two of them. Zevin accused Dick of having abandoned the fight for his people, to be a "big frog in a little pond," then went on to say how he was doing his best for the black cause himself by integrating blacks into the several hundred employees in his Cleveland, Ohio, printing company. Dick made a scathing reply about "you people flattering yourselves with these little gestures, when what's needed is a direct attack on the sources of American prejudice." Zevin reddened and I hastened to act as peacemaker, saying it was getting late and hadn't we better postpone this ticklish discussion until another day. As usual, no one paid very much attention to me, but Ellen and Lillian decided there had been enough contention for the night and the party broke up.

The next day Dick and Ellen took the Zevins to dinner and they made up, but I wasn't invited and didn't know of it until Ellen told me she had sold Zevin a novel by Simone de Beauvoir. Ellen had told me previously that she was conducting a literary agency with a Frenchwoman who was the wife of a minister. But it was the sale of this novel to Zevin that influenced me to let her handle the French rights to my books.

I had met a young man named Frederick Morton who had written a review of my book *Cast the First Stone* for the *New York Herald Tribune's Book Week*, on the Champs-Elysées one day; and I took him and Zevin to lunch at the barbecue restaurant near Pigalle run by Leroy Haynes and his French wife Gabrielle. Morton promised Zevin he would review *The Third Generation* when it was published, but other than that we had very little of consequence to say to each other, and I did not see either of them again.

Ellen took me to see Buchet and Chastel, co-publishers of the French firm Corrêa, who had published *La Croisade de Lee Gordon*. They told me the book had been a critical success and showed me clippings, but that it hadn't sold well and hadn't earned sufficient royalties to pay for the $250 advance. When I expressed my surprise at this, they became affronted and sent for the accounts. A young woman brought in a huge black leather-bound ledger and they invited me to examine it for myself. Ellen was becoming embarrassed by this, but when I opened the ledger and saw all the complicated entries in red and black ink in very fine handwritten French script, I confessed it didn't mean a thing to me. They assured me I could take their word, which I did, as I had no other choice.

The following day a woman from Martinique sought me out in the Café Tournon and said Monsieur Buchet would like for me to come to a cocktail party that afternoon in the offices of Corrêa given in honor of Henry Miller, whose books *Le Monde du Sexe* and *Plexus* had been published in the collection *Le Chemin de la Vie*, along with *La Croisade de Lee Gordon*. It was my first opportunity to attend a French publisher's cocktail party. The two front office rooms of Corrêa, which was located in a court on the rue Condé, about a half block from the Place de l'Odéon, were jam-packed with French intellectuals of both sexes and such mistresses and lovers as they had brought along. The Martiniquan woman, whom I gathered was the mistress of Buchet, and her grown daughter, a lovely young woman as beautiful as her mother, had elected or been assigned to stick by me in this gathering of impatient and arrogant French-speaking intellectuals, perhaps because the mother spoke a little English. The rooms were so packed that one could barely move, so we stood there rubbing against one another, unable to reach the buffet to get an hors-d'oeuvre or an apéritif, while my hostess pointed out various celebrities. Jean-Paul Sartre came in, but it seemed to me as though no one spoke to him and after a few minutes he had disappeared. I got a brief glimpse of the shaved head of Henry Miller, but I didn't get close enough to him to speak to him. Several people squeezed over toward me and spouted a few words in rapid French but when they saw I didn't understand they soon lost interest and moved on. An elaborately made-up middle-aged redheaded woman gave me her card and invited me to a cocktail party she was giving that Friday at her apartment on the Ile de la Cité, and shortly afterward I left to go to the Café Tournon and get a drink.

Someone, probably Mrs. Putnam, told me that this red-headed woman was a well-known art agent, and the man whose Dutch name was on the card along with hers was a famous art dealer from Amsterdam. I went to the cocktail party. As usual, I had difficulty finding my way about strange French apartment houses. I finally located the elevator, a small cage capable of holding three persons, in the well of the winding old-fashioned stairs, and ascended slowly to the fourth floor. That elevator moved as though people had all the time in the world. My hostess was standing beside a pedestal at the end of a long entrance hall, alone and statuesque in an off-the-shoulder evening gown. She greeted me cordially, extending her hand palm down, and I bowed and kissed it as I supposed was proper. She accepted the tribute graciously and asked me to write in the leather-bound guest book atop the pedestal, turning to a clean page. I signed my name in small letters and went into the salon, where a few guests had already assembled in groups about the period furnishings. I knew no one, so I sat down on a Louis Quinze chair and looked at the others. For the most part they appeared to be fashionable French couples in the late thirties or early forties clad in evening gowns, dark suits, or dinner jackets. But there was one old man with abundant snow-white hair and a fabulous snow-white beard, dressed in white tie and tails, with a resplendent tricolor sash diagonally across his starched white shirt, who struck me as being the most distinguished-looking person I had yet seen in France. Like me, he sat alone and looked at the others, while the room slowly filled with the fashionable people.

After a time, folding doors were opened to reveal a large buffet extending from wall to wall of the dining room, heaped with an assortment of hors-d'oeuvres, and presided over by four white-jacketed barmen. Evidently at a given signal, which, unfortunately I didn't see, the guests jumped from their seats and bore down on the buffet like a swarm of starving locusts. I had got left, and by the time I got to my feet and made for the buffet guests were surrounding it three and four deep and I couldn't get near enough to grab a caviar sandwich. I stood behind several guests and signaled to a barkeep for a dry martini, which he passed to me over the shoulders of some women and I backed off toward the door to drink it. In so doing I found myself beside a moon-faced young man in rimless spectacles, a shabby blue suit and a soiled white shirt with a dark greasy ring about the collar. He said in slightly accented English, "Want something to eat?" I hadn't seen him before and at first I took him for a servant, but then I realized he looked too dirty to be a servant, so I put him down as an eccentric intellectual, and said, "I wouldn't mind." Suddenly he burrowed through the guests about the buffet like a purse snatcher making a getaway in a mob; but shortly he returned with a plate piled with canapes and two dry martinis. I never knew how he did it. As we stood by the door gulping the canapes, no one paid us the slightest attention; everyone's attention was concentrated on the buffet as they snatched canapes from the trays and stuffed them into their mouths and washed them down with champagne. I noticed the old distinguished-looking gentleman standing with his belly pressed against the buffet stuffing tidbits into his mouth as fast as his hands could move and having his champagne glass refilled every thirty seconds. It looked like a scene from a movie on gluttony; I didn't believe it. My shabby companion said, "They're all like this. They got it from the Americans." "What?" I asked. "Cocktails," he said. Then he went on to tell me he hadn't been invited; he had seen the guests alighting from taxis outside the house and knew there was a cocktail party somewhere and had followed them. "I go to all the cocktail parties," he said. "But I am never invited." After a while he said, "All the waiters go to Gallimard cocktails; they got dinner jackets."

No one else spoke to me. Later I was to learn that some Frenchwomen think that blacks, or *métis*, as they would call me, have great sexual interest, and when a hostess invites one to a party he is for the pleasure of the hostess alone and no one interferes. But I didn't know that then, and after a time of being ignored by all save my *clochard* companion, I decided to leave. I couldn't find my hostess, so I left without saying goodbye, and I never saw her again.

The next morning I went with Dick to see his black marketeer out on the Champs-Elysées. At that time the official rate of exchange was 348 francs for a dollar, but one could get from 500 to 550 on the black market. That had been the reason Dick had advised me to bring my money in twenty-dollar American Express Company travelers checks, as they were more acceptable on the black market than checks of any other denomination or even cash. Pops was a small flat-faced man with curly white hair and youthful-looking blue eyes that belied the grim tale he told me on that first day of his escape from the Nazis. He had a single room on the third floor of a walkup apartment building off the arcade beside the George V movie theater on the Champs-Elysées. After reaching it through a maze of corridors, one had to stand outside the door to be inspected through an invisible peephole before Pops undid his burglarproof locks and permitted entrance. Inside was a bed built in one corner below a shelf along the two walls which contained a collection of the most fabulous female dolls I have ever seen, sitting in rows side by side. Piled about the bed on the carpeted floor were bales of ten-thousand-franc notes, like bundles of scrap paper. Years afterward I remembered that first sight of Pops and his room filled with dolls and money, from which I got my first idea for a detective story, but I never wrote it.

Pops told us he had hidden in that building all during the Nazi occupation and the neighbors had kept him alive by smuggling him food. But the Nazis had caught his wife in the corridor and after raping her en masse had killed her.

Annie Brierre had a picture of her sister in a frame on the grand piano in her salon; she said the Nazis had shot her on the last day of the occupation. Everyone from every class had his own story of the Nazi occupation, I was learning, and I was touched. But on the way home, Dick told me not to waste any sympathy on Pops. "He's been arrested a half dozen

times for raping young girls who go up there to get money
changed," he said.

I think that was when Dick told me about his experiences
with European publishers, especially the French and Italian.
"Get all you can for an advance, boy," he said. "That's all
you'll ever get." He went on to say that none of his books had
ever earned more, according to the publishers' accounts, than
the advance; and in the case of one, his Italian publisher, he'd
had to go to Rome and sit in the publisher's waiting room
until he was paid his advance. "I sat there for two days," he
said, "And whenever anyone came in to see the editor I would
ask, 'Are you trying to get your money too?' They paid me to
get me out of there."

On this particular day, however, Dick wanted me to change
some money so he could borrow a hundred thousand francs
(two hundred dollars) to pick up his ticket to Ghana. Sometime
previous the leftist Jamaican writer George Padmore had persuaded Dick to go to Ghana to write a book about his impressions
of the rising nationalism there and the dynamic leader, Nkruma.
In order to visit Ghana at that time, Dick had to get a visa
from the British Home Office, and the Home Office was loath
to have black American writers visiting Ghana. Padmore had
published a number of leftist books on the rising nationalism
in Africa and was well known in British political and literary
circles and had a number of influential friends. Between the
two of them they finally wore the Home Office down and
got his visa, and he had booked ship's passage through Thomas
Cook's, but the time had come for him to pick up his ticket
and he didn't have any cash on hand. I knew he had been
trying to get the advance from Gallimard for *The Outsider*,
but until he asked for the loan of two hundred dollars, I
didn't know it was urgent. Until this day, what happened to
the great sum of money Dick earned from the American editions
of *Native Son* and *Black Boy* remains a mystery.

We had to wait on chairs by the door while Pops continued
a conversation with a rugged-looking Frenchman sitting across

from his desk in his overcoat. My first impression was that this character was one of Pop's runners who took his travelers checks to Switzerland for conversion into gold, which was the way Dick had said he operated. But Dick was annoyed to be kept waiting, and seemingly to hurry the interview along he began telling me in a loud voice how he had changed thousands of dollars with Pops and at first he had got as much as six hundred to the dollar. Pops glanced once or twice at Dick disapprovingly, but didn't say anything until the man had left, then he said, "Mr. Wright, you must learn not to talk too much in France. Our transactions are not exactly legal, and that man who just left is an inspector of the police." Dick's hand flew to his mouth in a gesture which was to become familiar. He always spoke loudly and unrestrainedly in English, apparently under the impression that no French person could understand; but certainly he must have known better. I remember one evening we had stopped in a café near his house for a quick apéritif before parting for dinner, and he had launched into a long and explicit account of the sex orgies in the quarter. It was the dinner hour and the patron and his wife and daughter sat quietly at a back table, eating. We were the only customers. Dick became so graphic about various sex acts that even I became embarrassed and cautioned him to speak more quietly, but he merely said, "They don't understand English." When we left, all three, father and mother and daughter, said, "Good night, Mister Wright." Dick clapped his hand over his mouth. Outside he asked, "Do you think they understood?" "Damn right," I said. "What the hell you think they were listening so hard for? Getting a liberal education."

As soon as we got the money and I let Dick have the hundred thousand francs, we rushed down the Champs-Elysées toward Cook's on the Place de la Madeleine. As we were passing Place de la Concorde, near the corner of the U. S. Embassy, a studious-looking white man approached us and greeted "Mr. Wright" effusively. Dick introduced him as being connected with the embassy and he gave me a limp handshake and ignored me. "I understand you have two daughters, Mr. Wright?" Dick assured him that was so. "I wonder if you will allow them to come to the embassy tomorrow afternoon; we will send a car for them." Dick asked what was the occasion, no doubt thinking they were to be given some honorary citation. "We're having some people in from the States," his friend said. "And we're trying to assemble a choir of little colored children to sing spirituals." I saw Dick puffing up and I turned away to smile. "My daughters don't speak English," I heard him say curtly. He was fuming. But his self-esteem was repaired when we arrived at Cook's. One of the clerks behind the counter came up and said, "I've just read your book, Mr. Wright. Good job." Dick seemed pleased, but I must confess, when addressed to me, that compliment infuriates me. "What *one* of my books?" I always feel impelled to ask.

From then on Dick was busy with preparations for his trip— he bought a portable typewriter, camera, canned food, tropical clothing, and had himself inoculated against tropical diseases; and I saw very little of him. But Ellen asked me to go to the country with her the following Sunday to visit the couple I had met with Vandi at the cous-cous restaurant on rue de la Huchette. She picked me up at the hotel and, with a young white journalist she was taking along, drove out to the pleasant suburb or Saint-Germain, which she called the country, and parked in the driveway of what looked like a scale-model château with a manicured garden.

Our host and his pregnant wife had gathered an assemblage of Jewish intellectuals from all over Europe, it seemed, and we took our places in the grand salon and sat quietly. And as always happened in those days, the conversation veered around to Richard Wright, and these intellectuals began subtly to pick him apart. Ellen blushed and looked exceedingly uncomfortable, and everyone began casting furtive looks toward me, as I was the only black present. Finally a professor from Austria asked me point blank what I thought of Richard Wright. "He's a great man," I said. "We're speaking of him as a writer," the

professor said. "He's a great writer," I said. The professor looked
at me with indulgent condescension. "Are you basing your
opinion on the literary values of the world?" he persisted. I
felt my temper flaring. These people were getting on my ass.
"I'm basing my opinion on the fact that Richard Wright is a
great man and a great writer," I said. "What are you basing
your prerogative on to question me?" There was a silence. I
turned to my host and said, "Will you show me to the toilet,
please?" Ellen jumped up. "I'll show him." Outside on the
stairs she squeezed my hand. I thought she shouldn't let those
envious sons of bitches upset her, but I didn't say anything.
When I got back the conversation had centered on the dirty
habits of Frenchwomen. "They never wash," my hostess was
saying. "They just dab on some powder and perfume." I don't
blame them, I thought, as cold as these houses are.

This conversation was interrupted by the arrival of a youngish
couple in riding habit who were introduced as M. and Mme.
Dreyfus. Shortly afterward I left and took the train back to
Paris. I didn't fit in, I wasn't an intellectual and I didn't have
a title; I only had a bad temper and I resented these people
carping at Dick. Whatever his faults or deficiencies, Richard
Wright was the first American black writer to break into the
big time, and by so doing he had convinced the world that it
was possible for the American black descendants of slaves to
possess the talent and the intellectual capacity to contribute to
the world's literature.

Book III

1.

Suddenly Alva was there.

I had been in constant correspondence with her during all the three crowded weeks and then I had received the telegram for me to phone. In a tremulous voice she said she was leaving her husband and her daughters and her home and coming to me on the first of May, as we had planned. "You will be good to me?" she asked.

Although I had read her daily letters dutifully and had replied to them lovingly, I had not really thought of her as flesh and blood, as a woman who loves and trusts. Her letters had not recalled her image, the shape of her body, the vision of her face, and it had not come of its own accord. And suddenly I was shocked by the sound of her voice. I realized that I loved her. "I love you," I said. "I'll always be good to you."

She told me the hour of her arrival two days hence and asked me to meet her. "As though you had to ask," I said.

With frantic haste I searched for other rooms. I felt I should have a separate room for her. I wanted adjoining rooms with bath. Dick had several days remaining before leaving for Ghana, and he helped me. He persuaded me against taking expensive rooms in another part of town. He had decided he didn't like Alva. He thought that if she was going to leave her husband and children to come and live with me there was no reason why she shouldn't live like other American tramps in the Latin Quarter, in a cheap hotel room, and take public baths. He resented my considering her something special.

We made the rounds of the cheap hotels. The weather was typical for the end of April—overcast, with sunny periods. We both wore belted trenchcoats and dark-green Polaroid sunglasses. Seeing the apprehensive expression of a woman who ran a cheap residential hotel, I suddenly realized we must look like two North African gangsters collecting tribute. But Dick had a membership card for some French writers' society cut diagonally with a tricolor band which looked impressive when he flashed it and must have convinced some of the hotel proprietors that he was connected with some ministry.

Alva was to arrive at six that afternoon. In desperation I took two rooms in a cheap hotel, Hôtel Michelet, on the rue Michelet south of the Luxembourg Gardens; a small one for myself on the fourth floor and a larger one for her on the second. Neither had a bath, and the door to hers was not very secure, but it was the best I could do. The proprietor, a cheerful, tall, dark young woman with bedroom eyes and a seductive smile, was obviously puzzled by the two rooms, one of which I said I wanted for my friend. Why couldn't we share one room? her eyes asked. If my friend was a woman, the hotel was safe, she wouldn't talk; if he was a man, she shrugged, she was broad-minded. But she took the money for the two rooms, even though she thought I was a little strange.

Dick helped me move that afternoon, although he shared the proprietor's opinion, and he came back later to drive me to the Gare de l'Est to meet Alva's train, more out of curiosity, I think, to see this woman for whom I was going to all this trouble than from any real impulse to help.

We saw her as she alighted from her coach and came down the platform toward us, following a man carrying her big, old American suitcase, looking so small and fragile and vulnerable in a brand-new badly tailored light-gray suit with a little black hat perched defiantly atop her newly marcelled hair, that my heart stood still. At that moment I felt infinitely sorry for her. She didn't know what she was letting herself in for, I thought. And then I was rushing forward to take her in my arms.

The stranger relinquished her suitcase and we took her to Dick's waiting car. She held two bottles of choice Moselle wine, which she had brought with her and pressed them both on Dick, perhaps because he looked so disapproving. I realized it had been a mistake to let him come to meet her, but it was too late to rectify it.

The three of us crowded into the front seat and took her to the hotel, but she did not want to go up to her room. Perhaps she felt that he would come along. She said she would like to go to a café and have an apéritif. So we left her suitcase at the desk and started down the street.

She seemed hesitant, undecided, unsure. I wanted to hold her in my arms and comfort her. Perhaps that was what she wanted too. But Dick's presence constrained us. He had an air of coarse jocularity that made it obvious he regarded her as a tramp, but would tolerate her because of me. We passed his house but he did not invite us in. She felt his condescension like a slap and felt so sorry for me that she would have run away, she told me afterward. I became blindly angry, but I did not want to fall out with Dick because of her. The situation had grown tense and insupportable and it had become a question of who would give first.

Then suddenly with a show of boisterous good humor, Dick led us to the Café Monaco, where all the American tramps hung out. Alva gave it one look and declined to enter. I suggested the Café de la Suisse across the street from the Luxembourg salon of the Comédie Française. We sat at a table inside, stiff and constrained, and made inane remarks. Dick got up abruptly and left us, saying Ellen was waiting for him. I found myself making excuses for him while at the same time Alva was apologizing for coming between us. We were like strangers. She asked me to take her someplace where there was music. The only place I knew of in the neighborhood was a crummy bistro beside the nightclub La Romance, which featured a gypsy guitarist. It was the dinner hour, and several couples who looked like prostitutes and their pimps sat about eating the *plat du jour*. We felt ill at ease and conspicuous on entering and passed quickly through the long narrow room to a table at the extreme rear. Although we hadn't eaten we ordered Cognac, and at a signal from the shirtsleeved proprietor the gypsy guitarist got up and came back and began serenading us. The customers stared at us with hostility but the patron beamed at us with the indulgence all French café proprietors maintain toward lovers. We knew his indulgence was strictly commercial but at that moment we welcomed a kind smile from anyone. I leaned toward her and in sight of everyone embraced her and kissed her. She clung to me desperately and after a while she was all right and said, "Let's go home." I feel certain that guitarist had never got a tip like the one I gave him then.

She was embarrassed by her room—not so much by its appearance as by the fact I thought it necessary to get her a separate room. She wanted to come up and share my little room. I could see it was not at all as she had expected and I cursed myself for not doing as I had first planned instead of following Dick's advice. Our landlady sensed that something was wrong and hovered about, but Alva just wanted to go somewhere and hide.

It was better in my room on the fourth floor because there was only space to move around in bed. There was literally no space for upsetting thoughts and regrets. Her body was trembling violently as from a chill, and I opened a bottle of whiskey for her. She said it was only from reaction but she took a big drink of whiskey anyway. We hadn't eaten and I warned her against drinking too much. I promised to take her to dinner when I returned from the WC, but I found her in bed with only her head showing above the covers. She wore a curious little smile. "Come to bed and hold me," she said.

I undressed and got in bed and took her small, trembling body in my arms. She was so cold her skin felt rough with goose pimples and I could feel her teeth chattering when I kissed her. I turned out the light and she snuggled close to me as though to get inside of my skin. Soon I felt warmth coming from her body and her trembling had ceased and I found myself in her arms instead of she in mine.

We fused together in the hot passionate dark and became one, and the world didn't matter anymore. That was the moment we overcame our loneliness and shed our regrets and grew strong together. It was the way we had known from the beginning it would be, the two of us one now against the world, needing no one, and we had thought then it would be like that forever. "Come with me!" she cried. "Come with me, darling!" But I never did. She was always first. It didn't matter. What mattered to her was she had lost herself in the darkness of my race. She had hid from all her hurts and humiliations. In a strange and curious way, by becoming my mistress, the mistress of a man who'd never been entirely free, she had freed herself. That is a curious thing about race relations. We can free the white man's women, and they can find freedom in us, but we cannot free ourselves. Even her very glands became free with me. It was as though a dam had broke within her. She claimed never to have experienced such freedom of ecstasy before. On the other hand, neither had I.

Afterward I asked if she would like to go eat, but she said she was not hungry. But that was not the case with me. I got up and dressed and went down the street to a Chinese restaurant near boulevard Saint-Michel and ate a dish of chicken chop suey filled with splintered bones, alone and conspicuous among the amorous couples, and when I returned I found that she had been sick in the washbasin. But the next morning she was fresh and bright.

When I went downstairs for her suitcase, the proprietor offered to return the night's rent I had paid for her room, but I said it didn't matter.

After wandering around all day searching for a more comfortable hotel, we went out on Rue Montparnasse to take the Malartics to dinner. They liked Alva immediately, perhaps because, unlike Vandi, she spoke French. But there was not the slightest hint in their behavior that they had ever known another woman in my life. They welcomed her as my one and only love and made her feel at ease. It was not long before they discovered she was unhappy in Paris. They didn't ask the reason, perhaps they knew. None of us had made any reference to the Wrights, but suddenly Yves offered us the use of his villa in Arcachon for as long as we wanted it, at no cost whatsoever, with the exception of the summer months, July and August, when his sister's family went there for their holidays. With typical French gallantry he put the onus on me. "Himes, you are not happy here. I can tell, I am a—what do you call him?—*devin* in French." His offer came so suddenly we had to beg for time to think it over.

The next afternoon we ran into Ellen Wright on the street and she invited us to drop by that evening after dinner for drinks. We arrived at the appointed hour and found that Dr. Schiller, the VD specialist of the quarter, and his wife were the other guests. I had never seen Dick behave so badly toward anyone but I realized that I was at fault. I had praised Alva so highly as a lady, he felt self-conscious around her and was furious with himself for feeling so. This caused a resentment that might have taken a vicious turn had it not been for me. The only comparison I can make to his behavior that night is the characterization Laurence Olivier has given to Shakespeare's Othello. Perhaps Olivier has the key. Black people do show their resentment toward whites by accentuating the characteristics for which the whites judge them inferior. Ellen did nothing to help, but I didn't expect her to. It was Dr. Schiller who saw what was happening and came to Alva's rescue, by engaging her in a private conversation and ignoring Dick. With tears in her eyes, Alva said, "You are a kind man." I took her home. We stayed in bed. It was cheaper and more pleasant. I did not try to introduce her to any of my other soul brothers. That evening we gave the Malartics our decision: we would leave for their villa in Arcachon the morning after the following day.

I got a note from Dick the following day asking me to come

by and get the money I had loaned him. I went by that afternoon and found him in bed. He gave me a pinned bundle of notes the way they came from the banks and told me he was leaving the next day for Ghana. I did not tell him we were going to Arcachon; I did not mention Alva's name. I wished him a good trip and left. I hadn't sat down. I did not see or hear from him again until years later.

We went by Yves' again that night to get the final instructions concerning his villa and found that Yvonne had made a detailed plan of the villa and had typed the following *rôlet*:

ADDRESS: Villa Madiana, Rue Jules Michelet—L'Aiguillon, ARCACHON (department: Gironde) . . . Chez M. Lamour (Yves' real name was Jean Lamour), across from chez M. Cabarrou, almost at the corner of Rue Alexandrine.

AUTOCAR: Twice daily there is a bus which goes directly from the station to l'Aiguillon. For the Villa Madiana get off at the terminus.

THE KEYS: Ask Madame Besnard, who is the grandmother of our excellent friend, Louis-Gerard Begaud, engraver, water-color painter and great sailor.

In case of the absence of Madame Besnard, who lives at Chalet Fleurette, Rue Jules Michelet in l'Aiguillon, ask our nearest neighbor, Mme. Meulliets, for the keys.

Madame Meulliets is authorized to come and get water when she wants to. I am sure you will get along with her very well. She is charming. Her daughter-in-law, Mme. Meulliets junior, is also authorized to come and get water.

METERS: *BE CAREFUL!* There are two electric meters—both are probably closed. One of them is in the big room in between the books, the other one in a room which we call the bathroom—where you can find everything but water. This you will easily find.

WATER:	The general meter is near the grill entrance. We do not close it in order for Mmes. Meulliets can get water. But there is a tap which regulates the flow of water for the inside of the house. It is under the small sink which is on the kitchen balcony. (The light is in the large room.)

In the big kitchen you will find a butagaz lamp on an old table which you may put in the courtyard in order to use the "white cathedral" made by the master. |
BLANKETS:	I do not know where I put them but if you do not find them on the beds look in the wardrobe, and if you do not find them in the wardrobe, look in the last room overlooking the front of the house. They might even be in the "concentration camp" with the children's belongings.
SHEETS:	There are sure to be one or two pairs which are not torn in the wardrobe. You will probably have to buy towels and tea cloths, but Arcachon is a big town where one can find everything—even too many things.
HOUSEHOLD RUBBISH:	In all Seasons the dustmen only pass three times a week. You must put the ash can out in front of the door. If you have any questions about this please ask the neighbors.

In case of serious illness, ask our good friend, Dr. Thé, who will look after you with an umparalleled devotion and you can explain your sickness in English or French. His son, Jacques, knows the house very well and will come and see you. (Dr. Thé, the Villa Nemo, Allée Sainte Marie, Arcachon (Quartier La Chapelle) (He loves green olives)

The book store proprietor, Monsieur Bernoud (Librairie Générale—just in front of the Nouvelles Galeries) is a good friend. His wife is not really savage, she is very timid. I will ask her sister (who lives in La Teste) to come and see you. Her knowledge, as far as grammar and classical French are concerned, is perfect. (*Signes particuliers:* she doesn't spit on the rug)

GROCERIES: There are seven or eight in the district. Most of them sell bread, wine and vegetables. Our neighbour, Mlle. Cancalen, is charming.

BUTCHERS: Monsieur Dutin (at the corner of Rue Alexandrine and Boulevard de la Plage) sells excellent meat. It's a very nice family: two grown daughters, one with a certificate in English, the other one is preparing her examinations to become a teacher. If they need any books, you may let them have them.

BOOKS: You may also lend books to Gerard Begaud, to Dr. Thé and his son, *but please always note the title of the books which they borrow.*

BUTAGAZ: When the bottle is empty, ask Michel Lepicart, a tall young man who lives in the house in front of ours, to go and get another one for you. He is quite accustomed to this operation.

POSTMAN: Give him, on the day of your arrival, the names under which you will be receiving mail, because he has instructions to forward our mail to Paris.

LAUNDRY: Mme. Lepicart, who lives in the house in front of ours, will do the washing for you either in your house or hers.

We thanked Yves and Yvonne for their trouble and promised to take good care of their house and went home to pack. The train left early the next morning but Yves had said we could get tickets at the time of departure that early in the year.

Early the next morning I fetched one of those old hearselike taxis and bribed the driver to help bring my huge trunk down from the fourth floor. But we couldn't get it into the back of the cab. The horse butcher who was just opening next door gave us a hand, refusing the tip I offered, and we piled our hand luggage in the rack on top and went to the Gare d'Austerlitz. Those old taxis, many of which were among the taxis that transported troops to the front in World War I, didn't have luggage compartments, but they could carry large trunks inside and any number of suitcases on top.

We bought third-class tickets and checked the trunk, paying for excess baggage, and found an empty third-class compartment. In the course of time I was to pay more for carrying that trunk around with me on European trains than I paid for house rent during my first two years abroad.

It was a relief to get away from Paris, even in a close, hot, third-class carriage. I hadn't told anyone that I was leaving. I hadn't made it with my soul brothers. Dick was the only one with whom I had spent some time. But then I never had liked American blacks simply because we belonged to the same race; I had liked only the ones who had interested me—my wife, some racketeers around Cleveland, several fellow students at Ohio State University, several fellow convicts at the Ohio State Penitentiary, several fellow workers I had met here and there in my many occupations, and Richard Wright. I liked Dick. When I deliberately avoided him it was simply because I didn't want to have to hurt him. I felt that I didn't have to like blacks in order to identify; I was one. I didn't have to prove anything by talking about my hard times, my pain, all that shit. I had received my lumps, I had been to prison, I had worked at every type of flunkey's job imaginable; my dues were paid. I wanted to get away and live a different life. At times my soul brothers embarrassed me, bragging about their scars, their poor upbringing, and their unhappy childhood, to get some sympathy and some white pussy and money, too, if they could. It was a new variety of Uncle-Toming, a modern version. Anyway I was glad to be going to Arcachon to get away from Paris.

We arrived at about seven o'clock that evening. I don't remember whether we changed at Bordeaux for the train to Biarritz, but Arcachon is on the line. The porter helped me pile my trunk and hand luggage atop a ramshackle taxi and I thought it was going to topple over from so much weight, but we arrived at the villa without mishap. We didn't have to look for the keys; upon seeing the local taxi with its cargo of American luggage and a strange black and white couple, the neighbors came out in force. It was just before the dinner hour on a warm and sunny day and the men were at home, too. A buxom woman with a rugged French face came from next door and introduced herself as Mme. Meulliets and presented the keys without our asking, and several strong men whom I don't remember ever seeing again took my trunk and our hand luggage and carried them into the house. We ate in a restaurant and bar a block away across the street and I noticed a number of men about wearing bright-red pants. Later I was told they had something to do with the fishing boats, but I have forgotten just what. By the time we returned it was dark, and we occupied ourselves that first night in making up a bed. It was while we were thus employed that we had our first visitor. She was Mme. la Lune, whom Yves had referred to as Mme. Moon when he had told us of her. She was a small, sleek, black-and-white feline with huge green, limpid, incredibly sexy eyes, in an advanced stage of pregnancy and crawling with fleas. We had been told she came with the house. She came in and made herself comfortable in the middle of the newly made bed and began to lick herself, and in horror we saw the fleas leaving her to beat us to bed. We made love most of that first night as a distraction from the flea bites, but we were up early, feeling reasonably fresh, with excited anticipation. At least we had a house to ourselves for better of worse, if only for a limited time. The first thing we did in the early morning was look it over.

Originally the Villa Madiana had been one of those pleasant little stucco villas with a bedroom and combination living and dining room facing the street with a large shedlike structure attached to the back combining the function of back porch, kitchen, pantry, storeroom, and toilet, behind which was the back yard with vegetables and flowers. There was a separate garage and tool shed at the back of the drive. All in all, it was the kind of small house built to accommodate a thrifty French householder. But it had been expanded with additional rooms, first a separate bedroom with a modern "American-type" kitchen and bath on the side opposite the driveway for Yves' married sister, and then a series of summer-camp bedrooms (the "concentration camp") and storerooms completely enclosing the garden, which had been paved, except for a single small tree in its center. At the time of our arrival it looked like a typical summer camp in Sullivan County, New Jersey, except that the living room contained a roll top desk and several worn leather armchairs and the walls were lined with books in several languages.

Some neighbor had turned on the electricity for us the previous evening while we ate and that morning I discovered the bottle of butagaz and connected the hotplate in our kitchen. I took my two-burner Primus stove from my trunk and got it burning and with the combined four burners we could cook practically anything. Alva went across the street to Mlle. Cancalen's épicerie, and came back laden with two bulging string fillets—a shopping bag much used by the French—and we were in the business of housekeeping without having to ask for any assistance. Later we went down to M. Dutin's and got some meat for dinner. Yvonne had said there was an icebox in the garage but I did not recognize it. We took our time and unpacked leisurely and got ourselves arranged.

The Quartier l'Aiguillon was the fishing village of Arcachon situated at the inner tip of the huge bay, some distance from the commercial center of the city, and on the side opposite from the fashionable section where the celebrities lived. The street was unpaved and the intermittent stretches of sidewalk had been laid by householders. Only a few of the houses had water and city gas, but most had gardens and fruit trees for private use. The fishing fleet docked there, and at night when the tide was out the shores were lined with small boats sitting in the black mud. The larger boats for deep-sea fishing, which went to sea for days at a time, were docked nearer to the city, where the canneries were located. Fishing was a major industry, and the oysters cultivated in the bay of Arcachon are famous the world over. Acres of oyster beds were planted in the shallow dirty water that crawled with marine life, each staked out and roped off, and one could walk for miles down the corridors between them at low tide. The baby oysters are cemented to sections of convex roofing tile and planted in the black mud at the bottom of the bay and left to grow until the following year, when they are replaced by other baby oysters and changed to fresh tiles, the process being repeated yearly until they came of age.

The boats of the rich—diesel-powered yachts and sailboats— were kept in winter storage there to be painted and repaired; some were even made there. In its preoccupation with boats and fishing, Arcachon bears a decided similarity to Newport, Rhode Island.

In the evenings, tired fishermen plodded up the dirt streets and congregated in the dreary local bistros, drinking cheap red wine until they became loud and quarrelsome. The myriad of docked ships rocking gently on the swells, here and there the rotted shell of some abandoned derelict rising slantwise from its sandy grave, formed a weird picture against the sunset. Twilight was animated with barrages of provincial French shouted by the housewives leaning on the front fences to gossip. The amazon of a woman, Mme. Lepicart, the washerwoman who lived across from us, took down the lines of heavy unbleached sheets, similar in size and texture to the canvas floor covers used by interior painters in the United States, and romped in the street with her three youngest daughters, flashing her big bare football player's legs and giggling and laughing and singing like a child let out to play. She had another daughter about seventeen, exquisitely beautiful, shy and a little ashamed, and a beautiful son of about nineteen who was in the navy, doubtless the Michel Lepicart of Yvonne's *rôlet*. Mme. Lepicart was a widow, we discovered, which seemed not only reasonable but inevitable.

Darkness brought the muted whispering of young lovers, strolling along the darker edges of the unpaved streets beneath the trees, as though each word were freighted with destiny, laughing in muffled, restrained self-consciousness.

When the weather was favorable, our neighbors on the sea side cooked and ate dinner in a small court that was separated from our driveway by a high wooden wall. After dinner, which they completed in darkness, they turned on a dim outdoor light and drank in silence for a time; only the clinking of the bottle against the glasses could be heard. Then they quarreled as by common accord, the nasty sound of spiteful voices rising and falling in the dark, until around midnight they turned off the light and went to bed. Their quarreling always made us feel immoderately normal.

We liked it there. Our neighbors were curious but not offensive, and when we went down to the one clean sandbar at our end of the bay and lay in the sun, the neighborhood children would gather about and stare at us from big eyes of wonder as though we were freaks escaped from the circus. But when Alva spoke to them in French they became shy and embarrassed. It was pleasant in the late afternoon, walking down rue Alexandrine toward the city and watching the curious family groups come one after another from their houses and lean on the front gates to watch us pass. At that hour the setting sun would appear as though it were sinking into the end of the street, and the whole street was turned into a straight, fantastic channel of molten gold. And afterward turning into boulevard de la Plage and walking the long crooked fascinating mile along the shore, past the famous old cathedral, where the fishing fleet was blessed each fall by the regional bishop. There was a statue of Christ with outstretched arms atop its steeple as though he kept watch over the men at sea. Finally coming to the wide, brilliantly lighted promenade along the waterfront, with its borders and parks of dense gay flowers, and its rows of tiny decorative trees, the aquamarine foliage shading to a pale lavender at its tips, as delicate and fluttery as ostrich feathers. Alva said they looked sexy.

We would sit on the terrace of a restaurant overlooking the

plage and dine on the various seafood delicacies and sip white
wine and watch the moon rise over the bay. I learned how to eat
seafood in the French manner. The proprietors of restaurants
and cafés were very cordial in those days and food was not expensive. My favorite garçon was a little curly-haired Algerian with
the sneaky demeanor of a pickpocket who would always give me
a sly knowing look as though we had served time together in the
same jail. We were amused by him until once, while I was in the
WC, he tried to conspire with Alva to cheat me on the bill.

At that time Alva did not know I had been to prison, and when
she read my novel *Cast the First Stone*, she did not believe that
I had written it. But later when she became convinced of it and
I had told her all she wanted to know about my crime and my
punishment, it didn't make any difference. She might even have
respected me a little more as a writer because of the book.

About that time I wrote to my platonic black girl friend
Ruth who was working as a secretary at the embassy in Paris to
send me ten cartons of Lucky Strikes and she replied, "You must
be stark, raving mad. If they catch me getting cartons of cigarettes
from the Embassy commissary to send to you I'll be fired . . .
you just have to be satisfied with your love."

Alva began wondering what I had been doing those three weeks
in Paris when she'd been in Holland. I assured her I had been
thinking only of her. I don't know whether the answer satisfied
her, but she saw to it that I would no longer have the time,
energy, or inclination to think of anyone else from then on.

Although the city offered a variety of diversions, numerous cafés,
excellent restaurants, swimming, boating, excursions, gambling,
and nightly dancing in the casino on the quay, and numerous
young people of both sexes anxious to entertain and be entertained, for the most part we entertained ourselves. There were a
thousand picturesque and bizarre sights free for the looking.
Puritanical people often have a bawdy sense of humor in private
and Alva was no exception. She was completely uninhibited,
even exploratory, sexually. We bought a barrel of the local
Bordeaux *vin rouge* and prepared most of our meals in a spirit

of adventure. Down at the end of the street, along the bay, lived one of the prosperous oyster farmers who had a pool in his courtyard where he kept graded oysters for retail. Often we would buy a dozen of his largest oysters for eighty francs (twenty cents in American money) and once I bought two dozen eggs and made a tremendous oyster omelette with *fines herbes* and a dozen eggs. Alva thought the mess would be inedible but it was *formidable*, as the French say, and we shared it with Mme. Meulliets and it became a minor legend in the neighborhood.

When Alva received a trunk of clothes from her home in Kerkrade, I discovered how much she missed her daughters. She cried for two days and was inconsolable, and though I tried to comfort her in bed, I was the one who was worn out. She heard regularly from her aunt in Philadelphia, but it was only the love and respect of her daughters that she really wanted.

The bed in the master bedroom was so lumpy that going to bed became a torture. A few years previous a tidal wave had inundated l'Aiguillon, damaging much of Yves' furniture and books. The legs of the bed had been destroyed and had been replaced by a number of large rocks that had been washed into the street from the bay, which apparently had been pushed beneath the springs indiscriminately. As a consequence ours was a literal example of rocks in our bed. Soon after Alva's seizure of remorse, we moved into the independent bedroom on the other side of the house.

If we were not awakened at an ungodly hour of morning by the fisherwomen's plaintive cries of *poisson, poisson,* the curious tame pigeons of Mme. Meulliets would stomp noisily about the roof, pecking at the glass skylight, or bending an eye flush to the glass to try to see what we were doing in bed. We called them the New York gossip columnists.

There were two fisherwomen, one with a pushcart and the other who carted her fish in a box attached to the handlebars of her bicycle. Often they had violent quarrels over our patronage, calling upon the neighbors as mediators. Once, to demonstrate the freshness of a huge gray eel, the pushcart fisherwoman permitted it to romp about the yard. It got through the fence and took off down the street, and had it not been for the combined efforts of the neighborhood cats, dogs, children, and alert housewives, it might have escaped into the bay. We did not buy any fish again until the quarreling of the fisherwomen provoked a public hearing of housewives, and we were forced to yield.

By then I had identified the icebox and at noon each day the ice truck stopped to put a block of ice in the driveway. If we failed to hear it or were absent at the time, we would find only a damp spot on the gravel.

Mme. Moon had accepted us and permitted us to feed her and sometimes pet her when she wasn't otherwise engaged entertaining all the tomcats of the neighborhood or going through trunks, closets, dresser drawers, and anything left open which she considered suitable for her confinement. The French have a positive fetish for pregnancy. At that time if a French father sired enough children he no longer needed to work; the government would take care of him and his family. This attitude likewise extended to animals. Despite our neighbors' reluctance to sell us milk to drink ourselves, they were more than willing to sell us some for the pregnant cat. All during the day, whenever they passed, the neighboring housewives flung scraps of meat and fish into the front yard for Mme. Moon. This attracted all the cats of the neighborhood, many of whom had been enamored of her charm before. No more ugly, mangy, lean, and hungry collection of cats have I ever seen, even in Harlem.

Feeling the weight of unseen stares, often Alva would glance up from cooking and find several lean gray cats watching her silently through the partly open kitchen skylight.

Mme. Moon's legitimate spouse was a long lean ancient insolent tom with dirty white fur marred with patches of raw pink skin, which appeared to be marks of furious nightly battles. Except for fangs at the corners of his mouth, all of his front teeth were missing, giving him a curious look of a Cheshire cat without teeth. His name was M. Berdoulas.

In strict French tradition, he was seldom home during Madam's pregnancy. I first saw him several days after our arrival. He was in the paved court in the shade of the small maple tree, calmly eating one of the glistening white sole filets we'd left in the kitchen for lunch. I rushed toward him angrily and yelled, "Hey!" He gave me a brief cynical glance and continued calmly eating. I gave him a sound hiding with a bamboo garden rake, but he escaped through the loft of the garage and took the filet with him. The next day he returned and stole some fresh sardines.

I developed a great respect for M. Berdoulas. He took whatever he found that was edible, and accepted his beatings philosophically. Doubtless he reasoned if I derived as much pleasure out of beating him as he did out of eating our delectables, that made us even. In time he grew fond of me also, and would rub his scabby sides against my leg and give me a toothless grin.

He was absolutely fearless and instantly attacked any competitor he found lurking about the villa or peering over the wall. On the whole, however, he looked upon Madame's flirtations with indifference, considering them harmless no doubt in view of her condition. Ofttimes he'd lie on the roof of the house across the street hidden behind the chimney and spy on her with cynical indulgence.

The bathroom, as Yvonne had noted, had everything but water. We found a huge galvanized tub in the woodshed, the kind always employed by animals in children's books to sail upon the seas. We took this out into the paved court beneath the tree and there we took our baths. Should we want a shower, I would fill the Primus stove with water, pump up the pressure and remove the burner caps, and produce two fine streams of water which would serve for rinsing off the soap. There was the risk of being seen by visitors entering through the driveway, but we figured they would risk as much as we. Our argumentative neighbors could be heard whispering and giggling behind the cracks in the wooden wall but there was a certain poetical justice in the fact that afterward they quarreled more violently than ever. The other side was blocked off by the continuation of the bedrooms.

A considerable controversy, much of which was loud if not

bitter, raged among the neighborhood trades people for our trade. Yvonne had suggested we spread it out. But Alva had settled upon the épicerie across the street because Mlle. Louise Cancalen, an angular spinster who looked as though she came from Zola's novels, took the trouble to correct her French. Alva also gossiped a great deal with our neighbor, Mme. Meulliets, whose husband was a deep-sea fisherman and away five days a week. She exhibited a surprising talent for French curiosity, and bargained shrewdly for full value of all information given, which endeared her to the French housewives.

Yves had indoctrined the neighborhood to all the licensed eccentricities of the writer. In hushed tones, Mme. Meulliets told of his writing at the typewriter from midnight until dawn, and of his stomping through the streets clad only in his swim trunks, which no sober person ever did in that part of town where most of the people lived from the sea, looking neither to the right nor to the left and speaking to no one day after day. As a consequence, when it was learned that I was a writer in addition to being a black American, I was treated with the awed deference accorded a zombie. No one ever addressed me directly, which was for the best, but directed to Alva any remarks intended for me in the hope she would transmit them. Always they referred to me as *le monsieur*. "Does *le monsieur* eat only sandwiches? . . . Is *le monsieur* a Christian? . . . Bon! . . . Does *le monsieur* have money?" . . . This question always caused Alva to blush.

The first of Yves' friends to visit us was Gerard Begaud, the engraver, who lived down the street with his grandmother, Mme. Besnard. He was a dark, handsome, slender young man with thick wavy hair, a child's clear complexion and guileless brown eyes. He was a bachelor and very shy. He was fascinated by Alva.

He came around to the back one morning and found me clad in old corduroy trousers, naked to the waist, and he blushed.

During several years as a prisoner of war, he had learned engraving, and on his return had opened a profitable shop in his house, engraving name plaques for houses, professional people, and business firms. As with many Frenchmen who live near the sea, Gerard painted, but he was more talented than most. His landscapes, in both water color and oils, had a somber charm; but his paintings of the sunken derelict ships in the bay had a true, moving, lonely emotion. He was slyly amused by the generosity of an American woman novelist who paid him far in excess of the asking price for several of his landscapes to assist in French rehabilitation. The French are amused by American circumspection of the obvious.

Gerard was also an enthusiastic sailor of great excellence. He had a slim, very fast boat which he had made himself. Once he took us sailing on an inland lake where his club of sailing aficionados held races every Sunday afternoon because the wind in the bay was too strong and uneven for good sailing. Afterward, while we sat with his grandmother, Mme. Besnard, on the terrace and watched, he won the race of eleven laps about a marked course. His club owned its own clubhouse, a large, rambling wooden structure containing club rooms and a restaurant and café with a terrace extending over the water. We gathered that Gerard was the poorest of the members, he owned the smallest car—one of those Renault bugs—and the only homemade boat. All the others had sleek, factory-built boats, expensive cars, and stylish wives of that highly competitive species of young Frenchwomen. Gerard's grandmother was his only girl. Mme. Besnard was an energetic, roly-poly woman with an aggressive inquisitiveness, a complete absorption in Gerard, and an acid indifference toward his more affluent club members.

We had Gerard to dinner alone, and afterward recorded a brilliant conversation on our tape recorder which we later entitled *Ah Oui*, by Chester Himes. We arranged the mike, set the spools turning, and for a time Gerard spoke in rapid liquid French. He had a very pleasant voice, deep and clear. At the end of his discourse, he looked at Alva. Hesitantly, with a strange reluctance, as though debating whether to plead the Fifth Amendment, she spoke a few limping words in a tiny voice. They both looked at me. Having not the slightest notion of what either had said, I cleared my throat and said jubilantly in my blurred American

English, "Ah oui!" This procedure was repeated several times until Alva became hysterical and Gerard's inherent French courtesy could no longer restrain his laughter.

A few days later Gerard brought some symphony records and his record player, which we played through our loudspeaker; and in turn we entertained him with recordings of blues and jazz classics I'd taped at Dick's. While taping one of these recordings, Ellen had come in from the telephone, where she was discussing with Daniel Guerin my eligibility for his writers' colony, and asked Dick, "How old is Chester?" which came out clear and loud and startling on the tape.

Dr. Thé and his youngest son, Jacques, along with his huge, fat boxer named Vous-Vous (You-You), visited unexpectedly at about ten o'clock one morning, and doubtless gathered the impression that we were very interesting people. The day before I had received the galley proofs of my novel *The Third Generation*, and I had been up all night trying to dramatize the ending at the suggestion of my editor, Bill Targ. But I had met with complete frustration and I was still clad in my pajamas and old bathrobe, trying to finish a bottle of Cognac with Alva's help before eating breakfast and going to bed. Alva had just gotten up. The front gate was still chained and padlocked because we hadn't found the key, and Dr. Thé and Jacques were forced to come around to the back door through the driveway. Neither exhibited the slightest surprise at finding us in our night clothes drinking Cognac for breakfast, construing such behavior as perfectly natural for Americans. Graciously Dr. Thé partook of our Cognac with his good manners—and a certain amount of courage, I might add—although Jacques declined. Nevertheless we had a hilarious time, doubtless due to an almost total lack of communication.

I remember Dr. Thé as typical of the rich, provincial Frenchman, ponderous, heavy-set and well fed, owning a dog with identical attributes; he had two sons, I learned later, and an exquisite, well-kept, stylish wife. Curiosity about the human animal was one of his chief motivations. He owned his own clinic, two fashionable hotels, an estate in the city, and a vineyard in the wine country of Bordeaux. Nevertheless, he had a genuine respect for anyone with creative talent, despite his barely concealed astonishment at my unartistic tastes.

When I recall his gallant consumption of our really terrible Cognac so early in the morning, I think of Dr. Thé as a gentleman.

Jacques, however, was more interested in himself, no doubt because of his youth and upbringing. Gerard told us afterward that his mother, who had a great fortune of her own, gave him five million francs (about twelve thousand dollars) a year for spending money. This was believable. Jacques's favorite description of everything that claimed his interest was *"Très jolie."* At that time he was completing medical studies, for which he had no enthusiasm, preferring instead to manage his father's hotels and be a playboy.

What did we talk about? Frankly, our conversation hardly got off the ground. Conversation through a translator is always painfully embarrassing, laborious, disappointing, and extremely limited. Subtleties are impossible. The *bon mot*, the witty phrase, the delicate jest, the satiric twist, are reduced to flat statements of inanity. There's always a slight shade of idiocy over the most serious conversations.

"McCarthy?" Dr. Thé questioned, expecting an eruption of flame.

"Subverting the First Amendmentists," I replied.

He looks to Alva for the translation. She gives me a thou-too-Brutus look.

Dr. Thé notices the by-play and is quick to understand. We were afraid to talk about McCarthy. Confirms his worst suspicions. *"Très mauvais!"* he denounces fearlessly. "Very bad!" After all, McCarthy was not his senator.

For some inexplicable reason the American editions of my books intrigued Dr. Thé. He picked them up, one at a time—*If He Hollers Let Him Go, Lonely Crusade, Cast the First Stone*—hefted them in his hand, turned them one way and then the other as though they were newfangled gadgets. "If he hollers let him go," he read in English. This afforded him great amusement. He opened it at random and read a line: "'Ain't I beautiful?' she said. 'Pure white.' Ha-ha-ha," he roared, *"Pure white."*

I won't belittle Dr. Thé by trying to reproduce his accented English; I understood it about the same as I did his French. Both Alva and I considered him a charming man. However, I must confess that Alva was not convulsed by that particular line.

Jacques became friendly in a dictatorial manner, which required accepting his proposals immediately without dissent. He drove us about the fashionable end of town, along the scenic drive skirting the bay, pointing out the various places of interest, the most memorable of which were the resplendent villas belonging to Charles Boyer, Annabella, and Maurice Thorez, the leader of the French Communist Party, who had just returned from the two years of medical treatment in Moscow. He drove his Peugeot 203 in the typical French fashion, at moderate speed when the road was straight and empty, only accelerating in congested traffic or when going into a curve.

One stifling-hot morning shortly after their visit, I sent Alva down to the beach, locked myself in the library and drew the blinds, and wrote the last chapter of *The Third Generation.* When Alva returned and found me sitting in the red-hot darkened room, she thought I had gone crazy and for a moment was dreadfully alarmed. I could understand it. The thought of having left her home and family for a man who had gone crazy a few weeks later must have given her a dreadful fright. But when she became reconciled to the eccentricities of my creativity, she told me about the book she was trying to write herself. She had written a couple of hundred typed pages of what might be called notes, which she had shown to Donald Friede when she had been in the States—I don't remember what firm he was with at the time, but later he became editor-in-chief of World under the direction of Bill Targ—and he had told her that he thought a very good novel could be worked out of her story. I read it and was caught and promised to help her work it into a novel, and this, in the end, became the tie that bound us. She was so desirous of writing a successful book to gain her daughters' admiration and respect, and vindicate her leaving her husband.

We became so engrossed in this project that afterward we often learned more of what was happening to us from Yves' letters from Paris than what we observed firsthand. The first one, in typical French simplicity, read:

Dear Friends,

Almost two weeks since you left Paris, and I did not write. But we had some news about you from Jacques Thé who told us you seemed to be settling quite well in our hobo's palace.

Thanks for your letter. But you did not say anything about my beloved Lune and my dear old Berdoulas. Are they dead? I should never leave those little ones. It is a shame.

Is Chester writing? Summer time is not too favorable for artistic creation. But I hope you'll get along.

My sister-in-law, Carmen-the-Terrible (like Ivan) will probably go to Arcachon in July. From the 1st or about to the 14th she'll only have with her Francis (4) (Francis is a boy and Colette (14½). I am quite sure you'll manage to live together. But from the 15th to the end of the month she'll have her husband, Jean, too, and her eldest daughter, Miss Marie-Claude. Maybe you'll feel the house is a little crowded at that time but you'll be able to make all necessary dispositions before with Carmen Dupret.

few days later

So I had written a first and second page and my conscience was more at ease. "After all I wrote." But this morning I find this beginning and I feel writing is not enough and mailing is necessary.

What could I tell you about our life over here? It is warm (damned) warm, and I work a lot. But by the end of June I'll be a little *free-er* (is it possible 3 e's). Paris is wonderful at night. Yesterday I worked from 5 to 12 and at midnight I felt like sitting at a "terrasse" and staying there for the whole night that would never have ended.

Before that, in the afternoon I had lost a tremendous fortune.

Millions of tons of millions! "WE" were going to start the biggest franco-anglo-American newspaper every imagined "in the history of mankind." Alas! most unfortunately I found within a few minutes that my financier and prospective associate had the most horrid temper. That was a first nuisance, then he told me, definitely, word for word, "I am the only intelligent man on earth," and that was too much of a nuisance. So I abandoned all hopes of making any kind of deal with him. I knew very well he was wrong because *I* am the most intelligent man on earth.

So he paid for his café noir, I paid for mine, and he went straight to the English book shop to tell Miss Froger she is wrong to be a Catholic. He also told her his father's name is well and honorably known all over the States (Freedman!) and that, there fore, he could not make this newspaper with me. There he was right.

That is how I lost my 2,926th opportunity to get rich.

Thanks for the book (The man without a country). As you sent it perfectly well, my wife wants to ask you something.

She left "somewhere in Madiana" two dresses she feels like having over here.

1) one green cotton dress—green with big red and yellow flowers. The skirt is very large. There are no sleeves to that dress.

2) a gray dress with a long series of buttons up the front.

Could you and Alva find them and send them to us?

We have received a letter from Jacques Thé and another from Mr. Ludomir alias Louis alias Gerard Begaud, grandchild of Mme. Besnard. One says Alva had a sore throat, the other says it was Chester. It seems the one who had a sore throat is well now. My friend Ludo (mir) is reading "La Croisade de Lee Gordon" and feels he'll understand you better when he will be through with it. He also wrote that Lune is always young and graceful, and Berdoulas amiable but dirty. So there does not seem to be much change at Madiana.

We miss you, we'd like to be with you over there or have you over here and chew the rag a little—writing is so tiring when it is warm.

I hope (1) you'll understand this letter (2) you are well (throat, soul, heart, mind and everything) (3) that you still feel Arcachon

is a place where one can live (special addendum for "the young
lady from the patriotic association. . . . where one can live, even
one from "God's own country")—This man (1) is always a little
mean (but only a little, very little)

Salut et fraternité, Yvonne et Yves

When Gerard had finished reading the translation of *Lonely
Crusade*, he visited us to discuss it. I had written this book, which
contains a long torrid affair between an intellectual black man
and a white woman, while I was still married to Jean, and as I
have written previously in these pages no one in America liked
it; Jean hated it, my soul brothers hated it, communists hated it,
liberals hated it, capitalists hated it, reactionaries hated it, and I
must confess that Alva was no exception. However, Gerard was
convinced, despite my solemn denial, that the book was autobiographical, and seriously suspected that Alva was the white
woman of the fictional affair—Jackie was her name in the book.
Alva had always loathed this particular character more than any
other character in any of my books. I saw blood mounting to her
face as Gerard's skeptical expression remained unchanged. For
a brief spell they exchanged some highly charged remarks, but
Alva flatly refused to translate for me afterward. From that I
knew exactly how it went. By then Alva had begun to cheat a
little on translations and omit things she found too embarrassing.
Poor Alva, I thought. Thank God I don't know the language.

She finally steered the conversation on to other books. Gerard
said that *Out of the Night* by Jan Valtin was one of the best
books he had ever read, and that it compared favorably with
the *Odyssey*. I told him I liked it too. He was also very curious
about Ethel Waters, whose autobiography was on sale in the local
bookshops. It had a cover picture of Ethel in a sequinned evening
gown trimmed with ostrich feathers doing a blues number, and
Gerard asked if she really looked like that. I said that picture
looked to me more like a female witch doctor exorcising stub-
born spirits. Poor Gerard was shocked. By deft manipulation
Alva eventually got Gerard onto the safe subject of sailing.

Yves had an old-fashioned scabby sailboat stored in the garage. We had it caulked and painted a bright lemon-yellow and launched in the bay. But we had to write Yves to ask him about the sails. He replied:

Dear Friends,

The sail is "chez Claverie" who washed it and keeps it. Claverie makes sails, washes them in Autumn and keeps them in a dry place during the winter. He kept mine for three years now. I wrote this afternoon to M. Bretaux whom you call Bonnafaux and my nieces Bouaf, although his real name is indeed Bretaux, son-in-law of M. Bonnafaux who lives next to that little bistro where you went on your first day in Arcachon.

I explain to him where the sail is and I tell him to go and fetch it. There will be something to pay. I do not remember at all what it cost me four years ago. I think it was not much. There is another small sail with it. Claverie will probably give you both of them together. We'll settle the expense about this sail when we'll meet, and also the postage for the book and dresses. But I do not think I'll pay you back entirely because Berdoulas is indignant. "Only raw soles to steal in that house now!" he told me in one of my dreams. So please cook the fishes before leaving the kitchen door open . . .

Something else, not too urgent, but I'd like it to be done before you leave, and I thank you in advance. Amongst my American books, (I think they are on the right side when sitting at the big roller desk) there is quite a bunch of Upton Sinclair's novels. I'd like to have THE JUNGLE (Vanguard Press 1946). Somewhere, on the left side of the window probably, there are a few Marxist books. I'd like to have "Au dela du Marxisme" by Deman or de Mau (I don't remember the first name). It was a red book but I think it turned some sort of brownish red during these last years. So two books, "The Jungle" in English and "Au dela du Marxisme" in French. A young man needs to take them to the country during this summer because he believes he'll find something useful in them for a thesis he is writing about "public relations." I do not get exactly his idea but as long as he asks for them I don't want to disappoint him. So I thank you if you can send them before he leaves for his summer holidays.

Now, about that crazy Freedman. I must honestly confess he is far more crazy than it is permitted even to an American, far more. He left for Italy yesterday to make over there that paper he is dreaming of.

That damned little English Queen has been crowned today. I'm glad it rained because she gave me too much work, and I'll end this letter by

> Vive la Republique, nom de Dieu!
> Salut et fraternité a tous les deux
> et a mes chere enfants chats
>
> Yvonne et Yves

P.S. Next morning: Last night the cats told me they are well and you are good people. Good. Y

The large sail turned out to be as crude and enormous as those on Chinese sampans, making the shallow sluggish boat dangerous and unwieldy in a stiff breeze, and with the addition of the small sail it was too much for us. The young man whom Yves' nieces called Bouaf took us sailing the first time and showed us how to handle the boat, but he was an expert sailor and what seemed easy for him was impossible for us. We found that it was such a struggle to keep it from overturning and sinking that our destination became of minor importance. Once, to our horror, we found ourselves crashing through the rope boundaries into an oyster field, the one unpardonable offense in that section, and before we could get the boat turned and depart, the tide went out and left us stranded atop an oyster bed. We had to get out and push and pull the boat over the tiles to which the oysters were attached, doubtless scraping off enough infant oysters to start a school of their own, and then push and pull it through the thick mud of the channels, which resembled nothing so much as wet coal dust. Luckily no one noticed our offense, but the damn boat was as heavy as lead, and it was pitch-dark before we came reeling toward shore, black to our waists and stinking of chemicals and rotten fish. By then Alva had learned an entirely new vocabulary of swear words and my stock for originality had soared in her estimation.

All in all, our two months there had been exquisitely happy and satisfying, and for a short time I had become completely free of my soul brothers' envy and jealousy and intrigues, and my fellow countrymen's obsession with the "Negro problem." It wasn't so much that Alva was free of racial prejudice as that she simply did not think about race, or even politics. She was more concerned about domestic affairs—her daughters' schooling, her husband's infidelities, her aunt's and uncle's health, her own value as a woman. I had ceased to feel sorry for her; instead I had become imbued with a genuine respect and admiration for her. Gallantry is not generally considered a feminine virtue, but I know no other word to define what I admired about her. She was courageous, uncomplaining, adaptable, and congenial, and I never heard her speak badly of anyone except her husband, and she even rationalized his infidelities, which had hurt her so much, on the grounds that he was exceptionally handsome and that all women except herself claimed that he was a fantastic lover. She who had had four daughters by him and had been made pregnant five times. In the course of time I came to feel that he had hurt her so much that she would belong to him forever, but that was later, and even then it didn't change my love for her.

We hated to have to leave Arcachon, but we knew that the presence of others in our little paradise would spoil it for us, so we decided to leave the first of July, when Carmen Dupret and her children arrived. It was then we first considered going to Mallorca. An old friend of mine, Vandi's former husband, William C. Haygood, was then living with his second wife and young son in Puerto de Pollenso. For two years previous to moving to Mallorca for the purpose of writing a book, Bill had been in Madrid setting up a library for the USIS. Bill is a librarian of great distinction. I wrote and asked him about living conditions for the two of us there. I will quote his reply:

Dear Chester,

A quick note with hopes it will reach you in time. I just received your letter the day before yesterday and would have answered immediately except for two house guests and two very sick babies. The guests are gone now and the babies are well again and I will try to get this off in the afternoon mail. In a way I rather hope you went ahead and took the Writers Group [Daniel Guerin's writers' colony in La Ciotat] up for the months of July and August as they are fairly hectic in Mallorca, being the height of the tourist season with everything overrun and inflated, especially in Palma. Boat and plane reservations are difficult, and villas are very scarce. Of course, I only know the conditions out here in the Puerto where there is not a single house left and all the hotels are booked until September. By that time conditions begin to ease up, the weather is cooler, and thank God the French are gone. However, if you and Alva have already laid your plans you will be able to find something.

Now to answer your questions in order:

1) Villas will range from 1000 pesetas up, furnished, linens usually extra. Our house guests are a young couple who pay 1500 (about thirty-five dollars) for a very large place in the San Agustin section of Palma. This would be suitable for you and your friend. The Bates are planning to spend three months in another part of the Island and if their landlord will permit, they are willing to sublease to you. Their address is Brainerd Bates, Los Leones, Camino Vecinal de Genova, San Agustin, Palma de Mallorca. It has a lovely view and a wide terrace.

2) Hotels range from luxury to bad and prices from 300 ptas full pension to about fifty. Pensions can be had for about a dollar and a half a day, but frankly I do not know the names of any in Palma. The Catalonia, the Cala Mayor, the Hotel Londres are second class, clean, reasonable hotels where you could stop off until you got your bearings.

Short and Sons on the Borne downtown and Vich's Agency across from the Victoria Hotel at Plaza Gomila are English speaking rental agencies and reliable. The people who will accost you at the boat hawking hotels and pensions are honest and trustworthy. You can generally get by with a knowledge of French since the Mallorquin language has much in common.

3) Living conditions are good. The food is cheap, but the most expensive item, but still many times cheaper than France and a third less than its US equivalent. Living will cost you what you want it to. A carpenter makes about a dollar a day, to give you something to go on. Clothes are much cheaper than in France and many French come here just to replenish their wardrobes. Entertainment is cheap and life in general is as pleasant as it could be anywhere. Palma is rapidly filling up with the neurotic overflow from the Left Bank but there are many serious writers and artists who manage to keep clear of it. I would advise a village, but this would depend on your personal preferences and working habits, and what you decide when you get here.

4) The electric current is 115 and we have always just plugged in our American things with no transformers.

5) I don't know what else to say except that I think you would like it here, especially if you are tired of cities.

The place is so tranquil (outside of Palma) that there is an inescapable tendency to begin to deaccelerate and just give in to the pleasant life, but this has its points, too.

In any event, I hope this reaches you. When you and Alva get here, if you come, come out and see us and we'll do anything we can to help. There may possibly be villas in this vicinity of which I am not aware. There is a villa colony at Alcudia across our bay which has not yet been invaded.

In haste and apology
Bill

I don't know what it was about Bill's letter that repulsed me. It was cordial and informative and extraordinarily kind of him to take so much trouble with me. I don't think we had ever particularly liked each other. I had only met him in person a few times. I remember him best from a party in Chicago, when he had been director of fellowships for the Julius Rosenwald Foundation, and he had offered my wife Jean a fellowship to write my biography. But I must confess his letter struck me like a cold shower. Perhaps it was his exuberant praise for Mallorca, and his well-intentioned implications about what I was searching for. What I am searching for has always been my own private business. I don't mind saying now that all I have ever wanted and searched for is peace. And I don't like for anybody to try to sell me anyplace, not now or ever. I think this was my basic objection. It's a pity I'm like this. It has made my life difficult. But how in the hell could anyone know what I—a pariah, an American black, "alien corn," as *Time* magazine once called me—wanted from this world, this life?

Anyway, we decided to go to London. Why London? one might ask. Principally because we could both speak the language.

We received a letter in little-girl English written by Mme. Carmen Dupret's fourteen-and-a-half-year-old daughter, Colette, saying she and her mother and little brother, Francis, would arrive on July 5, and were looking forward to meeting us. We had every intention of awaiting their arrival, but we received a letter from the Malartics that made us change our minds:

Dear Himes and Alva,

You wrote recently that Mrs. Moon was preparing a litter of kittens. Trembling with fear, pleading on my knees, I beg you not to let these little innocents stay too long in this valley of tears, terrors and sufferings. Please, if you want to deserve my eternal gratefulness, please destroy them. I understand you do not wish to do so. So please find somebody to do it.

I know it is a most disagreeable task. But I know also that I am not even able to accomplish my duty towards Moon and

Berdoulas, so I am sure the fate of their children would be most sad if they lived. . . .

If you stall before the abominable murder I am asking you to commit, please ask Miss Cancalen, the grocer on the other side of the street, the one who looks like the last lady pirate, to send you somebody. If she does not understand, tell her some months ago Mrs. Quemener, the mother not Mimi, offered me to kill all the kittens Moon had born at that time.

Salut et fraternité

Yvonne et Yves

The fact is we could not commit the "abominable murder" or even bear to see it done, even to deserve the Malartics' eternal gratefulness. We knew that once the litter of kittens arrived, and we saw them squirming blindly at their mother's teats, we were stuck with them. We'd either have to remain there and raise them ourselves, or go to great trouble to pay someone to take care of them on their sacred oath they wouldn't kill them as soon as we were gone. And that would leave the solid thrifty French of that neighborhood an impression of our idiocy far in excess of that already established.

We explained the situation to Mlle. Cancalen, the grocer across the street, and left a letter addressed to Mme. Carmen Dupret atop Yves' desk, and left early the next morning, as Yves was later to say, "carrying our house on our backs, like snails." After transporting my huge wardrobe trunk, Alva's trunk, and four pieces of hand luggage, from Gare d'Austerlitz to Gare du Nord, we took a room in our old Hôtel Michelet in the Latin Quarter for the night, and spent the evening with Yves and Yvonne, bringing them up to date on the happenings at Villa Madiana. Leaving the hotel next day about noon, we ran into William Gardner Smith and a fat, sleepy-looking girl in the Café Suisse across the street, whom he introduced as Heather Chisholm, from Canada. When I introduced him to Alva, Bill gave her a glance and said, "Oh, there are lots of white American women around the Latin Quarter." Alva startled us all with one of her outbursts of laughter.

Bill said I'd written the book *If He Hollers Let Him Go* and Heather said, "Eenie, meenie, minie, moe—" and Bill interrupted, jokingly perhaps, "Don't you say it!"

When Bill discovered we were on our way to London he gave me the address of a rooming house in Sussex Gardens off Edgeware Road, where he had stayed, saying we could put up there until we found a permanent place. Heather suggested we apply at the KIWI Accommodation Bureau on Earls Court, run by a friend of hers, and use her name. Richard Wright was still in Ghana and I don't remember seeing any of the other brothers.

I telephoned Ruth at the embassy and asked if she could get me some cigarettes and whiskey and she made an appointment for that afternoon at Café Royal a few doors up from Maxim's. She brought me a quart each of Old Grand-dad, Pinch, Haig & Haig, and two cartons of Lucky Strikes. Back at the hotel we opened both bottles of whiskey and had a drink out of each to get them past customs and took them in a shopping bag along with our overnight case, to Gare du Nord, where we caught the boat train at about four-thirty that afternoon.

2.

At eleven o'clock that night, shaken up by a rough channel crossing, and bone weary, we arrived at Victoria Station. I claimed our luggage and had everything checked except two suitcases, which I left with Alva in the cavernous waiting room, in the company of other weary travelers, and, despite her uneasiness, sallied forth in search of a telephone. I found a row of booths in the entrance hall with the directories in a rack to one side. While looking up the number of the rooming house on Sussex Gardens that Bill had told me about, I placed my bright-yellow pigskin case containing both of our passports, seven pounds sterling, and my little address book, on the stand beside me. I forgot to pick it up when I stepped into the adjoining booth. Perhaps this foolhardiness was due to my overconfidence and the fact there was no one in sight. In any event, while studying the directions for making a telephone call, I suddenly thought of it. When I stepped from the booth to retrieve it, I found that it was gone. I had still seen no one.

I do not take any credit for not panicking, for my entire life had conditioned me to a constant expectation of catastrophe. But the short journey back to the bench where Alva was waiting patiently with our suitcases was the longest I have ever made. I was overcome with chagrin.

Alva had been in Europe long enough to know the extreme seriousness of losing one's passport, and she went sheet-white and began to tremble. Nevertheless, after a short time she composed herself and consented to stay with our suitcases while I went to report the theft to the police and the stationmaster.

As it always happens in such cases, the bobbies we'd seen patrolling on our arrival had disappeared, and after considerable exploration of that tremendous station, which I found every bit as large as the American Steel & Wire factory in Cleveland, Ohio (and as dark and ugly too), I found the stationmaster's office closed.

In my absence Alva had got hold of a bobby, who, after listening to my story, instructed me to report the theft to the Victoria Station police. I found their offices at the extreme end of a dark deserted passage to one side of the station, looking like a scene from one of Dickens' books. I reported the details of our arrival, the theft of our passports, and the predicament in which we were left without identification, hotel reservation, or English money, to a bareheaded, heavy-set uniformed officer who stood behind a long bare wooden counter making notes. He listened attentively and impassively without interruption. Then he asked for my full name, for Alva's maiden name, for our address in the United States, for the numbers of our passports, and where they were issued. Undoubtedly he must have thought I was a halfwit when all I could tell him was our names. The fact that we were not married did not seem to interest him, but the fact that I didn't know the numbers of our passports aroused his suspicion. Another officer clad in a baggy tweed suit and a battered tweed cap appeared from the interior. The son of Sherlock Holmes, I thought. He had a ruddy complexion, walrus-type reddish mustache and cold unsmiling blue-gray eyes, with the curved stem of a huge unlit pipe clenched between his big strong teeth. He asked about the same questions I had been asked at customs: Occupation? . . . Writer. . . . And my companion's? . . . Writer. . . . How long did we

intend to stay in England? . . . Three months. . . . What was
the purpose of our visit?

I must explain here that my first two novels, *If He Hollers Let
Him Go* and *Lonely Crusade*, had been published by the Falcon
Press in London. The Falcon Press, along with the Grey Walls
Press, had been owned by a Captain Peter Baker, the most dec-
orated English serviceman of World War II and later an MP.
Captain Baker was the nephew of a wealthy English industrialist
or financier, from whom he had embezzled seven million pounds.
He had been sentenced to seven years in prison and his publishing houses, among other possessions, had been confiscated by
the court. At the time of the seizure the Falcon Press had owed
me £114 in royalties.

I told the police officer what I had told the customs officer:
the purpose of my visit was to collect the £114 owed to me.
He studied me in silence.

I felt impelled to explain that our money for expenses was in
American Express travelers checks, which we could not get
cashed without passports, and we had no place to stay and no
money for food, adding maliciously that I would never have come
to England had I not been owed this money.

For the first time he smiled slightly. "You're in quite a fix, aren't
you?" he concluded. Then he said that he had already sent a
number of plainclothes detectives into the station, but there was
little likelihood of their finding our passports that night or ever.

The uniformed officer broke in to instruct me to report the
theft to the Metropolitan Police of the area, whose offices I
would find on a street some half dozen blocks distance; he jotted
down the exact address for me. He added that I might inquire at
the lost and found department in the checkroom, but he doubted
if it would be of any use.

The tweedy detective took me by the arm and ushered me out
into the middle of the dark cobblestone street. He pointed to a
red neon sign in the distance which read HOTEL WILTON. He said:
"That hotel is right across from the entrance. When you come
back from the Metropolitan Police, you and the lady might take

your suitcase and walk over there and get a room for the night.
The desk clerk has gone by now and there'll be only the night
porter left, and no one will ask to see your passports until tomorrow morning, and by then you'll have a good night's sleep and
some breakfast and things will look better. But be careful to tell
him that you're married."

When I returned to tell Alva I had to go to the Metropolitan
Police, I found the station crawling with bobbies, so I went to the
checkroom and pushed the button above the notice "Lost and
Found." The baggage attendant told me he was Lost and Found.
When I reported the loss of our passports he replied cheerfully,
"Americans are always losing their passports; during the corona-
tion hundreds lost 'em," adding that the previous night even a
Frenchman had lost his passport along with forty pounds sterling,
and as far as he knew no lost passport had ever been recovered,
but that was neither here nor there. With the latter, I agreed. I
told him that I had reported the loss immediately to the station
police. He nodded approvingly and said encouragingly, "You did
the best you could do, now, didn't you?"

However, Alva was somewhat cheered by the prospects of sleep,
and we lugged our suitcases across the street to the Wilton Hotel
like parched travelers approaching an oasis. We saw, to our relief,
that the night porter, a middle-aged bony man in a red uniform
with gold braid and brass buttons, was alone, and hastened
forward. But at the sight of us lugging our heavy suitcases toward
the desk, he came forward to meet us—and to take our bags, I
thought naïvely. I asked for a double room overnight. He flushed
blood-red and shouted in a loud voice that all the rooms were
taken. I stared at him stupidly and began telling him that the
Victoria Station police had suggested that hotel. He turned
abruptly and made off. I was blinded with a sudden rage. If it
hadn't been for Alva hanging to my arm, I would have followed
the flunky and clobbered him. However, fury needs food and rest
to subsist like any other emotion, with the possible exception of
despair.

So, weary and dispirited, we went back to the street and turned in the direction of a small sign a half block distant stating simply HOTEL. We soon discovered it was one of a group of hotels scattered about the vicinity and it was filled too, but fortunately the proprietor of the group resided there. He took us in his car around the corner to another hotel, a small four-story walkup over a restaurant, where we were given a surprisingly large, clean, comfortable room on the second floor overlooking a narrow street named Kings Scholars Pass, where an elementary school was located. The rates were thirty-five shillings for us both, inclusive of breakfast, and we were not required to register or pay in advance.

To round out a night fringed with hysteria, Alva was chased by a psychopath as she came from the toilet down the corridor. I heard her calling me and dashed out to find her running back toward the toilet, it seemed, being pursued by a heavy-set man in a white shirt and dark trousers. I shouted something, I don't remember what, and the man took a quick look over his shoulder and fled abruptly up the stairs. I followed wildly but he had locked himself in the room directly above ours. I hammered on his door. "Come out, and I'll cut your throat!" I shouted, not realizing the incredible idiocy of such a threat.

"Come on, please, and let him alone," Alva pleaded from the foot of the stairs, where she stood trembling from shock and fatigue.

We returned to our room and locked and bolted the door, and I fixed drinks of the fine old Haig & Haig. We had just about calmed down when the manager, an elderly sedate woman clad in a heavy gray bathrobe with her gray hair in curlers, knocked at our door and inquired the cause for the commotion. Alva informed her without mincing words, woman to woman I suppose, and for a bonus delivered her impression of London.

The manager apologized in a precise manner and unhesitatingly went upstairs and reproached the psycho. Through the open window we could hear her threatening to call the police and his whining reply that he was only trying to pass to get to his room and the "lydy was frightened." After she had retired he was silent for a time, then he began to sing ballads in a fine, loud baritone.

Suddenly he paused and, evidently sticking his head out of his window, he shouted the information that American-made cigarettes contained so much coal tar that they were giving American smokers cancer. When I made no reply to this he shouted, "Bloody furringers," and for some reason began throwing his clothes out of the window. Fascinated, we watched them fluttering past our window into the schoolyard below. Later a big black suitcase sailed by and plopped noisily on the pavement. I waited hopefully for him to follow, but he wasn't that crazy.

We were just on the verge of sleep when the police arrived. They talked to him at exasperating length and finally left; he remained quiet, and we got to sleep. The next morning we saw him down in the schoolyard picking up his things, being watched silently by the schoolchildren.

That was our introduction to London. In a way it was like laughter that's gotten stuck in your throat; it would have been funny if we could have only gotten it out.

Breakfast was brought to our room by a maid with a face like a movie actress but a body that was strangely bloated as though it had been blown up with compressed air, reminiscent of the reconditioned horse in Faulkner's *The Hamlet*. We dressed and went down and explained our predicament to the manager. She took it calmly. After all, it wasn't her hotel, and the owner had brought us there himself. Then we called the American embassy and reported the theft of our passports and were instructed to call back in several days if they hadn't been found. I telephoned the office of my London agent, Innes Rose of John Farquharson Ltd., in Red Lion Square, Holborn, but Mr. Rose was absent. However his associate, George Greenfield, told us to take a taxi and come to the office immediately and their secretary would pay the fare.

The driver took us by way of Buckingham Palace, Queen Victoria Memorial, the Mall, along St. James Park, the Strand, and Kingsway. It was a cold gray morning with a slight drizzle and those huge silent heavy stone buildings appearing from the low visibility impressed me more with England's permanence than all the pages of its history. Holborn, however, had been heavily bombed during the war because of the offices of the ministries that had been located there. It was strange and frightening to see the gutted shells of bombed-out buildings in the cold gray morning rain in the summer of 1953, eight years after the war's end.

The secretary was waiting in the rain to pay our fare. George Greenfield advanced me four pounds ten shillings, the extent of their petty cash, and provided me with this letter of introduction:

> John Farquharson, Ltd.
> 8, Halsey House
> Red Lion Square
> London, W.C.I.

TO WHOM IT MAY CONCERN:

This is to introduce Mr. Chester Himes, who is an old and valued American client of this firm, and who is the bearer of this letter.

His signature appears below:

Chester Himes

We shall be pleased to answer enquiries on his behalf.

8th July, 1953

> George Greenfield

By the time we proceeded to the American Express office on Haymarket Street to cash some travelers checks we were back to normal, which I might say we found always slightly subnormal in London. I cashed the checks and no identification was requested; all I had to do was stand in line and await my turn, which was my introduction to that postwar English institution known as the queue.

We decided to stay where we were while looking for a more permanent place. We discovered that rental agencies for self-contained flats and bed-sitting rooms were known as "Accommodation Bureaus." The first we consulted was the S.S. Accommodation Bureau on Edgeware Road, in Paddington, conducted by an elderly stiff-backed Polish military refugee whose socialized dentures presented a perpetual smile.

We were placed at a deal table and given a stack of filing cards listing vacancies. From the number of vacancies listed in his files, it seemed as though half of London were uninhabited. But about seven out of ten cards contained the notation, "NO COL." and three out of seven further stipulated "No children . . . No pets . . . No loud hobbies." At that time the Mau Mau uprising in Kenya was at its height and I naïvely thought that NO COL. referred to No Colonials, assuming that English landlords were leery of harboring African terrorists. In the ordinary circumstances of life I think so seldom of my racial origins that many times I find myself in ridiculous positions.

Disregarding this irrelevant trivia, I deposited the three pounds' registration fee and we made several selections for the secretary to call. She was a tall, well-corseted woman whom I assumed to be in her early thirties, with a dramatic streak of white through her sleek black hair (as one might find in the hair of young women in San Francisco), red-lacquered fingernails which had attained the length and curve of scimitars, and that sterling efficiency one sometimes finds in English secretaries which borders dangerously on officiousness. During the course of a telephone call, evidently in reply to a landlord's query, she gave us an appraising look and replied in all seriousness: "The missus is white but the mister is slightly colored." Alva let out a whoop of such outrageous glee it startled all of us. The secretary blushed. "You are slightly colored, aren't you?" she appealed to me. I assured her that her eyes had not deceived her. Tears flowed down Alva's cheeks.

Slightly colored though I was, we were sent to interview a Mrs. Mather on Randolph Crescent, not too far distant, who had a four-room flat in the basement of her four-story house available. The interview took place in an ice-cold, pitch-dark, musty-smelling parlor, securely curtained against the corrosive effects of the gray daylight and hermetically sealed against poisonous outside air, which the true Londoner breathes only when sleeping.

Mrs. Mather was a tall, thin, impressively bony woman with hair and face of such indistinguishable whiteness as to create the effect of some nocturnal cereus blooming in the black-dark chair. She informed us that the late Mr. Mather whose enlarged portrait was said to hang over the mantel on the opposite wall though it was indiscernible from where we sat, had been a highly respected Fleet Street barrister, and that she desired only the most respectable tenants. The admirable desire apparently had to do with Mr. Mather's peace and quiet in his grave.

We assured her that we were indeed as respectable as they come, and for proof produced Mr. Greenfield's letter of introduction. I doubt if my passport signed by Mr. John Foster Dulles would have created a better impression, but fortunately Mrs. Mather didn't ask to see our passports.

Her only doubt was expressed by the remark, "You are certainly very dark, Mr. Himes." I was surprised that she could see me. But her anxiety was quickly dispelled by Alva's saying, "Oh, we have been a great deal in the sun, and my husband has a slight bit of color. We have the world's biggest and best sun in America, you know."

"Oh, I wouldn't say that," she demurred. "We have a very bright sun in Australia," adding with that inbred caution of the English toward weather, "But we have some bright spells here too—when it's summery."

We finally agreed to take the flat at five pounds weekly with a guaranteed tenancy of three months and gave Mrs. Mather a deposit of ten pounds against a promise to pay monthly in advance upon moving in. Next morning we went to Victoria Station, took our trunks and luggage from the checkroom, and arrived at Mrs. Mather's before noon, to be presented first thing with a contract recorded in India ink on a large sheet of foolscap, which called for an additional payment of two pounds, nine shillings, and threepence for laundry, telephone, the use of two blankets and the services of a cleaning woman two hours twice weekly. I signed and paid accordingly, partly because of the foul weather, which necessitated heating, and partly because of our desire to get to work again on our book.

Our flat consisted of a small bedroom and a large adjoining sitting room with French windows opening onto a well-kept back lawn, which in turn bordered on a large green commons shared by all the houses on parallel streets, and a large bedroom at the front below street level with windows looking onto the carefully padlocked dustbins of all the tenants. Adjoining the master bedroom was a long-ceilinged windowless kitchen, which looked incredibly dreary, and the stairway that led to Mrs. Mather's flat. The water closet was beneath the stairway, and the bath adjoined the small back bedroom.

When we arrived on July 10, the flat was ice-cold, stuffy, damp, and musty-smelling as though it had been sealed for ages, and pitch-dark in the middle of the day. There were gas grates in each room with coin meters that took shillings and sixpences, and that first week we spent a pound daily to keep from freezing. There was a leather-upholstered divan and two leather-upholstered armchairs, on which we were requested not to sit, and a large, very heavy mahogany table in the sitting room, all of which Mrs. Mather prized dearly. When in danger of asphyxiation we would open a window, only to have Mrs. Mather tiptoe down the stairs a moment later and close it to protect her furniture. When it rained she closed the windows to keep out the damp, in fair weather to keep out the cats, and in bright spells to keep out the sunshine, which is known to deterioriate antique furniture more than anything else. She lavished more protection on her Victorian furniture than the British Empire on the Crown Jewels in the Tower of London. We were very docile, however, perhaps because of the devitalizing effect of the weather.

One morning we received word from the American embassy that our passports had been found by a businessman on a bench in Hyde Park. The money was gone, of course, along with the case, but the passports were dry despite the heavy rains, and in excellent condition. The young English girls at the embassy looked at us curiously, but no questions were asked.

Each morning we rode on the upper deck of a red bus via Edgeware Road, Marble Arch, Oxford, and Regent Streets to Piccadilly Circus, and from there walked down to the American Express Company on Haymarket Street to stand in line for mail, but chiefly to get warm. Riding the double-decker buses was one of our greatest pleasures. We also took exploratory walks along St. John's Wood Road, past the Lords Cricket Ground and the small quiet graveyard beyond where mothers wheel their baby prams and schoolgirls play among the tombstones and old men sit on the marble benches and wait their turns, or else went into Regents Park to sit like other English people on the deck chairs in the rain and watch the future admirals sail their toy boats on the stormy lake.

At the end of our first week, just as we'd become resigned to the permanent misery of life in London, Mrs. Mather floated down with an incredible story of the imminent return of her son and daughter-in-law from fifteen years' uninterrupted absence in New Zealand, and naturally she wanted them with her. And since all of her other tenants had been with her for years, she had to ask us to leave. She was sure that we would understand. I understood immediately. Mrs. Mather had become apprised of my slight coloration. I had wondered how long it was going to take her.

I refused categorically, adhering firmly to the terms of my contract, which I had been coerced into signing before being given time to unpack. At first she entreated, appealing to Alva's understanding of a mother's love; then she appealed to our fine American generosity; and finally she offered to pay the expense of our moving and reimburse one half of the rental fee that we would thereby forfeit. It occurred to me that complaints had come from her other tenants, and I became adamant.

She said her late husband had many friends in the legal profession who would come to her aid, and I reiterated that with that contract she had forced me to sign I didn't need any friends.

After that she floated down at every opportunity to annoy us. There is no other word to describe her descent. At home she always wore long loose shapeless grayish-white gowns that blended indistinguishably with her grayish-white face and hair, along with felt slippers. She descended soundlessly, her garments billowing as though from an updraft, emerging from the perpetual gloom of the staircase like the last of the Shakespearean ghosts, and, finding us absent or asleep, drew our shades, closed our windows, turned out our fires, closed our closets left open for airing, and read our correspondence assiduously.

Accommodation Bureaus we'd never heard of began telephoning to give us lists of vacancies; filing cards describing other available flats appeared miraculously on our tables. One fine morning, after she'd slipped down and closed our sitting room windows and drawn the shades against the first warm day of sunshine we'd had, I rushed upstairs and burst into her flat without knocking and told her we had no goddamned intention of moving and the next time she invaded our privacy she'd have need of all her husband's legal friends, for I was going to take her to court. The poor old lady must have had the fright of her life. A half hour later she knocked loudly at our door, and came in with a tray of cakes and tea, even though it wasn't tea time. That afternoon, while we were absent, she had a long telephone conversation with my literary agent, Innes Rose. And that night she informed us that she had just received a telegram from her son that he would not return that summer after all and she would have to wait another year for his long-postponed visit, so we could stay.

I decided instantly to move. First we went to see Douglas West, of the KIWI Accommodation Bureau on Earls Court Road, whom Heather Chisholm had recommended. The KIWIS did a thriving business at a three-guinea fee in a charming little house that had been converted into an office building. We found the reception room packed with clients and the staff of young men and women, who seemed recently escaped from the Actors Lab in Hollywood, dashing madly about. Doubtless one could have gained an audience with the Prime Minister with greater ease than we were having in seeing Mr. West.

But he turned out to be a pleasant young man with fair hair and a complexion like a baby's who could not quite conceal his thorough enjoyment of his success, somewhat to his embarrassment. He candidly confessed the difficulty in finding housing for colored people in London, and explained that it was due in part to the postwar influx of West Indians, who, unlike Africans, were demanding employment and prostituting white English girls, and in part to the natural English antipathy to all non-English peoples. However, he contended that there was no resemblance in their attitude to American race prejudice. "No, you are just more subtle," I said involuntarily, and Alva gave Mr. West a taste of her startling laughter, which caused his lovely complexion to turn fire-red.

This precipitated one of those very violent arguments which Englishmen conduct with voices pitched so low, faces so continuously smiling, in attitudes of such studied patience, that they give the impression of taped voices emanating from wax dummies. He contended that there never had been a lynching by Englishmen of a native in the history of the British Empire; and I contended that that was a matter of definition—in less than two years the British had killed more Africans in their native Africa than American whites had lynched American blacks in all the years since the Civil War. He retorted with smiling patience that Britain was conducting a limited engagement against an armed uprising of natives, who had lynched innumerable white settlers, in a Crown colony. I further retorted with as much smiling patience as I could muster that a lynching was a lynching by any name, whether by armed natives or by armed soldiers, as long as it consisted of the unlawful killing of a person or persons without benefit of trial.

He terminated the argument by providing us with a list of ten vacancies without accepting a fee. However, he declined to telephone the landlords and recommend us or arrange an interview, as was customary, asserting that our personal appearance might do more to allay any bias than his most ardent plea in our behalf.

We thanked him for his time and the list, which we did not use. Point of honor, that's all.

Two days later, through an advertisement in the *Evening News*, we found a second-floor flat in a house owned by two very old sisters in Glenmore Road, in Hampstead. I held Mrs. Mather to her promise of paying the expense of our moving and refunding half our rental fee; and we demanded and received the other half from the S.S. Accommodation Bureau. We had two rooms on the second floor front and a kitchen in the attic of an old private house identical with all the other houses on the street.

The neighborhood was exceedingly interesting and convenient. There was an excellent shopping center containing the widest variety of stores around the corner on Haverstock Hill Road. Although rationing was not officially over in July 1953, it was so near the end that we had no need of applying for ration books and had not the slightest difficulty in purchasing whatever we wished. We found the food good, cheap, and in abundance; indeed, favorably comparable to Paris, where the food overflowed into the streets. Prime beef, mutton, lamb, and pork were available in all cuts, choice or otherwise. Eggs, butter, cheeses, fish, fowl, game, dried and fresh fruit, canned and fresh vegetables, all manner of cereals, coffee, tea, and sugar were plentiful. Practically all products came in three varieties: English, Empire, and Imported. Imported wines were expensive, Empire wines reasonable. All gins and whiskeys were domestic, seventy proof, and expensive. At that time the best of all English-made products, whether food, clothing, or machinery, were only available for export.

We were only half a block from the Belsize tube station on the Northern Line, which went directly to Leicester Square which was a few minutes walk from the American Express Company. And we were within a half hour's walking distance from Hampstead Heath, Parliament Hill, Ken Wood, Chalk Farm and Hampstead Heath railway stations, Swiss Cottage, the Whitestone Pond, and Jack Straw's Castle on Spaniards Road—said to be the highest point in London—the zoo in Regents Park by way of Primrose Hill, and the Central Public Library of Hampstead on Finchley Road.

Alva always called London a complete city, but if you are not a walker you will never know what she meant. The true Londoner is a walker. We toured the night life in Soho, went barhopping on occasion, saw some of the shows in the West End. But one needs friends for London's night life, because its quintessence is mostly talk, basically similar to the life of the pub, only conducted in greater darkness with greater intimacy at much greater expense. We derived our greatest pleasures from walking in the Heath and feeding the swans and ducks bread smeared with bacon drippings, or watching the amateur cricket games, the football tournaments, and the kite flyers on Parliament Hill, or exploring the damp jungle of Ken Wood, or browsing through the zoo in Regents Park. Sundays we'd go to Everyman's Theatre to see the old movie classics and when the bright periods came in August we'd go up on Heath High and look at the outdoor art show similar to the May show in Greenwich village in New York.

Our ancient landladies had emigrated from Poland in the early 1930s. They had a sister, the stylish one, equally ancient, Mme. Galewska, who owned a house on the next street and gave piano lessons. Fifty years previous she had been a Continental concert pianist of great note, her sisters claimed, and we visited her occasionally for tea and made tape recordings of her renditions, which delighted her. We were rewarded with complimentary tickets to various concerts at the Albert Hall, which we seldom used.

We took library cards at the Belsize branch library, where I was pleased to find my novels, *If He Hollers Let Him Go* and *Lonely Crusade*.

And we worked on Alva's autobiographical novel of her love affair and nervous breakdown in Switzerland entitled *The Golden Chalice*. When we were not shopping, cooking, or walking, we were working. For relaxation we made love. We didn't have any friends or acquaintances at first, nor did we miss them. The weather had become bearable in August and very warm and pleasant in September.

Alva would write the first draft downstairs in the little sitting room, and I would rework it into chapters up above in the kitchen. We both worked at the same time. And as the story of her love and guilt and subsequent insanity unfolded, my pity for her grew again. Poor woman, she hadn't even slept with her lover, according to the story she wrote, and her husband, who obviously had learned of the affair, had set out to punish her with subtle sadism. It was simply the story of an innocent American girl caught in the complexities of European life, which impressed her from beginning to end as evil; a way of life that was traditionally evil, an evil that had existed for so long, for so many centuries, that it had attained the status of normalcy. Even I came to view this life, with its polygamy accepted by society but condemned by the church, its sadism accepted in usage but condemned on principle; this life of expediency but minus integrity, of *bien-fait* but lacking compassion, revealed in all its shameful detail in her book as evil. Perhaps it is described best by our own song, "It's Not What You Do but the Way That You Do It." She had gone from Bryn Mawr College to the University of Bonn as an exchange student at the age of nineteen, an innocent American puritan, and she had been caught and imprisoned in a form of legalized white slavery. Not just by her husband, but by his family, his class, his society, the whole cannibalistic culture of a continent. I became convinced that a nice, healthy, wholesome, innocent, and rich American white girl is as vulnerable on the Continent of Europe as a American black girl in the white South. No wonder the Americans grew up with a tradition of violence; it was their only defense against the Machiavellianism of their own European traditions. Her story enthralled me, fascinated me, and I employed all my ability and resources to shape it into a novel. Yet at the same time it hurt me. As a little boy I had seen a young girl student in Mississippi run over and crushed by the heavy wheels of a wagon filled with fellow students that was being drawn by other students at the beginning of the term. Her book hurt me as I had been hurt then, watching the blood spurt from the girl's mouth and nose. I didn't want to pity her; but I did.

Our three-month visas expired around the first week in October and we were granted three-month extensions by the Home Office. My money began running low and Alva didn't have any, and we began our headlong rush against time. Alva confessed that she had thought I had lots of money, but we had such high hopes for our book that she didn't feel the disappointment she might have when she learned that I was practically penniless. We scarcely noticed the life about us any longer. Our life was reduced to a fundamental routine: eat, work, and sleep. But living made its usual demands. When the weather turned chilly, we had to arrange for our winter's supply of coal, which was still rationed, and start the grate in our large bed-sitting room, and I had to move down from the kitchen to work.

We finished our book around the middle of December. We had a marvelous feeling of accomplishment. We were so proud and happy. There on our table lay our book, *The Golden Chalice* by Alva Trent and Chester Himes, consisting of 520 typed pages of manuscript. I thought it was a touching story with an American best seller appeal. To me it compared favorably with an American best seller of the time, *Dinner at Antoine's*.

But at about the same time we finished the book our money ran out. I remember going to the PEN Club in London to try to get money and was told the purpose of the club was not to aid writers financially but to make it possible for the writers of the world to become acquainted with one another. I didn't want to know any other writers; I knew all the writers I wanted to know and that was too many. So I decided if I couldn't get any assistance from the PEN Club in an emergency, there was no point in my being a member, so I resigned. I went directly to my agent, Innes Rose, and got twenty pounds on my promise to let him handle the English rights to the book, which he knew we were writing but hadn't seen.

I also tried to get an advance from my New York agent, Margot Johnson, but she wrote that they were agents, not bankers, and I took my account from her. When I think of my behavior in periods of financial panic, I am always reminded of the lines of a poem written by Francis Robert White, who was at Yaddo with me:

> *Want will assume a lost, Lysippan*
> *Animal proportion of man;*
> *Small of head and long of arm's reach,*
> *Whose knuckles break, break again*
> *In the brute contest for contested ends.*

There is nothing so panicking as to be broke and without friends in a foreign country. I took our manuscript to Innes Rose and he promised to read it as soon as possible. In the meantime Alva had made a contact with Macmillan publishers in London and wanted me to get the manuscript back. Rose hadn't finished reading it and wanted to keep it. Like amateurs, we hadn't made a copy. I averted disagreement by letting Rose keep it and promising Alva she could have it if he didn't find a publisher immediately. In the meantime I pawned my typewriter and Alva's diamond engagement ring for a pittance to keep us going. Finally I sold my tape recorder to Mme. Galewska for forty-nine pounds.

There was a heavy snow and suddenly it was Christmas and the city attained its traditional Dickensian Christmas aspect.

Previously, we had met an engaging couple we knew as Karl and Phyllis who conducted an Accommodation Bureau on Edgeware road called the K Agency. We had seen them on several occasions and had become rather friendly. Karl was a Hungarian refugee count, and in that Hungarian colony around Paddington Station he was revered for his stand against the Nazis. He had escaped from a Nazi prison camp and was a great hero to his fellow countrymen. He was an exquisitely dressed man of the type who owes thousands of pounds to his tailor but sets up the local pub. And his wife Phyllis was of that class of Welsh who recognize only the Romans as their equal in antiquity. Somehow they had discovered our address and invited us to Christmas dinner.

We went to Mass at Saint Paul's in the morning and to their flat for dinner that evening. Along with a Hindu couple, a Chinese couple and hordes of his Hungarian compatriots, many of whom couldn't speak English, we had the traditional English Christmas dinner of roast turkey and pudding, washed down with several cases of a light dry Hungarian wine which Karl had gotten from friendly importers. The wine helped greatly to alleviate the asphyxiating effect of that damn Christmas pudding Phyllis forced on us after we were all stuffed.

However, the most interesting event was furnished by a dark-skinned American who claimed to be a Mayan Indian who was loudly and insultingly indignant at the presence of the Hindu couple, the Chinese couple, and me among that assemblage of whites. His attitude created utter amazement among those who understood English.

I could have explained that Americans whose dark skins are not attributable to African ancestry must always assert loudly and continuously their distinction lest some white person call them a nigger, but I felt that my explanation would be more difficult to understand than his behavior.

Afterward some of us went to another Hungarian's flat to continue celebrating and there again was roast turkey and Christmas pudding, which I declined. But I remember drinking something and then dancing wildly with a large strong girl dressed like a peasant who had the finest figure and the bluest eyes I'd ever seen. Even now I still remember her from the few minutes of that dance, and wonder if it wasn't just a dream.

But after Christmas we were back where we were before. I tried to promote more money from Rose but he felt the manuscript needed much more work to be made into a salable book and he was reluctant to show it in that draft. So I took it back and let Alva try her editor at Macmillan but his opinion was about the same as Rose's—that the book, the story of a woman, told from a woman's point of view, was not convincingly feminine. I disagreed with that.

The extension of our visas expired January 7 and we again applied to the Home Office for another extension. The clerk who handled our application was inclined to refuse and I launched a loud and bitter diatribe—actually he could have seen I was in a state of panic if he had been more discerning. Anyway we couldn't have left the country because we didn't have the fare. Finally his superior entered the dispute and gave us an extension of one month.

The next day I telephoned Bill Targ long distance from our landlady's private telephone, and asked him to send me five hundred dollars and take an option on *The Golden Chalice* to be deducted from the advance if he accepted it for publication or be deducted from the balance of payment due from NAL for the Signet edition of *The Third Generation* if he rejected it. Bill said he would cable the money and for me to send him the manuscript and he would give me his decision as soon as possible. Alva and I celebrated. But we celebrated too soon.

Bill sent the money, which I received next day, but subsequently he rejected the manuscript. He too felt that the book was not convincingly feminine, although it was a first-person woman's story.

That January it became bitter cold in London and the streets turned black with frost. Suddenly the city became lost in fog. We squandered our ration of coal, trying to keep warm. It couldn't possibly have lasted the winter anyway. Our kitchen was without heat and we brought our meals down to the sitting room to eat before the grate. We closed off the little bedroom and slept with the windows shut, risking death from asphyxiation to keep warm. In the houses on that street the water and sewer pipes for the upper floors were outside and in several houses the pipes had frozen and burst. We kept ours from freezing by letting the water trickle from the kitchen tap. But it was too damn cold to bathe in the heatless bathroom. Concern for our novel took a back place to the necessity of keeping alive.

We decided abruptly to go to Mallorca. I don't remember how much money we had but there couldn't have been more than four hundred left from the five Bill had sent me. Perhaps Alva had received a little money from her aunt in Philadelphia as a Christmas present; I know that her aunt worried about her. But it couldn't have been much and I don't remember Alva having any money at any time.

3.

We bought third-class tickets through to Barcelona, and set out one cold morning with our houses on our backs. It was so cold in London that the automobiles stirred up frozen dust. We had given the remnant of our coal to our landladies, for which they were extremely grateful, and departed from England the last day in January looking forward to the hot sunshine on the sandy beaches of Mallorca. We had a rough Channel crossing and I was as seasick as I've ever been. I think we changed trains again in Paris but we did not see anyone we knew.

Before dawn we arrived at the border and passed through the French customs at Cerbère. When we came to the Spanish customs at Port-Bou we thought it strange that so many passengers were leaving the train; but we had our tickets to Barcelona and stayed put. Finally uniformed officers came into our compartment and motioned for us to take our luggage and get off. When I got the luggage onto the platform and went looking for a porter, I found all the porters occupied with passengers going through the Spanish customs in a large lighted shed. I had to find a hand trolley not in use and move our luggage myself, and we were the last through the customs. Alva wasn't very helpful; she had drawn into herself like a hurt animal and I had lost contact with her.

We changed to a Spanish train for the remainder of the trip. Later I was told the tracks were of a different width. We were passing along the seashore, skirting the Pyrenees, when the sun rose. The sun came out of a sea of molten gold and tinted the steep mountainside, where grapevines grew in serried rows. A Spanish peasant sitting between me and the window began to hum the high-pitched stirring melody of the corrida that goes up and up and up until it falls like the bull at the moment of truth; a tune filled with glory and blood and death, ineffably stirring. That strange golden sunrise ushered in by that mounting tune, the sea and the mountains, and Alva's withdrawal, became Spain for me, hurting, bewildering, heartbreakingly beautiful.

Alva had been hurt by the rejection of our book coming so closely on top of our sudden, frightening destitution. It had been too much for her. She had experienced many other hurts in her life but she had never experienced the hurt of helpless want, of suddenly finding herself in the world without money or friends. This happens to American blacks every day and we are accustomed to it, but it was shattering to a white woman of her class. I found it strange to see her trying to protect herself by her quiet withdrawal from the world that had hurt her. Perhaps that was why she had come to me in the first place. Now it was my turn to be the one to hurt her. But I didn't want to hurt her; I wanted to protect her. And I had never experienced the luxury of withdrawing from hurt. I sought to remain cheerful and capable. But I was inexperienced and untraveled. My greatest asset for coping with the situation was my ignorance. Perhaps my race helped, too. Not too much was expected of an American black. The Spanish people seemed to expect me to be ignorant; they wanted me to be ignorant so they could help me. It was a damn good thing too, because I needed all the help I could get. And I was grateful for it. That made me *simpatico*, as they called me. From the very first I was taken up by the Spanish people because of my ignorance and my race. Perhaps the French had done the same for the same reasons but I hadn't noticed it—maybe because I hadn't needed it.

When we arrived in Barcelona I discovered my trunk was being held by the customs in Port-Bou. I should have cleared it through the customs myself, but I hadn't known. People gathered about me in the station, spouting advice in Spanish, while Alva sat quietly to one side. Finally one of Cook's men asked me the trouble, and then said if I gave him the key and an order for Cook's to clear the trunk, he would have it forwarded to Mallorca for a fee to be paid at Cook's in Palma. With that settled, we took a hotel room for the night and to my good fortune the hotel proprietor was in the black market— as were all the little hotel proprietors, I was to learn later. The next night, after hours of red tape and clearing our luggage through another customs for the Balearic Islands, we took the boat to Palma. It was cold and we were still wearing our winter clothes, thinking Mallorca far to the south.

The crossing from Barcelona took about twelve hours, and when we arrived early the next morning we were greeted by big wet flakes of snow. Sunny Mallorca, I thought sourly. To escape from the chilled mob of hotel hawkers who were fighting over the few passengers like desperate slavers, I seized upon the first taxi I saw, an old dilapidated prewar American Chevrolet, and had the porter put the bags in the rack on top, as though I had hotel reservations. Evidently playing at the same game, the driver took off without asking for instructions, and went for what seemed like miles through the wide, maple-lined, snow-wet streets, past innumerable walled whitewashed villas, each with its several palm trees and clinging vines blossoming in the snow, until he came to a recently built white stucco hotel in the middle of what had previously been a goat pasture, bearing the brand-new sign: TANGIER RESIDENCIA. The surrounding earth was still raw, but the hotel looked pleasant enough and the gravel driveway looked reasonably firm and the green latticed entrance struggled to look gay.

Suddenly our driver let loose his vocabulary of English, "You like? Yes?"

Alva hadn't said a word until then, only looked at me as though wondering what was happening. "It looks clean anyway," she murmured.

"We like, yes," I said, and by then a mob of people were coming from within to take our luggage, and the proprietor, a stout young man in a dapper Spanish suit and red Mallorquin shoes, was welcoming us in voluble English.

It was pleasant inside, with many plants and flowers in pots, and open fires in the lobby and the dining room beyond, but that was all the heat there was. There was a basic rate of sixty-five pesetas full pension daily. Including the additional 15 percent service charges, the tips and extras, it cost us both about two hundred pesetas daily (about four dollars on the black market). We had a large ice-cold room on the second floor in which the plaster was still green, but the "señora" gave us a bundle of blankets and brought us hot-water bottles for our feet each night. While a bath was being prepared for Alva in another part of the building, I slipped out to the nearest liquor store and bought two bottles of Spanish brandy at about fifty cents a bottle. That evening for dinner we ate *Calamares Romano* for the first time and found it delicious, if you have a taste for hot fried rubber inner tubes.

We hadn't written to Billy Haygood, but we followed his advice and caught the Toonerville Trolley, along with assorted Mallorquins and their livestock, out to Plaza Gomila in Terreno to the Vich Agency. The Plaza Gomila was a small paved square to one side of Calvo Sotello, the main traffic artery through Palma to the southwest on which the trolley ran. Señor Vich was a little fat man with dandyish clothes and slick hair who spoke fluent English with an accent like a West Indian. He was a dead ringer in appearance, speech, and manner, to a bantam-weight, affected bandleader from the Virgin Islands named Eddie

Bonelli with whom Jean and I had once roomed in the Bronx. Señor Vich had a lot of villas but they were all too expensive for us, and after two days we decided to give up on Señor Vich and contact Billy Haygood. Our hotel proprietor telephoned to Puerto de Pollenso for us, but was informed that Mr. Haygood had left and that Mr. Short of Short & Sons on the Borne was the only one who could give information as to his whereabouts. Without difficulty we found the office of Short & Sons at the lower end of the Borne (officially known as Paseo del Generalissimo Franco) on the Avenida Antonio Maura.

Mr. Short told us that the Haygoods had returned to America but they had friends, the Kings who lived in Cala San Vicente across the island from the Bay of Pollenso, who could give us all the information we desired.

The Kings couldn't be reached by telephone so we decided to go see them. Our hotel proprietor, who had now become our information center, told us that the Cala San Vicente was on the extreme northeastern shore of the island and that we would have to take the train to Inca and change to a bus which would take us to the city of Pollensa where we could catch a bus to the Cala San Vicente; but we should plan on staying overnight, what with transportation as it was we couldn't depend on getting back that night. Cala San Vicente was about fifty-five kilometers from Palma in actual distance but to the Mallorquins a journey inducing tearful goodbyes, embraces by all the family, and much handkerchief waving—and damn right, too.

Following our usual custom, we took third-class tickets, and to our dismay found ourselves crowded into a tiny boxcar with compartments of rough board seats occupied by a mob of tearful, sinister-looking Mallorquins and their livestock—goats, pigs, chickens, lambs, and sheep with red backs which looked as though they had been liberally daubed with Mercurochrome. It was a tiny train made up of seven or eight other tiny boxcars similar to ours pulled by a miniature wood-burning engine like the museum pieces American millionaires collect as toys for their children to play with. At 7:30 A.M. the train moved slowly out of the station away from the wooden platform packed with furiously waving relatives, the engine pulling for all it was worth to mount the slight incline out of Palma, and blowing frantically to clear the right-of-way, sounding for all the world like a young shepherd whistling for his dog. Suddenly it began to snow, filling the landscape as far as the eye could see with big fat wet flakes drifting sluggishly through the red sunshine. We sat tightly together in our compartment with the peasant women in their black woolen dresses, fragrant with the smell of fornication and sweat and wet wool, and the peasant men in their black wet town clothes securely clinging to their wet nanny goats, the smell of wet peasants and wet chickens and wet goats almost but not quite asphyxiating in the ice-cold boxcar.

The train chugged along at about ten kilometers an hour, its shrill whistle screaming without stop as though there were danger of innumerable citizens being run over and crushed; but once it had surmounted the incline of a few yards in height it began running away down the narrow tracks at a flying speed of about thirty kilometers an hour which caused it to sway precariously and the black-clad women to cross themselves and pray, which well they might.

But when we left Palma and came into the flat valley of rich red earth that runs south of and parallel to the snow capped mountain range along the northwest shore, we saw literally miles of almond trees, laid out in geometrical design, so that they seemed to rotate lazily as we passed, their young leaves bright green against the red wet earth, their white and pink blossoms like overflowing froth. They were like fantastic powder puffs of pink and white rotating lazily in the snow-filled sunshine, as beautiful and intricate as Spanish lace; a pure and overwhelming mobile sculpture that I will never forget. Just that part of our trip that morning paid for our disappointment from our book. I took Alva's hand and squeezed it. The peasants stared, smiled slyly. We didn't care.

When the train stopped at Inca and most of the peasants got off, taking their livestock, we were so happy to see them go that we forgot that we should have gotten off too. So we rode on in comparative peace to La Puebla, where the line came to an end, and when we finally alighted we were surprised to find the station deserted and no buses in sight. The snow had turned to rain and it was raining cats and dogs—cold dogs and cold cats. We tried to find someone to give us some information, but it was the luncheon hour and the ticket booth was closed. Several of the peasants who had alighted with us stood watching us curiously, probably wondering what we'd do next. Alva tried her French on them, but no one understood. When I tried my English, they all became greatly excited as though I were a strange man from Mars and began to jabber and gesticulate. I could make neither heads nor tails of their gestures and certainly not their language. "Stationmaster!" I shouted. "Ticket agent!" Why is it that we always assume people will understand our language if we shout? They shook their heads. Others came in from the street. Evidently the word had gone about that a strange man had landed in town. I thought of that song, *"Mack the Knife is back in town."* Shortly we'd collected sufficient peasants to fill the waiting room. "Norteamericano?" someone asked. "Sí, sí, señor," I squandered my vocabulary of Spanish. Their answers I didn't understand. I saw we weren't getting anywhere. In desperation, I shouted, "Taxi!" Dark faces broke into sudden grins. "Taxi. Sí. Taxi." Taxi is taxi in any language, I concluded.

Several men rushed out into the rain. We waited for the taxi, not trying any more to communicate. A half hour later the scouts reappeared with another man in their midst who looked as though he had been snatched from the luncheon table. "You want taxi? I call taxi for you. I get you taxi from Inca." I was appalled. I remembered having passed through Inca miles back. "No, from here," I said. "No taxi here," he said. "Nearest taxi Inca." Alva felt it was time she took part in the discussion. "We'll take a bus," she said. "To Pollensa." The stationmaster shrugged and spread his hands. "No bus until six." Alva looked at her watch. It was shortly after noon. "Let him call a taxi," I said. He smiled happily. All of the spectators had been watching the conversation which they couldn't understand, their gazes going from one face to the other, hanging on every change of expression. When the stationmaster smiled, they all smiled. "Olé!" I heard someone say.

The stationmaster went into the ticket office, where he also presided as ticket agent, and telephoned Inca for a taxi, then he came out, carefully locking the ticket office behind him, and told us the taxi would be along soon and excused himself to go home and finish his lunch. We thanked him profusely. He said something to the spectators and a number of them left with him. However, some stayed to watch us to the end.

We sat disconsolately and waited. They stared at us without blinking. About an hour later a car horn bleated apologetically. Several voices cried, "Taxi," and they made for the outside, gesturing us to follow. Across the muddy street, about a half block's distance, stood a muddy sedan which vividly recalled the first car my father had owned in 1917 when he began teaching automobile mechanics in Alcorn College in Mississippi when I was a little boy. I noticed Alva's apprehension. "Anyway, it beats walking," I said. We followed our guides through the pouring rain and piled into the back of the taxi. The seat springs were broken, the upholstery had come apart, the lining of the ceiling had fallen off in places, and on one side the window was missing. I took the open side and turned up the collar of my coat and told the driver, "Cala San Vicente." He nodded and reached for the starter as though accustomed to going to Cala San Vicente every day. The engine coughed and spluttered into life and we moved off slowly, the old taxi rattling in every bone, while the peasants stood in the muddy street in the rain and waved.

Almost immediately we were in the country, going down a straight mud road between two low stone walls without space to pass a man walking. The road consisted of two straight ruts no doubt cut by the traffic of ass carts. We bumped slowly along through the rain. There was no danger of the car leaving the road, for it couldn't get out of the ruts. The surrounding countryside consisted of plots of red turned earth separated by the same low stone walls, but the mountains were now straight ahead of us and we could see white patches of snow all the way down their slopes, and there were patches of snow beneath the olive trees in the fields. There was nothing moving in sight.

Alva had no sooner remarked what a godforsaken place to be stranded than the engine stopped. The driver got out in the rain, standing in the mud beside the tracks, and raised the hood. He looked at the engine, I could see him shaking something, then he came back and got a screwdriver from beneath his seat and fiddled around with that for a time. He was bareheaded and protected from the rain and cold only by a thin cotton coat that had become wet all through instantly. His wet hair stuck to his skull and was plastered to his forehead and rain streamed down his face. Finally he gave up and came back to us and opened the door without a window to say, "*Mecanico.*" And without more ado he shut the windowless door and began trotting back down the middle of the rutted street in the direction from which we had just come.

I moved over to Alva's comparatively dry corner and we huddled in our wet clothes and looked out disconsolately at the raw red earth in the steady downpour, and said nothing.

Hours passed, it seemed. Actually it was only an hour and ten minutes according to Alva's watch, when we saw our driver returning, running down the center of the muddy road as he had left, but now with another man in wet greasy coveralls following on a bicycle. The man propped his bicycle against the stone wall and came over to the car and opened the door without a window and stuck in his head and grinned. "*Mecanico,*" he he announced and pointed to himself. Then he carefully shut the door and went forward to look at the engine. I looked at him in amazement. He didn't have any tools with the exception of one ball peen hammer in his rear pocket. After several moments of looking at the engine, he took out his hammer and struck it several resounding blows. Then he went around and opened the door to the driver's seat and tried the starter button. Nothing happened. Again he reached for his hammer and hit the dashboard several times. Again he tried the starter button. The engine coughed and sputtered into life. The *mecanico* turned to us and grinned broadly. "All she needed was a good beating," Alva quipped, and I couldn't help but say, "Some *mecanico!*" He didn't understand the words but he understood the meaning and when he got on his bicycle he went off grinning cockily in the rain.

We arrived at Cala San Vicente without mishap and without seeing another soul, and found the streets of that picturesque little village as deserted as the countryside and swept clean by wind and rain. Our hopes suddenly fell. It seemed as though the residents had abandoned the whole north end of the island, fearing a tidal wave. As yet we hadn't seen the sea but from where we stopped we could hear the surf booming on the rocks; the sound dominated the steady downpour and seemed to grip the shuttered houses and empty streets in a sinister atmosphere of terror. But our driver, though soaked to the skin, seemed strangely cheerful and was not the least put out by what seemed to us the total absence of inhabitants. He got out and trotted off in the rain, returning shortly with a man wearing a coat draped over his head. The stranger said in pidgin English that he spoke English and asked if he could help us and when we told him we were looking for an American couple named King, he said, "With a little girl," and directed us to a *residencia* nearby. Our driver took us there and waited while we went in and asked for the Kings and were told by the English-speaking proprietor that the Kings had only stayed there for a short time after they had given up their casa and had moved to a casa of a friend of theirs named Haygood in Puerto de Pollenso and we should ask for them at a café called The Sands.

We felt like fools. With the proprietor translating, I asked the driver how much would the whole fare be if he took us to Puerto de Pollenso and he said two hundred pesetas and I said that was all right. He turned around and took a short cut to Puerto de Pollenso and we arrived to find another deserted city without a soul in sight. When he turned into the quay, we saw a row of bars and cafés and restaurants side by side, occupying the whole front, all closed and shuttered and silent in the steady downpour. But we found the sign of The Sands between two other cafés and the driver parked in front while I got out and went to the door, hoping I could get someone up. I found the shutters unlocked and opened them and found a curtained glass door. I opened it and sound burst over me with a shock. Jazz was being played loudly from a jukebox and the room was filled with gaily dressed people dancing madly. I felt gripped in an hallucination. I stood in the open door with my mouth open and stared like an idiot.

A young blond woman with pink cheeks and a very pretty face detached herself from two men at the bar and came forward to me. She was smiling so engagingly I felt another shock of embarrassment. "Come in," she said. "Don't be afraid."

"I'm looking for the Kings," I said. "I didn't expect to find anybody here. It looks deserted outside."

She kept smiling without saying anything and I said, "I was looking for a friend named Billy Haygood and I was told he'd gone back to America and I'd have to see the Kings and we've been to Cala San Vicente looking for them and were told to ask here. Do you know them?" I asked.

"I'm Mrs. King," she said. "Come in and have a drink and tell me what you wanted."

"Well, I have someone waiting," I said. "And we're looking for a house."

"Oh, you'd better come home," she said. "They're having a wedding celebration here. We live in the casa that Bill had."

She got in the taxi with us and we drove down to the back of their casa, which fronted on the sea, and went inside and met her husband, a young man who looked as if he'd only recently gotten out of the Army, and their little girl about four with gold-blond hair like her mother's. Husband and wife discussed our problem. I gathered that a woman named Catalina was the big landlord and owned most of the places for rent. They got her on the phone. She had a place, a first-floor apartment in a two-story casa beneath an English couple, a retired captain and his wife, for 750 pesetas, extra for gas and telephone. I said we would like to see it. All of us went to meet Catalina at the casa. As we walked along Mrs. King walked beside me. Unthinkingly I took her hand in mine. I wasn't thinking of making a pass. It's just a pleasant feeling walking hand in hand with a pretty and attractive woman. If I should reach for a woman's hand while walking beside her, she can always know I think she is attractive. It really meant nothing to me. But Alva had noticed it and became upset. I didn't know what was troubling her. Besides, I had to deal with Catalina.

She showed us the apartment. It was in a relatively new and modern casa called "Cala Madona" and consisted of an entrance hall with telephone, two front bedrooms with windows on the street, a back bedroom looking out onto the walled patio, a large sitting room with English-type fireplace, a modern American-type toilet and bath, and a kitchen beyond the sitting room with an electric hot-water tank and city water but an indoor well for drinking water. It looked pleasant, private, and convenient, and I took it on the spot.

Doña Catalina Rotger Amengual, the proprietor, was a buxom widow of about fifty, tall for a Spanish woman, with thick reddish-black hair, which she wore long, and a large sensual smile. Later I was to learn that her brother, Don Ignacio Rotger Amengual, operated the large general store (vaqueria) patronized by all foreigners. She was the only true cosmopolitan Spanish Catholic woman I ever came to know; she had traveled extensively, and what she hadn't seen wasn't worth seeing; she didn't believe for a second that Alva and I were married (in fact she had her reservations about the marital status of the entire English-American colony), but she was immensely sympathetic and a little curious too, perhaps, for they hadn't had many American black tourists there before, if any.

We had to stay in a local hotel overnight, but it was agreed we would move in the next day, February 1, 1954, at which time Doña Catalina would give me a signed contract. Mrs. King invited us to stay with them for the night but Alva wasn't having any, so we took an ice-cold room in a pension near the *vaqueria* and for supper had half-done cutlets from a baby pig sprinkled with red pimiento powder, along with the perennial cauliflower. Alva was sick. I was up half the night filling wine bottles with hot water from the kitchen to place on her stomach and when we set out for Palma next morning she was white and drawn.

When I remember how intensely I always desired to make love to Alva, whether she was gay or melancholy, well or ill, I suspect I have a streak of sadism in me. But it always turned out to be the best cure for whatever ailed her. In a strange way she reveled in the sensuality of the sex act, and yet at heart she was a puritan. Perhaps it was the contemplation of living in sin with an inviolable American white woman that incited my sexual desire. In any event, while nursing her I made love to her since it was all part of the same process.

She was unable to help in moving so I had to do all the work myself. Fortunately my trunk hadn't arrived and I had sent my stove and typewriter in a separate package through the post, so we had only our hand luggage to move.

On our arrival at the Cala Madona I started a tremendous fire in the sitting room then went to the store and bought food and started a charcoal fire in the braziers in the kitchen. Shortly after dark while we were sitting before the fire, Alva suddenly turned sheet-white and sort of gasped, "Oh, Chester, I'm going away, I'm passing away, oh, Chester!" I leapt to my feet and caught her just as she fell from the chair. I carried her into the back bedroom. She was so white I thought for a moment she was dead but I didn't take the time to find out. I rushed to the telephone and called Catalina; unconsciously I must have felt Alva wouldn't want me to call the Kings. I told Catalina I thought Alva was dying. Within a few minutes Catalina arrived at the house, in a state of anxiety, with a short, fat, bald-headed doctor who didn't speak a work of English. He asked a few questions about Alva's health in general, especially if she had a history of a heart condition, which I answered with Catalina translating; then he went into the bedroom to examine her. Catalina told me I should go with him as it was the custom in Spain, and tardily I followed. He examined Alva with his stethoscope, pulled back her eyelids, put away his instruments, and rejoined Catalina. They conversed briefly in Spanish; both of them looked at me curiously. I asked Catalina what was the trouble. She said the doctor said nothing.

I suffered one of those blind fits of rage in which it seems that my brain has been dynamited, and when I could speak I said it must be something. The doctor said she had just fainted; it appeared to him to be a sort of self-hypnosis. I had nothing to say to that. He prescribed some pills he said were nitroglycerine to be put beneath her tongue and said that she should stay in bed for several days until she felt better. Catalina stayed a few minutes after he left and offered to help in any way she could. I could see that she wanted to ask about Alva, she was curious about her background and how we had met and what we were doing together, but I didn't give her the opportunity. I wasn't about to share Alva's problems with anyone else. In some way Mallorca had aggravated her sense of guilt for deserting her children; perhaps it had recalled the happy times she had spent with them.

For the first month we kept pretty well to ourselves. The English captain and his wife who lived in the flat above had returned to England for a vacation, and according to Catalina they had taken a shipload of Spanish oranges back with them to sell, but their maid would come around to clean a couple of times a week and when she first saw me downstairs in the patio she dropped some of her nylon panties she was washing. I was amazed to see the panties dropping at my feet and looked up to find a young Spanish woman smiling at me, but when I offered to take them up to her, Alva said she'd do it. The upshot was that the maid had to come down and get them from Alva.

Mrs. King called with her little girl, but afterward Alva said, "I fixed her for good," and I was astonished to learn that she was jealous of our holding hands the first night we had met. Anyway, Mrs. King did not call again, and I was acutely embarrassed, for I felt indebted to her for finding us a house. Furthermore, I had expected her and Alva to become friends, but that ended the matter.

Ever since the last rejection of *The Golden Chalice* Alva had shown a marked antipathy toward the manuscript. She did not wish to submit it again; in fact she did not wish to look at it. I knew nothing more to do with it, so I began working on a novel of my own, tentatively entitled *The End of a Primitive.*

Alva finally settled into the household chores while I spent my days in the small walled patio, writing. It was a beautiful little patio with rose vines covering the entire wall, and sometimes when I wrote the village cats would line up by the dozen atop the wall, side by side, to watch me. There was one wild young black tom I had begun to tame, putting food out in the patio for him, but initially he wouldn't let me get near him. However, he would let the other cats come to eat, and after a time I noticed they had a well-organized hierarchy for eating. He would eat first, then sit back and let the females eat in a special order which was repeated each day, and always a little was left for him and he would eat again last. By that time I had learned there were no other toms participating. I named him Tom and on several occasions I had to protect him from other older, larger tomcats of the neighborhood, most of whom were black. I would see him in the distance, hightailing over the rooftops, being chased by a big black tom, steering for the safety of his patio, and I would run out with the broom and chase the enemy cat away; they were so vicious, on occasion, that they'd spring right down in the yard and make for my little Tom.

In the early stage I strayed far afield with my story of Jesse and Kriss in *The End of a Primitive,* and it was always Alva who would pull me back. She was fascinated by my writing process and watched this story of an affair between an American black and a white woman emerge, page by page. I didn't know what she was thinking; it didn't occur to me to ask; and I didn't tell her it was the story of Vandi and me. Somehow I'd become committed, and writing that story absorbed me completely, although it took shape slowly. Alva kept me toning it down to prevent it from becoming pornographic. But the very essence of any relationship between a black man and a white woman in the United States is sex, and generally sex of a nature which lends itself to pornography. To describe a black man, the blackness of his skin, black sexual organs, black shanks, the thickness of his lips, the aphrodisiacal texture of his kinky hair, alongside the white breasts, pink nipples, white thighs and silky pubic hair of a white woman, no matter how seriously intended, is unavoidably pornographic in American society. Given the American background, the bare colors create a pornography of the mind. Just to put a black man into a white woman's bed is to suggest an orgy.

But that wasn't the point of my book. I had been made furious by the hypocritical respectability of white people feigning outrage and indignation at sight of me and Alva together, while all the time smirking and leering and revealing sick envy of our perpetual orgy that took place in their minds. Then, too, I was trying to express my astonishment at this atitude and say that white people who still regarded the American black, burdened with all the vices, sophistries, and shams of their white enslavers, as primitives with greater morality than themselves, were themselves idiots. Not only idiots in a cretin manner, but suffering from self-induced idiocy. Obviously and unavoidably, the American black man is the most neurotic, complicated, schizophrenic, unanalyzed, anthropologically advanced specimen of mankind in the history of the world. The American black is a new race of man; the only new race of man to come into being in modern time. And for those hackneyed, diehard, outdated, slaverytime racists to keep thinking of him as a primitive is an insult to the intelligence. In fact, intelligence isn't required to know the black is a new man—complex, intriguing, and not particularly likable. I find it very difficult to like American blacks myself; but I know there's nothing primitive about us, as there is about

the most sophisticated African. The problem was, how to make
the point?

As I wrote *The End of a Primitive,* an aura and a smell of
sensuality emanated from me like a miasma which intrigued and
attracted all manner of white perverts and puritans too, for that
matter.

One day a tall, dark, hairy young man dressed in the typical
uniform of an American socialite going native—worn-out espa-
drilles clinging to his dirty feet, strained and bagged white cotton
trousers, sport shirt open to the waist showing a mat of black
hair covering his entire front, and wearing an invisible sign as
big as a door reading I AM A HOMOSEXUAL—came to visit us
and sat out in the patio, trembling all over as though locked in
a cage with a male gorilla, and invited us to dinner with him
and his lover. We had heard of them before; they were known
in the Puerto as Bob and Mog and from the stories I had heard
they were the most extroverted, exhibitionistic homosexuals in
all the Mediterranean island life. They lived in a second-floor
apartment beyond the Kings on the quay facing the bay in that
strip between the end of the esplanade where the cafés and
restaurants are located and the wired enclosure of the Spanish
Air Base.

Puerto de Pollenso is in the northern curve of the Bay of
Pollenso at the foot of the tip of the mountain range which
separates it from Formentor made famous to American tourists
as the residence of the guide-book compiler Fielding, who was
there at the time. Between the Puerto and Formentor was the
air base, housing a number of Spanish soldiers and no doubt
pilots too, and while it seemed equipped with a number of
trucks and bicycles, the main thing it seemed to be lacking was
aircraft. Although I must confess on two occasions I did see an
old seaplane ascend a few hundred feet from the bay; or perhaps
there were two that looked alike.

Why shouldn't we go to dinner with them? I thought. Homosexuals can be interesting, and from what I had heard these two
were not only interesting but rich. So we had dinner with them

on their second-floor terrace overlooking the bay. Bob was from a socially prominent and wealthy family in Boston who were perhaps richer but not of the same social class as Alva's family in Philadelphia. Bob had been to Harvard, as had the rich homosexual who was a minor character in the book I was writing, and I gathered he was the female of the couple. Homosexuals have a hierarchy of genders just like heterosexuals; there is the female homosexual and the male homosexual, although whether there is a difference in function or just in state of mind I couldn't say. Mog was the male. He was a tall, Hitler-type blond second-generation German, who had been a Princeton University fellow to Cambridge (or Oxford) and had returned to teach English literature at Princeton before joining the American State Department. He had been chargé d'affaires for a United States Embassy somewhere in Europe when he was dismissed during the McCarthy purge, upon which he got in touch with Bob, whom he had never met before and they had come to Mallorca on their extended honeymoon.

During the course of the dinner, served by their Spanish maid, Maria, they took off their shirts and invited Alva and myself to do likewise, but we declined. The conversation turned to literature, Mog's forte, and I learned he was a great admirer of Swinburne. Henry James came into the conversation and I said he was too "precious" for me and Mog said belligerently that was why he liked him, because he was "precious," that literature should only and could only be written by the upper classes and I excused myself and went to the toilet. When I returned I found the scene had changed; seemingly Mog had hit Bob because Bob resented Mog's attentions to Alva; but it all became peaceful upon my return and I think we started a game of Monopoly.

The "boys," as I always think of them, got their gin in glass bottles of a size and likeness to the water bottles once installed in the water fountains in American offices, and of course they had all the limes they could use, many of which came from the Kings' garden. We were drinking very strong Tom Collinses in tall glasses with plenty of gin and ice and at some time during the afternoon I had my first blackout. As I have explained previously, no one could tell when I was blacked out because I continued acting the same as I had been doing before, or at least I thought so. And the only way I knew was from the lapses of time.

I remember playing this game on the terrace with Alva and the boys and the next thing I knew the sun had set and the house was filled with people and I was standing in front of Mrs. King, who was sitting on the sofa trying to feed the boys' pregnant Siamese cat some caviar canapes, staring bemusedly down at her breasts. There followed a series of blackouts in which people kept disappearing and I kept getting ideas about Mrs. King and then she disappeared too and I escorted Alva carefully down the dangerous stairs and along the walk by the bay back to our house and safety, although my trouser legs and her stockings were wet when we arrived from wandering out into the bay. And while I was in the kitchen trying to cook some kidney stew at three o'clock in the morning, Alva fell in the bathroom and dislocated her shoulder blade and bruised her temple, giving herself two enormous black eyes.

The next day I took her to see Doctor Gomez, a young orthopedist, who was the official doctor for the air base. Fortunately his public office was on our street, Calle General Frutos, and we got there without too many people seeing us, but even so word got around over the Puerto that I had beat her up. Although still in his thirties, Dr. Gomez had contributed several articles on bone surgery to international medical journals which had won the acclaim of the world's medical profession, according to Catalina; and from the barber who came to cut my hair we had learned that Dr. Gomez had performed bone surgery on our Spanish neighbors' daughter to provide her with knee joints, which she had been born without.

Dr. Gomez examined Alva through his fluoroscope and said her shoulder was fractured but the black eyes and facial swelling were caused by the blow on her temple and would go away in time. She had been as drunk as I was, and I gathered she had tripped on her skirt while trying to step out of it and had fallen against the sink. Anyway, Dr. Gomez put her arm in a black cloth sling and taped up her shoulder and told us to come back and see him in a week.

Catalina got us a maid to do the household chores and several people of the Anglo-American colony called to offer their sympathy and satisfy their curiosity; first the boys, looking contrite and apologetic, and an elderly woman whom we had never met who had voluminous praise for Dr. Gomez, who was treating her son for leukemia. She was a rich widow from Texas and she said she had come to Mallorca for the sole purpose of seeing Dr. Gomez, whom she had been told was the only doctor in the world who could save her son, who unfortunately died a short time later anyway.

Others came, among them an English couple, Mr. and Mrs. Baker, who lived on the third floor of a small apartment building on the quay owned by Catalina. I liked Mr. Baker. I remember once, before Alva's accident, when he had stopped by during one of his customary walks and I had just come back from the Puerto with a liter of grain alcohol, which I had cut with some well water. I made us cocktails from the gin with sugar and lime juice. He gulped his down and said, "Tastes better than castor oil," and then, "Well, I must be going," and when he stepped from the shade of the house into the sun of the street he became so suddenly drunk he turned around several times and began walking off in the wrong direction. I telephoned his wife and told her to go and get him.

And the Kings called and were very correct and sympathetic and offered to help in whatever way they could. But we would not accept help from anyone. The Spanish maid cooked such dishes as dried fish and beans, cauliflower, potatoes and eggs, using an abundance of the red capsicum powder which sat about the stores in crocus sacks, shopped and cleaned.

I don't remember our exact financial state, but at that time we weren't desperate. I got several small advances from World, and an advance of eight hundred dollars for a book of short stories to be called *Black Boogie Woogie*. At some time I had borrowed money from my brother Edward, who lived in Harlem —one or two hundred dollars—which I had had World repay, and he had written advising me to make a quick trip back to the United States and get my business affairs straightened out, concluding with the classic statement that "every good soldier should stand on his own two feet," which caused me to quit writing or speaking to him for nine years.

When Dr. Gomez found no improvement in Alva's shoulder after a week he sent us to the village of Pollensa, about twelve kilometers from the Puerto, to have it X-rayed. The X-rays showed nothing. All that bother and expense for nothing. He untaped it and took away the sling, and in a few days she was back to normal. I hoped I would never have to deal with him again.

Alva's accident propelled us into the consciousness of the foreign colony. It had become a *cause célèbre*. It had given all the bored, frustrated, perverted, curious, condescending English and American residents an excuse to call, to look us up, to see the inside of our house and how we lived, close-up views of the white woman who dared to live with a nigger and was beat up by him as her reward, and the nigger who had beat her up, and a chance to consider whether taking him to bed was worth the risk, and a few perhaps who felt genuine sympathy, Catalina, for instance, who was genuinely fond of Alva, and the boys, who themselves were of an oppressed minority, and the local Spanish artist, Roch Minué, and his wife, whom we had met sometime before.

During the season from about the first of March to the end of October, Roch Minué lived in an old stone house at the very end of the esplanade. He had a large terrace at the front of the house facing directly down the esplanade which could be seen all the way to the main road to Palma. When the weather permitted, which was most of the time, he would take his easel alongside the quay and paint the fishing boats, or he would go inland and draw the old Spanish houses and wells and wind-mills in the white-hot sun with India ink on dead-white paper, and these were the most dramatic of his works. He was a journeyman painter but I always had the feeling he could do better if he wished. But he merely wanted to make a living and he kept his paintings within the limit of appeal to American tourists, who bought enough in season to keep him living the year round.

Roch Minué had a new Vespa that he had bought with money he had won in a national lottery—everything that ran on wheels and had a motor was very expensive in Mallorca—and he could be seen with his easels strapped on his back, his black hat pulled down over his eyes, along any road on the island. When he learned that we were approaching the end of our lease and didn't want to remain in the Puerto during the summer when it became overrun with German and American tourists, he offered to try to find us a house somewhere else. He said his favorite village in all of Mallorca was Deya, and that when he died he would like to be buried in the little cemetery on the promontory in front of the church there, explaining how the graves had sunk down the steep embankment over the years and new graves had been dug on top of the old ones until they were four, five and six deep.

Roch Minué spoke neither French nor English, but his wife spoke French, and all our serious conversation was done through her and Alva. He told us he had been born in Ibiza and had been a childhood friend of Garcia Lorca and that the inhabitants of Ibiza did not like Elliot Paul's book *Life and Death of a Spanish Town*, which was exaggerated and untrue for the most part, and that Elliot Paul in person had got the hell away from Ibiza long before the invasion.

We liked Roch Minué. Although he wasn't one of the greatest artists in the world he was one of the greatest humans. But we didn't depend on him entirely to find us a place. We looked ourselves. Catalina, who understood our desire to leave, told us the accepted procedure in the small towns was to contact the local postman, who would know all the places available and would recommend us to the proprietors for a fee.

We went across to Alcudia, the Port of the Bay of Alcudia to the south of the Bay of Pollensa. It was not very fashionable at that time. Much of the surrounding country was comprised of uninhabitable marshes infested with mosquitoes. But we contacted the local postman and he took us first to see a large, brown gypsy woman with flashing black eyes, a strong stink, and a mouthful of dangerous-looking teeth, who, he said, had a few rooms in her casa we could get for about two hundred pesetas a month. She took us in, showed us the three rooms on the second floor and flashed her dangerous-looking teeth in a smile. She said we could have the rooms for eight hundred pesetas monthly. I didn't understand but I saw the postman's face. He said to Alva in French, "She has rented them." But Alva understood enough Spanish by then to get the drift of the conversation. Afterward we conjectured as to whether she was high on hashish, disliked Americans, or was trying to exploit the racial angle, thinking that as a mixed couple we were desperate for somewhere to live. But we never learned.

The next place the postman took us was on the second floor also, with four small clean and pleasant rooms, and a large wooden terrace at the back with a distant view of the bay. But the terrace was piled with hay and the three brown nanny goats from the proprietor's pasture below were allowed upstairs to eat the hay at the end of the day. The price was all right, too, but we didn't want to share our terrace with the landlord's goats; the next thing they would be coming into the house.

In the end Roch Minué found us a house in Deya through a friend he had there, Gaspar Sabater, who combined the duties of principal of the elementary school and justice of the peace. He told us it was more primitive than where we were then living and it faced a small square, but it was protected from the main highway and there was a small garden at the back which was quiet, in which I could write.

We took it sight unseen for six hundred pesetas a month

and Gaspar Sabater made the arrangements with Pedro Canales, the proprietor, neither of whom we had met. Roch Minué arranged for one of the empty provision trucks to take our luggage as far as Palma, where we could have it taken atop a bus the rest of the way, and he went ahead into Palma to arrange transfer.

We hated to be moving again; already during our short acquaintance we had moved four times, but we were glad to be leaving the frenetic life of the colony in the Puerto. In a way I was accustomed to it; all of my life in the United States, except for the seven and a half years I had been in prison, I had moved continually from place to place, at first because my father moved from post to post in the colleges for blacks throughout the south, and later Jean and I had been constantly on the move from pillar to post to keep alive. I had moved in prison, too, from company to company, from cell block to cell block, from dormitory to cell and back again, from the prison to the prison farm and at the farm from job to job, from the idle house to the correction cells and solitary confinement. And although I did not know it at that time I was never to stop moving, always one jump ahead of disaster, always a hair's breadth away from destitution; until I can truthfully say there has been nothing permanent in my life but change.

But Roch Minué was right about Deya. Deya touched my emotions more than any city, any town, any village that I have known before or since. It was an old, old town without a single hotel, built originally on a rock that rose steeply in the valley of surrounding hills to a sheer promontory, housing the church and Roch Minué's cemetery, and then dropping steeply a thousand or more feet to a narrow valley running a torturous route through terraced olive groves to the cove, with the sea just outside stretching to the horizon. The surrounding hills are composed of pink stone and when touched by the red rays of the setting sun from early afternoon until ten o'clock at night, the town is caught in a pink glow, so it gives the impression of a white lump of sugar at the bottom of a conical pink wineglass, for it is a pink town. The lemon trees in the gardens of the great hacienda that looked down upon the square from across the main road from Palma to Soller were in bloom, and their sweet-perfumed, aphrodisiacal scent at sunrise or in the moonlight was like nothing else of my experience. Deya was a town for lying in the cool perfumed dark of a shuttered room during the heat of the day and making love.

We moved on Saturday and Roch Minué had to return home from Palma. Deya is directly north of Palma and the road from Palma circles through Valdemosa, Deya, Soller, and Bunola and returns to Palma. We were met in Deya by our landlord, Pedro Canales, who took a high-wheeled pushcart from the bus terminal to move our luggage up the hill to the square abutting the Palma road. Our hearts sank at the sight of our new home.

Like many other houses in Spain, it was divided in a haphazard fashion between two owners. Our side, owned by Pedro Canales, faced the square which had a public fountain for drinking water beneath the stone staircase leading to the upper town and the cathedral. While the other side, which was owned by an attorney from Palma, Damien Caubet, fronted on the highway and was unseen from the square. It was occupied only on weekends and holidays.

Our front entrance opened from a cul-de-sac onto a typical Spanish hallway flanked with rows of straight-backed chairs, which in turn led directly into the master bedroom. Unfortunately our master bedroom penetrated the other side of the house, cutting it in two, and our bedroom windows opened onto the highway also. As a consequence we could hear our neighbors on two sides through the thin walls and hear strangers passing along the street through our shuttered windows. In the early evening during the promenade hour our bedroom sounded like the lobby of Grand Central Station, but we were seldom there then. We made love during the siesta hour and slept late at night.

Going toward the rear of the house were several tiny rooms whose purposes I never learned, terminating at a primitive kitchen. It was a large kitchen, but with the back door shut it was black-

dark even in the middle of a hot sunny day. It was paved with
flagstones that might have been taken from a Roman road, and
it had one small opening which served as a window but looked
more like a stone missing from the thick stone wall. There was
a shallow sink scooped from a crude block of stone and two
charcoal braziers built into the wall. A well was located beside
the door that opened onto a tiny fenced-in garden with a grape
arbor, an almond tree, and a fig tree.

The toilet was located in the basement of the apartment house
next door and could only be reached by going through our
kitchen and garden and along a narrow walk behind the apartment house. It was dirty and stinking and crawling with dark
squirming things. But in the garden beyond was another, separate,
toilet owned by the proprietor of the garden; it was kept padlocked when not in use. However, we found an earthenware
urn, which we placed on the kitchen floor for use at night,
although it wasn't intended for that purpose.

What depressed Alva most was the lack of running water and
sewers and a bathroom and indoor toilet. But as soon as Pedro
Canales had delivered our luggage and departed, we got out of
the house too. We went walking down the road toward Palma,
unconsciously trying to escape, no doubt. Before returning we ate
supper in a small restaurant near the bus terminal and stopped
in the general store on the way home and bought candles and
two bottles of brandy.

The days had become long and warm and we took some
chairs from the kitchen and sat out in the garden inhaling
the perfume of the lemon blossoms until it became too dark
for comfort among the small slimy animals of our imagination,
then went inside and locked the doors and shutters and looked
with dismay at the single droplight in our bedroom. About ten
o'clock the light shimmered and began to fade. It faded slowly
until only the filament showed and gradually it darkened and
disappeared and left us in Stygian blackness. We finished a bottle
of brandy, passing it back and forth but carefully wiping the
neck before we drank lest some slimy insect had clung to it

in the interim, and went to bed, clinging to each other for comfort. But we didn't make love that night; it was all we could do to sleep.

When we awoke next morning about seven o'clock, the sun was high and bright and we flung open the windows and the shutters and the place looked different, more cheerful, even habitable.

Our landlord came early with the receipt for the first month's rent typed neatly in purple ink, and we learned that our address was Plaza del Porche.

Pedro Canales was a large man with a fair complexion, blue eyes, and brilliant plates, with the pretentiousness of a small Spanish property owner, and very proud of his English. When Alva expressed her deep concern at the lack of bathing facilities, he flashed his white dentures in a patronizing smile and said she could bathe in the cove, it was only three kilometers distant.

It was Sunday morning and soon we saw the black-clad natives climbing the steep ascent to the church. And a short time later our neighbor, Damien Caubet, came around to visit us. He impressed me from the first as looking like a shrunken Englishman. He was a small man with an amused unruffled attitude, dressed fastidiously in old clothes. That morning he was wearing a slightly soiled white linen jacket, a starched blue shirt with a frayed collar, a red tie with a flowered pattern, gray flannel trousers slightly bagged at the knees, and the highly glossed red shoes so greatly prized in Mallorca. He smiled ingratiatingly. Crevices calipered from his nostrils and slanted down his cheeks as though his face had become shrunken from a prolonged illness. The skin puckered about his strangely shaped gray eyes when he smiled, giving them the appearance of two oysters on the half shell. His thinning hair was neatly parted on one side and slick with oil.

He had come to invite us to an afternoon tea given by Gaspar Sabater, our sponsor, whom we had not met as yet, and his wife, Jeanette, at the home of his father-in-law near the bus terminal where they lived.

We opened the other bottle of brandy in his honor and he sat around a great part of the morning, asking us questions about our lives and telling us of his. In view of the frank manner in which he discussed his wife, we couldn't find his questions offensive. It seemed that his wife was related to Sabater's wife, whose father had been a wealthy doctor in Deya but had suffered a stroke that had left him paralyzed and speechless; and Gaspar Sabater, who was from a poor family, lived in his house and took care of him. We gathered that the family didn't think much of Sabater, but Damien spoke of him with amused tolerance.

Since it was our first invitation into Spanish society, I dressed in my beige gabardine suit, white shirt, black tie, and my Cordovan crepe-sole shoes, while Alva wore her pink ensemble: pink linen dress, pink pearl necklace and earrings, and pink shoes. She had become quite brown and I liked her in pink with her brown skin and brown eyes and brownish-black hair of the same color as Spanish hair but finer. It was a lovely suit dress, cut in severe straight lines that flattered her slender figure, giving it a semblance of voluptuousness. I was very proud of Alva's chic appearance that afternoon. She looked like what she was, the best of American society, assured and distinguished. Perhaps she didn't feel it but she looked it, and I was proud of her. I felt as though a great honor had been bestowed upon me, as though I had been given the exclusive care of something infinitely precious; and I was as proud of the honor as I was awed by the preciousness of the charge. I had rubbed my hair with olive oil to get rid of the dust that caught in the kinks, and we both felt gleaming and beautiful when we went down to the tea.

It was a large two-story house entered from the street. I had noticed the house only because it was not at all the kind of house one expects to find in Spain; it was more like an English house of stone and mortar and bays with leaded windows from the last century that are not quite large enough to be pretentious. But I didn't have a chance to see much of it, for as soon as the maid had let us in a pretty dark-haired woman with a thin subtle face and a stomach bulging from pregnancy came in from the garden and introduced herself as Jeanette Sabater, then led us beyond the dining room to the garden, which was separated from the street by a high thick hedge as effective as a wall. It was a small formal English garden with an oval-shaped gravel walk and was filled to overflowing by gaily clad women and dark-suited men sitting on straight-backed plush-bottomed dining room chairs holding messy-looking slices of green-and-white-frosted cake in small gilt-edged plates and drinking either tea or brandy.

Damien, now changed into a dark suit, came quickly forward with his ingratiating smile. I could see why he was so attracted to Alva. His wife had once had a very pretty face with a cupid's-bow mouth and perhaps a good figure, but her face had hardened and her figure had become bloated and shapeless from neglect. She tried to look pleasant, but that only emphasized the unpleasantness by contrast, and gave to her mouth a sort of puckered petulance.

Then Sabater approached and my first thought was that he was married to the wrong woman; he should have been married to Damien's wife. I'm sure they both looked at the world through the same kind of glasses, but whereas Damien's wife felt she was going down, Sabater thought he was going up. He wore an elegant dark English-tailored suit with vest, but spoiled it with his red Spanish shoes. He was tall and beginning to grow fat and his hair was beginning to thin. His dark eyes looked slightly protruding behind polished rimless spectacles as he scrutinized us curiously. But he was very much the affable host and man of good will who had done his artist friend a favor and he hoped in his best English that we had found everything suitable and in good order. Alva assured him that it was suitable and thanked him for his trouble. Damien said we should find seats and have some cake and tea.

Then a young American in a gray flannel suit, the shoulders of which were liberally covered with dandruff, rushed up and pounced on us like long-lost friends. Even before I had heard

him speak, I knew he was from the American South with rich
cracker parents, probably an alumnus of Ole Miss or Alabama U.
He introduced himself as Binum and was careful to address
us as Mr. and Missus Himes. The first thing I thought of was
jimson, the name of a stinkweed that grows in the South, I
don't know why. He had asked if he could visit us and got an
affirmative reply before we could get away to the other end of
the oval walk and grab the only available seats side by side.
Damien squatted down beside us and Jeanette came past with
some soft, spongy cake that looked as though it had been caught
in a snowstorm, and we were forced to take pieces and paper
napkins, although what I was going to do with mine I didn't
know. Damien whispered something about Graves and I
noticed Alva look up with interest, but I was trying to determine
what to do with my cake and paid little attention. But suddenly
I heard an English voice say firmly, "No, thank you. No, no, I
insist."

I looked around. I saw the long bony frame of an angular
Englishman with a thick mop of dark curly hair just touched
with gray and a prizefighter's face, clad in a white shirt open
at the throat, and well-worn khaki shorts exposing white, almost
hairless legs and knobby knees, draped negligently over one of the
straight-backed chairs. He noticed us looking at him and grinned.
"I hate cake," he said in a loud positive voice, I think more
for Alva's benefit than for mine. I'm sure Jeanette must have
heard his remark, but she didn't look around.

That was our introduction to Robert Graves, and whenever
I see his name in some newspaper or on a book I always
remember him saying "I hate cake." Oh, how I wished I could
have said it, instead of sitting there like a damn fool holding
that messy slice. Finally I just wrapped it in the paper napkin
and held it, and I noticed Damien smiling tolerantly.

The couple beside me got up to leave and a vivacious dark
young woman with beautiful flashing eyes took the seat beside
me and Damien took the seat beside her. She smiled at me and
said something in Spanish which I didn't understand and Damien

said, "Don't flirt, that's his wife." They smiled at each other knowingly and she said we must come down to the cove and swim as soon as we were settled. Alva missed all this because she and Robert Graves were talking to each other. I had noticed before that her pink dress not only made her look voluptuous but made her feel voluptuous, too, and at times it brought out a little of the slut in her.

But Jeanette, our hostess, came back and began talking to us and Alva had to give her attention to translating, because Jeanette could not speak English. Robert Graves left, telling us to telephone his wife when she returned from England the following week and make a date for dinner. Then when we prepared to leave, we were surprised to find Binum waiting for us in the dining room and we had to walk up the hill with him. Damien and his wife stayed on; they were having dinner there.

That Sunday night as I was making love to Alva I began thinking seriously of our sex life. Since our fiasco with *The Golden Chalice* I no longer needed Alva to inspire my work. Before I had needed to make love to her in order to work on her book. But now, that I had begun to work on my own book, the sex act was enough in itself. Any woman would have done. The sex act had always stimulated my thinking—not necessarily my thoughts—and of course relieved my tensions. But in that respect love was not necessary. But I still loved Alva, even though I did not need her. And although she read my manuscript page by page as it was written, she didn't share in the writing of it. And writing was my life, and the very essence of our relationship underwent a subtle change. I only wanted to give her courage and reassurance but it seemed as though she had got past expecting that from me. And all material things she could have wanted she could have gotten from members of her own race. It had occurred to me suddenly that night, probably because of her byplay with Robert Graves, that she just wanted to lose her identity in the soft exquisite darkness of sensuality, which was all I had become to her. No thought, no past, no needs, no future. Just to be free from all anxieties and despair, and the pride and responsibility that spawned them. She had already thrown away everything that mattered to a woman of her class and her race, and it had seemed to me as though all she wanted was to creep underneath my black skin, where she could hide. When I was with her, thousands of thoughts passed through my mind; thoughts about everything under the sun. With the possible exception perhaps that I seldom thought of being oppressed because I was black, perhaps never. I had done enough other things in my life for which to be penalized. I felt good about the fact that white people didn't have to hate me just because I was black; I had given them plenty of other reasons. All while I was writing *The End of a Primitive*, this thought was uppermost in my mind: I'll give them something to hate me for; I'll give them this book, because this is the kind of thing they can really hate me for.

But strangely, I never included Alva in "they." No white man has ever felt more protective toward his wife than I toward Alva. And yet I felt an enormous, moving pity for her that she had given up her place in the white world for me.

But Monday morning came. Back in the days I was contributing to *Esquire* magazine, I had written a short story called *Monday Morning Always Comes*, but it was never published. Too depressing, I suspect.

Our first problem was the flies in the kitchen. Unless you have lived in a fly country you cannot imagine flies in such number as to cast a shadow. They got into Alva's hair. We tried hanging flypaper about the kitchen, but that didn't reduce the number of flies and afterward sticky dead flies got into Alva's hair. So we set up the Primus stove in the garden and ate all of our meals outside. There were just as many flies, but there was more space to shoo them away.

The next problem was the toilet, and in time that proved to be the major problem. The only light came from a tiny hole high in the wall and during the night slimy slugs crawled up from the pit, and one was apt to sit on them in the dark. But with the door open we were exposed to the view of all the peasants who passed along the walk. I poured kerosene over the seats and into the cesspool, but that only caused the slugs to come out onto the cracked concrete floor. I thought Alva was a brave woman to put up with that house.

But I soon established a routine that took my mind away from it. I would get up at five, and by the time I had made coffee the first rays of the rising sun would strike our garden. I used the kitchen table for a desk and by the time the first peasants passed along the walk several feet below the embankment of our garden, humming the rising crescendo of the death song of the bullring, I would be typing happily, writing *The End of a Primitive*. I still had a good supply of Dexamyl. In fact, my tranquilizers sealed me inside of my thoughts so that I was almost completely unaware of the peasants and the flies and the movement in the distant street and could only experience the sweet, sensual, almost overwhelming scent of the lemon blossoms and the nearly unbearable beauty of the blossoming day far in the back of my mind. I wrote slowly, savoring each word, sometimes taking an hour to fashion one sentence to my liking. Sometimes leaning back in my seat and laughing hysterically at the sentence I had fashioned, getting as much satisfaction from the creation of this book as from an exquisite act of love. That was the first time in my life I enjoyed writing; before I had always written from compulsion. But I enjoyed writing *The End of a Primitive* (which was published as *The Primitive* by NAL in paperback); for once I was almost doing what I wanted to with a story, without being influenced by the imagined reactions of editors, publishers, critics, readers, or anyone. By then I had reduced myself to the fundamental writer, and nothing else mattered. I wonder if I could have written like that if I had been a successful writer, or even living in a more pleasant house. But one can write under such conditions for only a very limited time; in fact under such conditions one writes with the driving inspiration to get the hell out.

During the heat of the day I would sit in the shade of the fig tree—even though the natives said the shade of a fig tree was deadly—and write until the effect of my pills wore off. Then I would sit for hours and watch the behavior of the ants, of which there were many varieties, and sometimes I would kill flies to watch them move the carcasses. On such occasions I was always reminded of the Marquessa in Thornton Wilder's *Bridge of San Luis Rey*, which I had read for the first time recently on the recommendation of Roch Minué, who said he thought it was the best novel ever written.

Binum visited that first week and persuaded us to stop by his big house and have a drink. He lived on the ground floor of a casa on the steep mountainside of the road to Soller beyond Robert Graves' estate. His proprietor was an elderly woman, of some unrecognizable nationality, vainly trying to stave off old age with heavy applications of make-up; she had long tangled hennaed hair and wore garments which I can remember only for their violent colors and slightly obscene display of her wrinkled emaciated shoulders and dried breasts. She lived above him and fed him when he would eat, which was seldom; she complained bitterly about everything as she fluttered about the three of us, archly intent in drawing attention to herself. We only had a fleeting glimpse of Binum's sitting room with his typewriter on the table, and the floor littered with unnumbered pages of manuscript and empty wine bottles. His proprietor said disapprovingly that when he finished typing each page he would snatch it from the machine and throw it over his shoulder onto the floor; and when I asked Binum how he hoped to reconstruct the continuity without page numbers, he said that was the point. What point he didn't say and I didn't want to reveal my naïveté by asking. He led us into the room to drink some wine, walking over his manuscript uncaringly, but after examining the scores of empty bottles he discovered he didn't have any. His proprietor, who had followed us, said she had some upstairs. Naturally Binum knew the "boys" in the Puerto. Later I learned that Robert Graves had written a film script about the American Civil War, using Binum as a prototype for the principal character, but that was after I had left Mallorca.

His proprietor served us some cheap bitter wine, confessing

that she was a painter, and showed us a number of her paintings, which had religious themes showing pornographic Christs painted in such colors as to suggest that she was confused about the ultimate.

By the end of the week we had become convinced of the lack of edible food in Deya, and had learned from Jeanette Sabater that many residents did their shopping in Palma. The bus departed for Palma early, arriving at ten o'clock, and didn't start the return journey until three that afternoon, which gave sufficient time to shop in the central market and have lunch before starting back.

There was a large bar-restaurant in the plaza in Palma where the bus parked, serving as a terminus, where all the shoppers deposited their baskets of food while they went out into the town and had their lunch. The bus driver, a solid citizen of Deya, owned the bus line, and his son, who helped him, would load the baskets atop the bus before departure, so all the passengers had to do was get on board.

Our first trip was on a Saturday and we bought a beef tongue and two pork roasts. As we had no means of keeping fresh meat, I salted the tongue and one of the roasts in an earthenware urn we found in the storeroom, and we ate the other one that night.

Damien called for us early Sunday morning to take us fishing with friends in the small rocky cove at the end of the deep gorge that ran down to the sea from the cathedral promontory in Deya. It had very clear water, showing the smooth rocks at the bottom, and several boulders high enough to dive from. The entire northwestern coast of the island is one high, continuous cliff, broken by small *calas* and the Bay of Soller. The surrounding cliffs were very steep and accessible only to amateur mountain climbers and the goats of Mallorca, which one saw picking their way over the peaks, outlined against the sky. Damien's friend hadn't arrived but there was a pleasant little shaded café-restaurant extending over the boathouse where we sat and enjoyed the view. We had brought our swimsuits and after lunch we went into the water, and after the siesta hour a number of middle-class Mallorquins from Palma and Deya, some of whom had been at the tea the previous Sunday, came out in swimsuits to lie on the small pebbled beach and wade into the water. I saw the young woman whom Damien had told not to flirt with me, and she took up where she had left off. One of her girl friends asked me where I got such a deep tan, and she said, "Oooo, it's his color." Alva swam out some distance, showing off, no doubt, and I watched her, feeling envious because I didn't know how to swim. It had been a pleasant day and we went home about ten oclock when it was still daylight, tired and happy.

Following that day the sequence of events became dreamlike. We went to the *cala* many times by ourselves in the early morning, returning late at night in the bright moonlight to the scent of the lemon blossoms and undressing in the warm, dark, impossible house and making love. There couldn't have been a house so primitive, nor sunsets so enchanting. Neither the pink mountains nor the swarms of flies in the dusty city could possibly be real, I thought. Only my book was real.

We had eaten the salted roast in time but when I unpacked the salted tongue I found it had spoiled. But I boiled it anyway, unwittingly attracting all the flies of Deya, and put it out for the cats to eat, hoping it would make them sick for a night or two and give me a brief respite from their nocturnal yowling, fighting or mating, and their sly efforts to break into the house, rousing me in alarm thinking they were burglars. But they devoured it with relish and afterward I had twice as many disturbing my sleep.

It was the next month before we got around to visiting Robert Graves. We had met his entire family in his Land Rover once as we were getting out of the bus from Palma, his young wife and new baby and his son and daughter by a previous marriage. Graves asked us to stop by some night and have a drink. When we dropped around at ten o'clock one night we found his wife had gone to London and he was alone with his secretary, who lived apart with his own family in a small new house by the gate. The main house was big and comfortable with a front view of the distant sea and a back view of the surrounding mountains. It was screened from the highway by a high wall covered with climbing roses that were in full bloom, but there was a large area in back planted with grapes, limes, lemons, date palms, and avocados, in addition to a vegetable garden. When he sent his secretary home he said jokingly, "He writes all my books." During the conversation which followed Graves said he hadn't written *I, Claudius* as a historical novel, as most critics termed it; his intention had been simply to write a domestic story of the times. After a few drinks we all began feeling a little gay and soon he and Alva began speaking conspiratorially in German. Graves noticed immediately that I had become resentful and tried to draw me into the conversation by asking what musical instrument I played. That always makes me angrier than any other question a white person can ask me. I told him I played the radio. He said he played the drums himself and had thought perhaps we could get together sometime. I told him he'd have to get together with Alva—she played the piano. He pointed to the piano but she quickly begged off. It hadn't been a catastrophe, but when we left we weren't on as good terms as we had been when we had arrived.

It had always been like that with the Americans and the English. I got along all right with people of other nationalities, the French and the Spanish. I forgot that I was black with them. But the Americans and the English always made a point of reminding me I was black, as though it were a stigma, which brought out the worst in me.

I have nothing but the highest respect, even veneration, for jazz musicians. Most of the good ones are black and jazz is a contribution by black people to the world's culture. But, unfortunately, I am not a jazz musician, and I resent white people using it to remind me I am an oppressed black man. Of course I knew Robert Graves had no such intention, but my reaction was spontaneous.

That night Alva and I had our first quarrel. It wasn't really much of a quarrel. I simply told her that if she could find such rapport with men of her own race, why use up me? She said I couldn't expect her to keep away from the world. I said why not, she wanted it. We went to bed, silent and withdrawn. And when she tried to mention Robert Graves the next day, I said she could think of him all she wanted but I didn't want to hear her speak his name.

When the summer tourists began to appear, the *residencias* and restaurants on the road to Soller along the sea opened, and excursion buses came up from Palma to Valdemosa, Deya, and Soller. We never went to Soller, but we passed through Valdemosa on the way to Palma and we had been shown the monastery where Chopin lived with George Sand. It was said she used to walk into Palma to shop, but it was twelve kilometers in each direction and the way back was uphill, and I thought she must have been a strong woman.

A tall, lithe Swiss woman appeared one day in the *cala* wearing a white swimsuit, and Alva said enviously that she had to be a good swimmer to wear a white suit. She turned out to be a fantastic swimmer and loved to swim out of the *cala* into the sea and out of sight. Alva approached her and discovered she was from Bern in the German-speaking canton of Switzerland, where she taught in an elementary school, and was vacationing with a woman colleague in one of the *residencias*. Alva loved to speak German, although she denied it, and she invited the two teachers to stop by one evening for drinks. The one she had spoken to spoke perfect English, and when we were gathered in the garden, she looked at me curiously and said, "I wonder what goes on in your head." If only she knew, I thought. Her friend was a fat German hausfrau whose English was very limited and for the most part she sat quietly and grinned stupidly, as I suppose I did myself under similar circumstances.

I was getting near the end of my book when I had a strange dream. I dreamed that four young Chinese men whose wives had committed crimes while they were away to war were being taken with their wives in chains through a teeming street in a great city in China so that the Great Judge could judge all eight of them impartially for their separate guilt; and one of them had cried out: "Oh, what great wrong have I done?" while another cried: "Lay me lengthwise upon the everlasting water of the sea and let the stone wheel of Time roll continuously over my body until a channel is worn into the surface of the everlasting water but no dent is made in the everlasting wheel of Time."

The dream disturbed me, although I couldn't imagine what it meant, if anything, but I didn't tell it to Alva—least of all to Alva. She had enough to disturb her as it was.

When July came I had my first confrontation with my proprietor, Pedro Canales. A Spanish family, vacationing from Palma, moved into the apartment house above our toilet. On the day they arrived, as I was sitting in the toilet, a trap door was opened above, and a paper sack of garbage was thrown down on my head. Looking up through the trap door I saw someone industriously sweeping trash down into my toilet. I let out with a volley of English epithets and the door was quickly shut.

Señor Canales came by later that day for the rent and I explained what had happened. He shrugged and said the apartment didn't belong to him, only the toilet was his, and he couldn't stop them from dropping garbage into the toilet because half of the toilet was a garbage pit that went with the apartment. I said in that case I just wouldn't pay him until he provided us with another toilet. He said I had to pay him, I'd signed a contract. I said no. He said he would cut off my electricity. I told him if he tried to cut off my electricity I'd cut off his head. He went away in a great huff, but he returned that evening with a ladder and approached the house from the cul-de-sac where the electric lines came in from the street. I was in the kitchen at the time. Alva told me that Canales had come with a ladder to disconnect the electricity. I snatched the large kitchen knife and ran out through the garden and told Canales that if he put that ladder against the house I was going to cut off his head. Several men gathered about and looked on with grave faces. Canales started to move the ladder and I started toward him. No one else moved. After a moment he thought better of it and retired into the street with the ladder and shook his fist at me threatening to call the Guardia Civil. Later that evening the *comandante* of the Guardia Civil puesto in Deya stopped by the house. He was a pleasant young man with a black-winged mustache and fresh complexion, who spoke French rather well. He was polite and somewhat apologetic and seemed self-conscious in his uniform with the big black pistol in the holster at his side. Alva explained about the toilet and I took him out and showed him what I meant. He told Alva not to worry and for her to tell me not to pay Canales anything and make him take his complaint to the supreme command of the Guardia Civil in Palma.

That was all I needed. I didn't pay Canales and didn't permit him on the property. So Canales went to Gaspar Sabater, who had rented the place for me, and told him I had refused to pay my rent and he would have to pay it. Gaspar Sabater came up to the house and told me I was letting him down. He said that if I didn't pay the rent, he would have to pay it himself, since he was the justice of the peace and the superintendent of the school and a responsible citizen. Alva was translating as usual. I told her to tell him to go ahead and pay it, because I didn't intend to. I don't know what Alva told him, but they had a long discussion, ignoring me, which concluded with Sabater asking if I would pay Canales if he built a wall to keep the garbage out of my toilet. I said I would pay him after the wall was built, and not before.

The next day the *comandante's* wife came to visit Alva and reassure her. It seemed that Canales had been gathering support from all his friends in the city and she told us not to worry, they could do nothing. After I had showed her the condition of the toilet she told us not to pay anything until it was fixed and renovated and if Canales tried to make any trouble we should report it to her husband. We learned from her that her husband, the *Comandante de puesto*, was named Pedro Tous and her name was Carmen and she was French. She was seven months pregnant, like Jeanette Sabater, and there was much speculation as to who would have her baby first.

Jeanette also called to offer her reassurances and tell us not to pay any attention to her husband, Gaspar; that he was just letting himself be bullied by Canales. But Gaspar, like Canales, was of a lower social order, and Jeanette was from the Spanish aristocracy. She and Carmen knew one another, as did everyone in Deya, but they had no social contact. However, both had formed a close rapport with Alva and felt as protective toward her as I did.

The day after Jeanette called, masons appeared and began building a wall of concrete blocks about the garbage pit. But the incident had split the city into two factions—those who took Canales' side and those who took ours.

Damien dismissed Canales and the whole affair with a wave of his hand. It was nothing, Canales was nobody, Sabater was an ass, Pedro Tous was a good boy but only a corporal. Why worry? Worry made you old.

Robert Graves was in London.

During all this controversy, I had finished my novel and sent it off to World publishers in New York. Evidently it had come back immediately, for I find a copy of this letter to Yves:

Deya
Mallorca, Spain

20 July, 1954

Dear Yves,

I think publishers all over the world are going crazy. Perhaps this is the year of the publisher's moon. I know my publishers in the U.S. are crazy; they rejected the book Alva and I did together and then this one, both of which stand a better chance of sales than did THE THIRD GENERATION; and in England there is a great "clean-up" campaign going on in the publishing business. I'm going to make a study of this for my next book.

I am sending you the manuscript under separate cover. So be on the lookout for it. I will have it registered. Since first writing to you I have retyped and revised it. And I find it a much better book than I first thought. In fact it might be the best book I've yet written. I can say that I like it best of all. And the nice part about it is that it's short: 251 pages. A little package of dynamite.

No, I have not killed Alva. I found that I was able to do with my imagination in creating the murder scene. So she is still here. I figured it would be better to save her to cook and eat if things get any more critical, than use her up just for experience to write a murder scene.

And how is Yvonne? I notice you didn't mention *her* in *your* letter, so I assume that during the course of your rejections you threw her out the window on the head of a passing publisher. Alas, such is this profession.

I have been planning to go to Daniel Guerin's colony in La Ciotât for August, but at the present moment I don't even have enough money to pay our fare off this island; and if things keep on like this Alva and I are going to pick out our plots in the cemetery behind this church.

Give my regards to (ignoble) Nadeau and ask him if he has any extra copies of LA CROISADE DE LEE GORDON. I would like to have three mailed to me here to explore the possibilities of getting it published in Spain. I've come to the conclusion that your translation is a much better version than the original, and also the Spanish read French more easily than they do English.

Give our love to Yvonne. Alva did the bulk of the typing of the book and she says if she has to do it again she will be dead for sure.

Affectionately

In God We Trust
(Damn right)

Shortly afterward, near the end of July, we had a run-in with the proprietor of the bus company. I don't remember his name; he owned the two buses that ran daily from Deya and Valdemosa to Palma, along with a big garage housing other dilapidated old buses, old relics of motorcars, and related junk in Deya. To one side was the big frame house where he lived with his family, a veritable clan, which also contained the booking room that served as terminus. He was a self-made success, probably the richest citizen of Deya, and he always drove the Deya-Palma bus himself, generally with a young son of about fifteen as helper.

Alva and I always took the front seat, directly behind him, as he sat there in his American sport shirt with his big head always neatly barbered, looking solid and sturdy as he wheeled the old bus around the myriad curves. We had always thought of him as part of the scenery, like the bus itself. On that morning, he turned around and spoke to Alva in French. Alva had such a strange expression that I asked what he had said. She said that he had accused us of behaving badly. He interrupted to say something else which Alva translated without replying. The gist of it was that he claimed that Canales had treated us nicely; Canales had taken our trunk and luggage from the bus to the house on arrival, for which we hadn't paid him, and had always spoken of us well; and that we had repaid him by turning the gentry against him and being ungrateful. I hadn't thought about him before but suddenly I realized that he and Canales were the same type and it was natural they would take each other's part.

But all this contention had been going on for some time by then, and Canales had built the wall in the toilet and I had paid him and I was sick and tired of the whole business and didn't feel like entering into a controversy with the bus driver about something I considered was none of his business. We just moved to another seat.

While in Palma we shopped at the central market, deposited our shopping bag in the terminus, and went to have lunch with Damien and his wife and mother. When we arrived back at the terminus and found all the shopping bags loaded atop the Deya and Valdemosa buses, we did not give ours a thought and boarded the bus along with the other passengers.

When the bags were unloaded in Deya, ours was not there. We were standing alongside the bus like the other passengers, waiting for it to be passed down, when the top was emptied the boy

climbed down and turned away. By then the bus driver was surrounded by a number of his sons and employees. I told him in
English that we had had a shopping bag and he asked in English
if I had a ticket for it. I said that we'd never been given a ticket
for our shopping bag and no one else had as we'd seen. He said
that was all right for people he liked but we'd have to have a
ticket. Suddenly I realized that all of them were in on the joke. I
was trying to keep my temper. Alva said something in French
and the young man sneered a reply in Spanish. I asked what he
had said. She said, "He called me a liar." I hit at him. He ducked
beneath the blow and backed off. Everyone stood frozen and
became suddenly grave, as the Mallorquins do when a tragedy
is imminent. Alva had turned sheet-white. She was pulling me by
the arm and the mob of men were looking on silently, unmoving.
Some women came out of their houses. Suddenly I became
frightened.

I took Alva next door to the house of Gaspar Sabater's, but
the maid who answered my ring said in Spanish that he'd gone
to Palma and the Señora was not there. As we walked up the hill
toward our house I looked back and saw all the men on the
street gathered closely about the bus driver as though they were
plotting something. So instead of going home, we took a short cut
to the home of Pedro Tous, the comandante of the Guardia Civil.
He was out but his wife, Carmen, was very upset by our story and
sent a neighbor's little boy to the puesto with a message for him to
return home immediately. I would have felt safer if I'd had a gun.

When Pedro returned, Carmen was very indignant as she re-
counted the story. Pedro looked grave. I understood his predicament. The bus driver was a big man in the city, unlike our landlord, Canales. He probably had the ear of authorities high up in
the Guardia Civil. And Pedro was a young man. That was only
his second post as comandante. But he told us to go home and not
to worry. We noticed when we approached our house there were
two Guardia Civil militiamen with rifles on opposite sides of the
square.

We locked ourselves in the house and didn't go out again. Later we learned that Pedro Tous had gone down and told the bus proprietor to get our bag and when the bus proprietor had argued that we hadn't had any bag and were just trying to make some trouble, Pedro told him to get into his car and go get our bag of food, wherever it was, and not to come back to Deya without it.

At ten o'clock that night, shortly before the lights went out, we heard a timid knock at the front door. I armed myself with a kitchen knife and went out of the back door into the garden and saw the bus driver's son with two companions. He had our bag of food. I beckoned for him to come back to the garden. It was dark out there and he was as afraid as I was. He came forward timidly and handed the bag over the top of the fence.

The next day I wrote a detailed account to the U.S. consulate in Barcelona, to which I received no reply.

It all sounds a little silly from this distance, but at that time it was very serious.

Canales asked us to leave at the end of July and we had every intention of doing so, but we had not begun to look for a place. Any writer must of necessity be an optimist, and I had been waiting for our finances to improve before beginning house hunting. But after this latest controversy the bus driver refused to let us ride on his bus, so we didn't have transportation. In addition, our six-month visas were soon to expire. Damien did not appear that week, Robert Graves was still in London. Mail was slow and time was the essence. And we couldn't confess our predicament to the comandante of the Guardia Civil, no matter how friendly we were. We realized that we needed friends like anyone else.

Fortunately Carmen had a deep genuine sympathy for Alva and she wormed enough out of her to realize our situation was desperate. It wasn't hard to do. Alva looked it. And I suppose I did too. And again it was Pedro who saved the day. He had a married cousin living in Terreno, a suburb of Palma, who had a room in her house that she would let us have, but she was in another part of the island on vacation and wouldn't return until September, and we'd have to look after ourselves the month of August. However, her husband, Antonio, was still there and he would feed the dog, and her eldest daughter, Magdalena, would be back and forth.

We were glad to take it, although we had no way of getting into Palma to see it. Pedro wanted to confront the bus proprietor again, but we assured him we'd find a way to move. It wasn't as easily done as said. We telephoned Damien. The only suggestion he had was to appeal to the Guardia Civil. We avoided Sabater, and both Jeanette and Carmen were eight months pregnant by then. But the proprietor of the *vaqueria* where Alva bought a few things from time to time had heard that the bus driver refused to accept us as passengers, as had everyone else, and he promised Alva to arrange for one of the provision trucks from Palma to move us on a return trip, and that very same day he arranged for a truck to pick us up at six o'clock on the morning of August 1.

On the 27th of July I received a letter from Yves:

Dear Chester,

Just finished reading your book. I am very worried because I think it is a masterpiece and editors very seldom agree with me.

Tomorrow I'll have it given to Nadeau. But he does not know English. Who will read it for him? Maybe an imbecile. There are many in France too.

Maybe I'll give it to him myself to explain this:

When he read my translation of LONELY CRUSADE, he was disappointed because he had been told it was dynamite. Now he's got the dynamite. Therefore he has to publish it.

Believe I'll do my best. I want the book to be published, even if I do not translate it, although I'd be proud to do so.

I am jealous too, because you write the books I'd like to write and am unable to. This jealousy justifies the following reflection:

There is no negro problem. Jesse is not a colored man. He's an unsuccessful writer. White ones are just like him. I know it.

I am one and don't need to be colored to understand his reactions. They are exactly like mine. I thought, "How does Chester know I am and think like that."

Bons souvenirs a tous les deux

Yvonne et Yves

P.S. I'll write soon. Let us pray that Ignoble Nadeau is not on his summer vacations. These editors go vacationing a lot.

Y.M.

On the 29th July I was forty-five years old. I looked ten years younger and had the physique of a prizefighter. I was the color of new bronze in the sun. I had a nice smile, showing two faint dimples, and tiny laugh wrinkles from the corners of my long-lashed brown eyes. I had wide shoulders and narrow hips, and Alva always said she envied my legs. I had an almost unlimited vitality. All in all, I was an attractive man.

Alva had taken on weight and her small body had become rounded with curves in the right places. Her breasts had filled out. She had completely lost the harried, distraught look she had had when I had first seen her, although it had been replaced by one of anxiety. The desperation of our predicament had drawn us closer together again. Our only escape from fear was in sexual oblivion.

I woke up that morning, filled to overflowing with my love for Alva. In two days we would be leaving Deya to live with other people for the first time. Despite all the annoyances, the desperation, the disappointments, the outside world hadn't touched our love and our life together. We had at least been able to keep ourselves invulnerable to prying eyes, and now, we were on the brink of an existence which would make us vulnerable to curiosity. It frightened us. We clung together and wouldn't leave the bed.

But eventually we had to get up and face the day. We had to pack. I had some letters to write to notify all my acquaintances of change of address. Alva had to write to her daughters in Kerkrade and her aunt and uncle in Philadelphia. It is strange that I can't remember her daughters' names.

Late that afternoon when we had finished, Robert Graves called. He looked upset and concerned. We took him into the garden. He said he had been away and hadn't heard of our difficulties. He would have done something. He offered to help then. He would lend us his Land Rover to move. We thanked him but said we had already made arrangements. He confessed he felt extremely guilty. We said he shouldn't; after all, he wasn't there. He said we could have contacted his secretary. We said we didn't know his secretary, and changed the conversation, making a joke of our predicament.

Alva had a romp telling of all the shortcomings of the house. When she told him about the water seeping up from the floor in the bedroom, he exclaimed in astonishment, "But don't you know, this is the 'House of the Bleeding Jesus.'" It seemed that everyone in the city except ourselves knew the legend of the house running with the blood of Jesus. Some of the more devout inhabitants considered it something of a shrine. Alva whooped. "All this time we've been walking in blood and didn't know it."

Graves said that engineers from Palma had come to examine the phenomenon and concluded that there was a section of an old Roman sewer beneath the house dating from the time the Romans occupied the Balearics. At least we were able to relieve him of his distress before he left, but our resentment toward Canales had intensified. When the provision truck stopped for our luggage at six o'clock that morning, the proprietor of the *vaqueria* appeared in his own little car to drive us to our new home. I felt depressed. I hated to say goodbye to Deya. It was such a beautiful village, pink and perfumed, and despite all of our misfortunes we had been happy there. As there had not been many places where I had been happy in my life, I could not go away from any one of them with indifference. And, too, I was so very afraid of the future, afraid it would render me incapable of protecting Alva and making her happy.

4.

Our new address was *En casa de D. Antonio Sureda, Plaza de Son Catleret No. 9, Terreno.* It was about a half mile southwest of Plaza Gomila, on the same side of the dangerous thoroughfare, Calvo Sotello, with its loose brick pavement and deep potholes and disconnected streetcar tracks and overcrowded buses, that led out of Palma to the southwest. Plaza de Son Catleret predated all the tourist hotels along the Paseo Martimo and Calvo Sotello, and went back to the time when Mallorca was for the Mallorquins. It was not really a plaza but an unpaved area of baked dirt, like an amateur bullring in some remote village, which was reached by concrete stairs from the thoroughfare. The blank stone faces of the whitewashed houses with the small barred windows, joined by the high stone walls with the solid-oak gates, enclosing the bare red dirt of the plaza, gave it the appearance of a prison courtyard where condemned men might be taken out and shot. Tethered goats and burros hitched to carts dozed in the muddy gutters and swarms of butterflies buzzed about the patches of dried vomit in front of the wine store, where the beatniks sat in the sun and made themselves sick off the two-peseta wine.

No. 9 was a green-painted carriage entrance with two huge solid wooden doors, one of which contained a small pedestrian door. Beyond to the rear end of the plaza extended the white-washed wall of the two-storied house. The ground-floor wall of No. 9 was without windows onto the plaza, but at its end was another green-painted entrance to No. 7, the apartment above.

A young Spanish woman answered our ring and opened the pedestrian door and we entered from the glaring white plaza to a cool fieldstone walk beneath a thick-trellised grape arbor. She was Magdalena, the eldest daughter of Antonio Sureda and Maria, who was the cousin of Pedro Tous. She was twenty-one, as we later learned, and a very pretty young woman, but she had dark circles underneath her eyes that morning and her pale white face was bloodless as though she had spent the night, or early morning, in torrid lovemaking. I got the impression that time was of the essence for her too.

After a moment we heard the hysterical barking of a dog and I looked quickly about in alarm, but Magdalena only smiled and said he was chained up in the kitchen. Stepping from the cool shade of the arbor we were overwhelmed by a riot of color in the blazing sunshine. A flower garden extended to a stone wall along the distant street. It was sinfully neglected, like a tropical garden. It was the front yard of No. 9; all of the rooms on that side opened onto a brick walk between the house and the garden that formed a terrace. We were taken to a room at the rear with a separate entrance. Our door opened onto a wide back porch enclosing two sides of another small, neglected garden which sat atop the back of another house below with its own garden sitting atop another house and garden ad infinitum terraced one atop another from the high bluff of Plaza Son Catleret to the muddy bay of Palma below.

We were separated by a deep ravine, containing a shipyard, from the end of Paseo Maritimo, the fashionable quay of luxury hotels fronting the bay, and the high promontory of Plaza Gomila and Plaza Mediterraneo and the Mediterraneo Gran Hotel. From our back door we had a breathtaking view of the Bay of Palma with the sun shining on the rising white walls of the old town and the stained-glass windows of the cathedral of Palma across the bay. The apartment's toilet was also on the back porch.

Then we were shown into the kitchen, which we had already passed coming from the arbor, where the dog was chained to the stove. The dining room was to one side with windows looking out onto the front garden. We were permitted to use both.

We liked the room but the dog frightened Alva, although she tried not to show it.

Shortly after our baggage had arrived and we had finished unpacking, Antonio came home from his first job, expressly to welcome us. As a rule he worked from six o'clock until two o'clock as an engineer in an aircraft factory on the outskirts of Palma, and from then on until midnight in his sister's restaurant in the old town of Palma, traveling back and forth on a huge black 250-cc. Harley Davidson motorcycle.

He was a short powerfully built man with rock-hard over-developed muscles, thinning hair, and eyes that were always bright red from lack of sleep. I never learned their real color, I never saw him rested and relaxed.

He had lost his life's savings speculating on a number of old American trucks he had bought for reconditioning to sell to the Guardia Civil, but the deal hadn't gone through and he had been saddled with millions of pesetas' worth of junk. And he had a sick wife and three daughters and an adopted daughter to support. All very pretty and lively girls, wanting to get married—needing it, in fact, needing it badly. And he had to provide dowries for them or they might never get married. His adopted daughter, who was twenty-two, had come to the conclusion that he'd never be able to afford a dowry for her and she was doing the best she could with her good looks, her vitality, and her sex. No doubt she derived her abundant vitality from the tremendous amount she ate, and while she was pretty and vivacious, she could be very funny, too, sometimes in a manner so coarse and crude that Maria and the other daughters would blush from shame.

But despite all his troubles and responsibilities to these five women, Antonio was a very sympathetic and congenial man. He was surrounded by women most of his waking days, at home and at the restaurant of his sister, who was a widow. And yet he took time to be kind and considerate to Alva.

He noticed immediately that she was afraid of the dog and took it to the back of the garden and chained it to an olive tree. He kept the dog for protection for his wife and daughters, but he was the only one who could handle it and he was seldom there. It was a huge brutish dog as tall as a great Dane but heavier and with a bigger chest and I imagined more powerful. It had a gray mottled coat like a dappled horse, black points, and eyes as red as Antonio's, but senseless. It would pounce on everything that moved and destroy it. At night it was chained to the heavy wood- and coal-burning stove in the kitchen and the doors were securely locked, but I have no doubt that if it had run amuck it could have gone through one of those doors, dragging the stove behind. During the day, when it was chained to the olive tree beyond the end of the back porch, we had to pass it every time we left or entered the house and at each time the barking of that idiot animal shocked me so intensely that bile ballooned into my mouth. Alva attempted to slip by without being seen, but was never successful, and she dreaded having to leave the house.

It was a lovely house and for the first month we had it practically to ourselves. But I don't think Alva ever really enjoyed it because she had begun to grieve. Ever since our desperate situation in Deya I had realized that a part of her had gone away from me.

I tried desperately to get us away from Palma before Maria and the other three girls returned, but I could not get one cent from anyone I knew.

Damien took us under his wing, in a limited fashion. He didn't have much money either. His mother, a Puerto Rican, had married a rich Mallorquin and come to live in Mallorca. But his father was long dead and she lived alone in a big, old, cool, pleasant house on a large estate and did not help him financially. She became very fond of Alva and invited us to dinner several times, both with and without her son. She was a smart old lady and knew damn well we weren't married, and sometimes Alva talked to her about her daughters, but she always preserved the myth that we were man and wife and demanded that others treat us likewise. Damien's wife didn't care for us and his mother's attitude irritated her, but she had to put up with us. On most occasions when we stopped by Damien's apartment she had other places to go.

Damien had little business and lots of time. He was always happy to be with us and would stop whatever he was doing to go out with us. He had a couple of famous Spanish gun dogs, and did a bit of hunting in his leisure. His mother had an apartment directly above his, which she seldom used, and he used to keep his dogs there on her terrace.

He told us that in English his name would be Damon Corbet, or Corbett, and explained to us the complicated system of name-taking in Spanish marriages, and how the male and female children were named—all of which I have forgotten. Occasionally he would refer to the Spanish prejudices. He told us how when he was a little boy, his mother caught him picking on the Jewish children in the playground. It was a great sport among the Spanish youths to spit at the Jewish kids. His mother was very angry and took him home and reprimanded him severely. "You shouldn't do that," she said. "But everyone I know spits on the Jews," he said; "we don't mean anything." "But you shouldn't do it, you are a Jew, too," she said. He told us, smiling, "I didn't feel any different. I still wanted to spit on the Jews. But then if I was one too I figured it didn't make any sense."

After he had told us that he was part Jewish, I understood his wife's attitude better. She was a Catholic anti-Semite, and felt superior to Damien, but she couldn't feel superior to Damien's mother, who was not only a Catholic but controlled the money. Poor woman, she was in a hell of a fix with all her insupportable prejudices, I thought.

We had news that Jeanette Sabater had had her baby, but Carmen Tous was long past due and kept getting bigger and bigger, to the consternation of her doctors. It seemed as though her baby might grow to manhood inside of her.

We were still in the house when Maria returned with her brood of daughters. Alva had not drawn into herself as she had done on previous occasions of doubt and anxiety, but now she seemed distraught and intent on throwing herself away. It is a terrible thing to watch the woman whom you love try to throw herself away.

It became obvious that Alva was grieving for her own lost daughters. She grieved in public. Not that she cried—she was too well bred to cry in public—but she grieved. It was obvious. Even Maria saw it. And like all Spanish women, Maria had an overwhelming sympathy for her.

Damien was puzzled by her erratic behavior. I could see in his eyes that sometimes he wondered if her behavior was due to an overwhelming attraction for him.

I became afraid to leave her alone, as one dreads leaving alone a person who is likely to commit suicide. I could not trust her to keep herself alive. It hurt me terribly to see her hurt. I felt a sense of failure. I hate to fail. And I've failed as a thief, as a student, as a writer, even as a person, and now I was failing with Alva. The greatest failure for any man is to fail with a woman. No one will ever know how much that hurt me, how much it hurt me to watch helplessly as she went away from me, to see her grieve for her children, her family, normality, security, her white world. I had failed with my black wife in my native country and now I was failing with the white woman whom I loved in a foreign land.

During her terrible grieving, all the comfort I could offer her was sex. Is sex the ultimate that a black man can offer a white woman? I wondered. I didn't want to believe it. Alva didn't want to admit failure, either. She had run off with me in defiance of her tradition and her race, leaving her husband and her

children, and she didn't want to go crawling back penitent
and defeated.

We worked on our manuscripts as though they were our only
hope of salvation, which in fact they were.

We retyped both the manuscripts of *The Golden Chalice* and
The End of a Primitive, working turns on my typewriter until
we were exhausted. The family was impressed with our industry
and did all they could to help.

Alva did most of the shopping in the neighborhood stores
and cooked our meals when the kitchen wasn't in use, which
was seldom. For serious shopping we'd walk down beyond the end
of Calvo Sotello to the old market and shopping center of the
Mallorquins on that side of the bay. Occasionally we'd ride the
Toonerville Trolley across to the new market in the old town
and stop for lunch in the restaurant of a cousin of Damien's
where the *calamares* were so good.

Maurice Nadeau, the director of the collection *Le Chemin
de la Vie*, in which the translation of *Lonely Crusade* had been
published, rejected *The End of a Primitive*, mostly because he
couldn't understand it, I thought, but he didn't admit that;
he gave his reason that it was too sadistic for the French taste.
That left a bitter taste in my mouth. I wanted to remind him
that the Marquis de Sade, who gave the word to the language,
was a French national, but I couldn't write him in French.
And Alva flatly refused to help me write insulting letters to my
editors.

The Sixth Fleet of the U. S. Navy was moored in the bay of
Palma for several days, and at night, when the ships were lit
up, they looked like Christmas trees floating on the waves. The
appearance of so many American sailors all at once gave the
impression of a bit of America having come to town. From our
house, high up on the bluff of Terreno, we had a grandstand
seat of all the activity in the bay. I don't suppose that alleviated
Alva's homesickness very much, but I didn't offer to take her
into town—I wasn't confident of her composure. We stayed
indoors until they had gone.

I don't remember meeting any of Antonio's relatives except his sister at the restaurant where we went to eat occasionally, forcing down the oily Spanish food out of politeness, but many of Maria's relatives lived in the neighborhood and we saw them at the house from time to time. The one who made the greatest impression on us was Maria's father, the grandfather of the girls, who had been the official carpenter for the Palma bullring when he was younger, but at that time he was very old and was a sort of honorary carpenter.

He was always clad in faded denim overalls patched on both knees and his dried yellow skin also looked patched with brown splotches. He had one brown tooth in his brown-stained mouth, and his bald skull was covered with an almost imperceptible fuzz of gray hair that must have been a second growth.

He liked Alva. She made a show of flirting with him whenever she saw him about the house. Each evening he brought over the daily paper for Maria or Antonio to read to him, and he'd stop and joke with Alva if he found her in the kitchen cooking dinner.

"Why do you drink so much wine?" he'd ask.

"It's good for me," she'd say.

"Does it fill you up, like food?"

"No, but it makes me gay, and then I'm not hungry."

"I think I'll try it."

One week he fell ill and everyone expected him to die. When next she saw him he was frailer than ever. He told her he was just alive on the tip of life (*propina de la vida*).

It was following his illness that he got his dentures. They were ghastly-looking plates of China-white teeth and very painful. Alva had been a dentist's assistant for her husband and for her husband's friend, who had gone to the United States to set up practice. She advised the old man of a new American type of dentures to get with natural-looking teeth and so molded to the gums that they were painless. When he finally got them he was as happy as a lark. He could scarcely believe it was possible. They looked like natural teeth and he could eat anything without inconvenience. He said that if he had known such plates existed, he would have had them for years.

He obtained passes for us to the next corrida and we went on a bright hot Sunday and sat in the sun and I saw my first and last and only bullfight. I was deeply moved. I have always been moved by any type of solemn pageantry, whether high mass in a Catholic church, a Baptist funeral in Mississippi, or the march of the toreros in the corrida in Palma de Mallorca. I was moved by the music and the toros and the toreros and the sweating spectators and the hot bright sun. I had read Hemingway's *Death In the Afternoon,* and since the prison fire in the Ohio Penitentiary on Easter Monday, 1930, where I had so narrowly escaped death, I have always been moved by the forced contemplation of death. Alva was caught up too.

Bullfights, or rather the death of the bull, have an intense aphrodisiacal effect on some women. Alva had worn her pink linen suit that day, and I think the deaths of the bulls affected her strongly.

On the way home in the Toonerville Trolley I caught her flirting surreptitiously with a handsome young German, and that night she engineered our sexual activity to the point of exhaustion. And then she began to cry hysterically and disconsolately.

It hurt me to see her cry like that, so hopelessly. From then on I became obsessed with wanting to get her back safely to her aunt in Philadelphia. I became desperate. All I wanted in the world was to get her safely home. I would have lied, cheated, robbed, killed, just to get her home to Philadelphia *safe.* I had fantasies about it. I remembered the bales of ten-thousand-franc notes I had seen piled about the bed of Pop, the black marketeer who lived out on the Champs-Elysées. I made up a fantasy in which I had got her back as far as Paris and we had run out of money and I had gone out to Pop's with an empty suitcase and strangled him and stuffed the suitcase with ten-thousand old-franc notes and bought her a plane ticket to America. I had taken her out to Orly and just as she was about to go through the gates onto the tarmac to board the plane I had

kissed her and said, "Be happy, Alva. Be safe." When I turned
away from watching her walk up the boarding stairway into
the plane, two dark-suited Frenchmen with the brims of their
hats pulled low over their eyes took me by the arms, one on
each side. One of them spoke to me in French. I knew immediately they were from the Sûreté. I thought bitterly, I haven't
even learned the language.

The family was very kind. The daughters were well behaved
in a Spanish Catholic fashion and very obliging—too obliging.
They believed in the Catholic church and marriage and giving
birth. They were soft, lovely, obliging female animals.

I gathered that the youngest one reminded Alva of her favorite
daughter, and the nineteen-year-old behaved like her eldest
daughter.

The daughters, too, were fascinated by Alva's clothes and her
jewelry, especially the pink pearls, and her American manners.
She had got a lot of summer clothes from her home in Kerkrade
and from her aunt in the States, and although most of them
were old-fashioned and quite out of style, they must have appeared rich and opulent and the lastest American fashions to
those clothes-conscious, husband-hunting daughters of Antonio.

All the girls were very beautiful, but the outstanding beauty
was the second youngest. She was vaguely tubercular with large
limpid eyes and had the ethereal type of beauty generally ascribed
to Camille. I remember an incident that occurred shortly after
the family had returned from their vacation. Antonio had some
trapeze bars and rings installed in the concrete ceiling of the
back porch in front of our room, which he used to keep himself
in shape and which no doubt accounted for his well-developed
muscles. One evening when all the family had gathered in the
back to see if we were comfortable and take a good look at us
and our things, the daughters started showing off on the trapeze
bars, competing for our attention like little girls. As they turned
somersaults on the bars, showing their legs and panties, they
got carried away with themselves. Antonio had to stop this
daughter on account of her health, and she suddenly burst into

tears. They were the most feminine and sensuous girls I had ever known.

Once when all the girls and Antonio and Maria were congregated about the dog, I said facetiously I was going to write a book and call it *The Vicious Dog and the Four Virgins*. Alva could speak enough Spanish by then to communicate with anyone who wished to understand. She translated for me. The girls looked at me as though appraising my seriousness and Maria looked suddenly ashamed in the way of a Spanish mother.

How could anyone think they were virgins, I thought, who had smelled the strong alkaloid odor of stale semen when they went to wash in the mornings?

The tree to which the dog was tied was surrounded with tremendous bones which Antonio had brought from the restaurant and one could imagine a lions' pit where the Christian martyrs were thrown.

To distract our attention from his daughters, Antonio released the dog and bade it lie down while he rested his foot on its head—I suppose to show us how manageable it was. It didn't prove a damn thing to me. I had once seen that dog pounce on one of the hunting falcons the family above us bred. The falcon had got loose and flew down to investigate its hill of bones. That insane dog had pounced on the falcon as quick as the bat of an eye.

At the time all the daughters and Maria were sitting in the garden in front of the house, with the interminable crocheting of bed linen, which occupies Spanish girl children from the time they are born until they are safely married; and all the señoras and señoritas from above were looking down. When the dog pounced on the bird, the girls ran and beat at him with chairs, and the people from upstairs joined in their screaming until my brain was shattered and my hair stood straight up like magnetized iron filings. But that dog didn't let it bother him a bit. With incredibly vicious-sounding growling and slavering, he gobbled that bird down.

Alva wrote very often to her aunt in Philadelphia. She wrote every day to her children. She heard from them and sometimes from her husband. She sent them a copy of *The Third Generation* to show them she hadn't gone off with a tramp. I don't think it impressed them very much; their subsequent letters did not seem to cheer her.

Then suddenly the end of the season had come upon us. The sea turned green and sinister and all the smart tourists left. Damien said, "In the winter Palma is silent and mysterious, like the nature of the Mallorquin." The city filled with Germans, who seemed to time their vacations after the departure of the others, as if humiliated by having lost the war. They showed their humiliation by the loudness of their talk and the shabbiness of their clothes, by defiant drunkenness and permeditated insolence.

They behaved in the way white Americans accuse the black Americans of behaving. Alva hated the Germans, partly because they had had so much influence over her husband during the war, and consequently over her.

When the first rains came and the sea turned a muddy red and the cathedral was blotted from view, I remember putting on my plastic raincoat and hat and sitting on top of the abandoned well in our little garden in the driving rain. But it was silly and I didn't get anything out of it. That was the time we were seeing Damien so often because it was something to do. We had stopped working. Our typewriter remained silent.

Then I received the collection of short stories that Donald Friede, the editor at World, had selected from the batch I had submitted for a book of short stories. I had been paid an advance of eight hundred dollars for a book to be called *Black Boogie Woogie*. When I read the stories again, in that atmosphere of my hurt and isolation, they all seemed wrong and there was scarcely one that I felt proud of having written. And when I considered the fact that World had rejected both *The End of a Primitive* and *The Golden Chalice* and wished to publish this trash, I hated the stories. I didn't want my name attached to such a collection. I wrapped them up one morning and took them down to the bay and threw them into the sea.

When I told Alva what I had done, she looked startled. I
think that was the first time she really lost confidence in me.
She had always thought of me as a "complete person," to use
her own words. "You're the only complete person I've ever
known," she had said. And now she had suddenly discovered
that I was far from being complete. I think it must have
frightened her, too. For not long afterward she went to the
Palma office of the American Export Line to try to get a job
working her way back to the States. I didn't learn this until
a long time afterward but at the time I noticed a definite
change in her attitude toward me.

I remember a conversation we had one rainy afternoon lying
in bed, drinking cheap wine to pass the time.

"You want to leave me," I said.

"Should I?"

"You're bitter."

"What about you?" she asked.

"I'm not bitter," I said slowly as though sounding out my emotions. "I feel something like I felt when the judge sentenced me to
twenty years in prison. Not so much shocked or bitter. Just very
strange, is all."

"I don't have your advantage of having been to prison,"
she said. "But don't you think I have a right to feel bitter?
After all, I don't want to leave you."

I got up and dressed and walked outside in the rain.

Alva came to hate Palma, the very sight and smell of it. And
the last of our money was slowly running out and we had no
more coming from anywhere. That was when I first thought of
the title *Winter Coming On*, which I took from a line spoken
by a hobo in a James Cain novel, "Fifty cents in my pocket
and winter coming on."

And then came the day we were completely broke. We didn't
even have three pesetas to buy a bottle of wine. It was impossible
to borrow ten or twenty pesetas from anyone we knew. The
official rate was forty-two pesetas to the dollar. One just can't
borrow twenty-five or fifty cents from friends, not from the friends

we had in Palma. They wouldn't have understood that we didn't
have any money. We might have been able to borrow five or
ten thousand pesetas from Antonio or Damien. But Antonio
needed all the money he could get, and Damien might not
have had that much cash, which would necessitate his getting
it from his mother, and his wife would bitterly disapprove. It
was the second time since we had been together that we had
been completely without money. The first time had been in
London when we had hocked Alva's diamond engagement ring.
And that again was all we had left. But we had never seen
a pawnshop in Mallorca. The three gold balls of legend were
unknown there, or else I would have tried pawning my typewriter
and my clothes. I thought of Mr. Short. Billy Haygood had
first mentioned him in his letter to Arcachon and I had stopped
by his office when I first arrived in Mallorca to get Bill's address;
besides, we passed his office every time we went to Viajes
Marsans on the Borne for our mail. But I scarcely remembered
Mr. Short. However, I remembered King in the Puerto saying
that Short cashed personal checks for him and others whom he
knew, and if I ever found myself short and needed a small check
cashed on my American bank account, no doubt Short would
oblige. I didn't have any money in an American bank, but when
I had visited Bill in Vermont the winter before I left the States I
had opened a bank account in the Merchants National Bank of
Burlington, Vermont, and had been given a bank book showing
a deposit of $1250. I had never taken it back to have the with-
drawals entered. While packing my trunk some vague instinct
of survival had prompted me to bring it along to Europe for
just such an emergency.

I didn't tell Alva what I had in mind. I told her I intended
to pawn her diamond ring. I had her wear her pink linen dress
and I put on my beige gabardine suit and stuck my bank book
in my pocket and we set forth. We didn't have one peseta for
carfare. We had to walk. We went down the steep stairway from
the Plaza Mediterraneo to the Paseo Maritimo and kept on
around past the Yacht Club and along Paseo Sagrera past the

entrance to the Muelle and turned left into Avenida Antonio
Maura, where Mr. Short's office was located. I will never forget
that afternoon. For me it had seemed like the end of the world.

"I'll always hate this city," Alva said.

"We'll soon be away from it," I promised.

Before reaching Mr. Short's I parked her on the terrace of a
café in the sunshine. I didn't want her to run the risk of being
humiliated. A sprinkling of leftover tourists, looking seedy and
discontent, either homeless or stranded, stared at us with envy
and malevolence.

A waiter rushed up and I ordered a vermouth for her and
a pernod for myself and took a gulp without sitting down.

"Don't be long," she said. "I don't like to sit here alone in
this pink ensemble."

"It'll only take a minute," I said.

I continued along the Avenida Antonio Maura to a storefront
with a faded sign reading SHORT & SON—ENTERPRISES. Warped
boarding, once painted green, framed plate-glass windows opaque
from a heavy coating of light-gray dust. A sun-stained strip of
cardboard, obviously a shoebox top, on which was written OPEN
in runny red paint, hanging from a string on the inside of the
door, was barely visible through the dust. I took a deep breath
and went inside.

The main room at the front was filled with an assortment of
ancient luggage containing personal effects which had been stored
for safe keeping and had accumulated over the years. Each was
properly tagged and addressed to persons by then dead or per-
manently disappeared.

On one wall was an old blackboard covered with time-yellowed
cards advertising articles for sale and exchange: *Brindle boxer—
fine pedigree—perfect pet* . . . *Ski suit—almost new—for aqua-
plane* . . . *Primus stove—good condition—needs burner.* . . .

I picked my way through the debris toward the doorway at
the rear. Everything was coated with gray dust. I was careful
not to touch anything or to get dirt on my suit.

The back room was as crammed with relics as the front was

with abandoned luggage. Stuffed birds sat on a dusty mantel above a disused fireplace. Rusty swords, faded capes, motheaten hats, warped pics, bloodstained *muletas*, dried-up *banderillos*, souvenirs of *corridas*, all coated with gray dust, covered the walls. I wondered briefly who had been the matador. A stuffed sheep with red wool stood in one corner; in another was an antique olive oil press.

The man behind the scarred and littered desk was as much a relic as anything else. Feeble light from a fly-specked globe hanging from the ceiling fell softly through the dust on a grizzly gray head with a tan leathery bald spot in the center. Beneath was a broad bloated face with inconsistently white skin splotched with brown spots and peppered with tiny sores. It surrounded a big red nose indented with enlarged pores. He wore a navy-blue cotton shirt, yellow tie, a black-and-white cowskin waistcoat, and an ancient tan tweed jacket. For an instant I had the impression that he was stuffed too.

Suddenly he looked up through bleared blue eyes coated with cataracts. "What is it?" he asked in a cockney voice.

"It's like this," I began. "I'm short and—"

"No, you're not," he cut me off. "*I'm* Short."

I realized instantly it was his stock joke. I laughed dutifully. "You're *Mister* Short," I corrected. "I'm just plain short."

Mr. Short leaned back in the squeaking swivel chair and hooked his thumbs into his waistcoat pockets. His bloated belly stuck out. "What can I do for you?"

I had my story all made up. "My friend, Dave King, in the Puerto de Pollenso, told me if I ever found myself—er—in need of money."

"Did Dave find someone to take his boat?" Mr. Short interrupted.

I was stymied for a moment. I hadn't known King had a boat, I'd never seen it, never heard of it. But I didn't want Mr. Short to become suspicious that I didn't know him.

"I think he found an American to take it," I said. It was

a good safe answer. One could always find an American to take anything. "The last time I saw him he said it was all lined up."

"Glad to hear it. Didn't want him to get stuck with it. I sold it to him."

"Yes, he told me."

"So what is it you want?"

"Well, as I said, I'm—" I caught myself again. "King said you loaned money." I took Alva's ring from my change pocket. "I'd like to borrow a hundred dollars on my wife's ring."

I laid the ring on the desk, but Mr. Short didn't even look at it.

"No, I don't take anything in hock; I only loan money to friends."

I couldn't tell whether he was just saying that to protect himself against the law or whether he meant it. But I didn't want to press him.

"Do you know if there's a pawnshop in town?"

"There's a state loan office somewhere, I think," he said slowly as he searched his memory. "In the old town—on Plaza Cuartera, near as I can remember."

I looked at him uncertainly wondering whether to spring the check.

"But I'm not sure it's still there," he continued ruminatively. "That was before the war."

"That's not ten years," I said.

Mr. Short looked perplexed. Then he chuckled. "I meant these people's war—what you call the Spanish Civil War."

"Oh."

"I've been here thirty-seven years—except when they sent me back to England during the war. I don't know anything about the other wars, only hearsay."

I didn't give a damn how long he had been there or what he had heard about wars. I was wondering how to introduce the check. I regretted ever having shown him the ring.

"Well"—I made as though to leave, but I had no intention of leaving; I couldn't leave—"thanks for the information."

"They wouldn't give you anything on it," Mr. Short added.

I felt an idiotic impulse to burst into hysterical laughter. For that brought to mind a half-remembered fragment of conversation from the past: "Bessie sells 'em . . . she got bombers like what you like . . . but she wouldn't sell you none."

"It's not as though I'm a pauper," I said. "I got money in the bank in the States, but it takes two weeks to clear a check from here and I have a number of urgent debts."

"Do you have your bank book with you?" he asked.

"Yes, but I've run out of checks."

"How much do you want?"

"Just a hundred"—the instant I said it I regretted not asking for more—"and fifty," I added.

"I think I might be able to manage that," Mr. Short said.

"But I haven't any checks."

"Oh, I've got plenty of blank checks," Mr. Short said. "It's just money that I'm lacking." Comedian, I thought. He took a book of blank checks from the top drawer and slapped it on the desk. "Make it payable to E. C. Short," he said.

I took a long, deep breath; Mr. Short had avoided danger. I leaned forward and opened the checkbook on the littered desk and he handed me a pen.

"Sit down," he said, indicating a straight-backed cane-bottom chair covered with the inevitable gray dust.

I looked at it with distaste and said, "This is all right."

As I spelled out the name of the bank in block letters I was thinking that it would take ten days at least for clearance and by the time it had been returned marked "Insufficient funds" I'd be gone from Spain. I didn't think they could do anything to me in France. But anyway, when I got hold of some money I'd send him a money order to cover his loss, I promised myself. I filled out the amount and signed the check and held it by one corner to let it dry.

Mr. Short reached for it and carefully blotted it on the spotted desk blotter, then he put on a pair of horn-rimmed glasses and looked at it.

"*Chester Himes*—is that right?"

"Yes." I reached inside my coat for my passport, Mr. Short waved it aside.

"Now if you will let me see your bank book."

I showed him the bank book containing the one entry of a $1250 deposit, thinking at the time how I'd spent the last of it to pay my income tax in the spring of 1953, when I'd barely had sufficient income to tax. He opened it and looked at the one entry.

"You haven't drawn from the account at all," he said. I thought he sounded slightly suspicious. I tightened up.

"I haven't needed to," I said.

"May I ask you what is your occupation, Mr. Himes?"

"I'm a writer," I said.

He seemed satisfied.

"There's a little commission."

"Oh, of course," I agreed.

He reached into his drawer and took out a stack of five-thousand-peseta notes. He hadn't been acquainted with any American writers as poor as me, I thought. But I was tremendously relieved by the sight of the money. I refused to think of what I might have done if he hadn't cashed the check. Only the two of us were in the entire place and there was little likelihood of our being interrupted. The season was over and the day was bad. Alva was sitting in a café with an unpaid bill . . .

Later I wrote a version of this incident wherein I had strangled the old man and robbed him. It was the same version in which I had strangled the black marketeer, Pops, in Paris and robbed him too. In fact I had strangled three persons in that version before I finally got the money to get Alva safely home.

When I sat down across from Alva in the café, she asked, "Did you get some money?"

"Yes," I said. "We're going to Cook's just as soon as I pay up. We're leaving the island in the morning."

She looked at me inquiringly. I gave her back the ring. Her eyes widened in alarm.

"I wrote a check," I said.

"Oh!" she exclaimed but I could see she didn't understand. Her eyes were filled with questions, but I rushed her away without explaining.

I took her up the street to book our passage on the boat to Barcelona, but the clerk said it was too late to get places on the boat next morning. But, at my insistence, he telephoned the Compania Transmediterranea and was told we could have places on the deck, which meant we wouldn't have cabins in case of rain or bad weather and would have to sit in the public rooms or on deck for the entire twelve hours. The clerk said they would have to send down to the ships lines' office on the Muelle to pick up the tickets, which would take several hours, and advised us to come back around nine-thirty. But I said we had a lot to do and that would be too late. When he learned that we lived in Terreno he promised to send the tickets to our house before ten. We went home and paid our bills and began to pack. The family was extraordinarily shocked and disturbed over our leaving on such short notice and wondered if we'd gotten into any trouble. Maria sent one of the girls to telephone Antonio at the restaurant and tell him to come home. He came around to our room and asked me if I'd had any difficulty with the authorities or with anyone. I suppose they had heard all about our controversy in Deya with Pedro Canales from Carmen—I couldn't see Pedro telling them—and thought perhaps I'd gotten into some sort of controversy in Palma. Alva had to translate, and it was very embarrassing for all of us, but when I had convinced them that our leaving so quickly had nothing to do with anyone in Palma but was due only to a sudden decision about our writing by editors in France, they were all greatly relieved. They hated to see us go, but the girls were so excited that they crowded into our room and we could scarcely pack. They paid little attention to my things but they stared greedily and intently at every item Alva picked up— lingerie, suits, dresses, stockings, shoes, toilet articles.

Ten o'clock came and the tickets hadn't arrived. Antonio took me on his motorcycle down to Cook's, and we had to knock them up at the back door. They said they had sent the tickets an hour ago, and for us to be sure and be at the Muelle at six-thirty. On the way back I stopped at a taxi stand near Plaza Gomila and ordered a taxi for the next morning. Antonio spoke to the driver in Mallorquin and turned to me and said, "Okay."

When we got back, Antonio's three daughters were going wild trying on Alva's clothes. They scarcely noticed me. They were running about, all stark naked and smelling excitedly musky. Alva gave each of them a dress—she had numbers of dresses she would never wear again—and she gave Maria a suit in gray shantung silk that her aunt in Philadelphia had once sent to her in Kerkrade, no doubt thinking she was pregnant with quadruplets, for it was slightly large even for Maria. There was so much smooth young activated flesh around I could hardly pack.

The messenger turned up with our tickets at midnight, drunk and argumentative, but Antonio made short shrift of him. I had been so intrigued with the naked girls I hadn't noticed the passing of the time. When the girls caught me staring they just grinned as though at some nice compliment. After all, Alva was there and I supposed it was a compliment.

We didn't sleep a wink all night. We considered telephoning Damien but thought better of it, partly because of the inconvenience—there was no telephone in the house and we would have to go to Plaza Gomila—and partly because of his wife. Antonio helped us load the trunk and other luggage atop the taxi next morning before he went to work, and we kissed Maria and all the girls goodbye and left the island.

5.

We headed for the Villa Madiana, which Yves had told us we could have any time we wished with the exception of July and August. We hadn't had the time to notify anyone of our arrival or write to Yves of our coming—we just went, from Barcelona to Bordeaux to Arcachon. We arrived in the late afternoon, dirty and weary, with about nine hundred pesetas (twenty dollars) left and greatly in need of sleep. We hadn't slept for three days. But it was such a relief just to arrive. I felt like the friend who, at our all-day party in 1939 celebrating the end of WPA, went out in the late afternoon to get some whiskey and returned two hours later, pants hanging down, shoulders drooping, dragging himself into the room seemingly on the verge of exhaustion with a bottle of John Paul Jones whiskey in each hand, exclaiming triumphantly, "I made it," and then falling on his face in a dead faint. We had "made it."

We engaged an old dilapidated taxi similar to the one we'd had the year before and loaded our luggage on top, and after changing my nine hundred pesetas in eight thousand old francs (eighteen dollars) we climbed aboard and set forth for Villa Madiana.

We arrived to find a strange woman watering the lawn. But

our arrival was also a signal for all the neighbors to rush into the street and welcome us back. However, the woman watering the lawn informed Alva that her husband had bought the property and they had just moved in. There we were, with all our possessions in the world loaded atop a taxi in the middle of the street, with no place to go and no money to get there with. But I was consoled somewhat by the thought that at least I'd gotten Alva out of Palma.

I couldn't get into any more trouble than I was already in, I thought, so I told the driver to take us to the Hôtel Saint-Louis, Dr. Thé's swank hotel on the quay. Even if I didn't have any money, I reasoned, I was known. But the Hôtel Saint-Louis was closed. Fortunately there was a gardener about, who informed us that Dr. Thé's pension in another part of town was still open. We had the driver take us there. I was afraid that if we didn't get out of that taxi soon I wouldn't be able to pay the fare. Dr. Thé's son, Jacques, was managing the pension, but he was absent, and the housekeeper in charge said they'd be closing soon and weren't taking any more guests. I had Alva call Dr. Thé at his residence and tell him our predicament about Yves' house but not to mention that we had no money. Dr. Thé said they were just keeping the pension open to accommodate a Spanish doctor and his family, but we could put up there until they left, and no doubt by that time we would have made other arrangements. We moved in and remained there nine days, at three thousand old francs (six dollars) a day including service. Dr. Thé and his elegant wife took their evening meals there during the first week of our stay, and the food was excellent. But when they left for their vacation in Spain the quality of the food dropped off. We seldom saw Jacques.

After our first good night's sleep we got up and got busy on those things necessary for survival. I wrote Yves and told him we would be in Paris soon and wanted an immediate decision on my manuscript The End of a Primitive, which he had submitted to some publisher who was a friend of his. And Alva wired her aunt in Philadelphia for some money. It was unseasonably cold the first of October and we had to dig out our winter coats. My huge gray burberry, which came almost down to my ankles, was still like new, but Alva had left her fur coat in Kerkrade and had only a gray mohair coat without buttons that I'd bought her in London, and it didn't impress me as being very warm. But she didn't complain.

Dr. Thé had left by the time Alva got the reply from her aunt and the fifty dollars she sent. It wasn't enough to help. I decided to go to Paris and try to raise some money. Jacques Thé was also out of town and there wasn't anyone left with authority but the housekeeper and I gave her notice we'd be leaving after lunch on our tenth day. The bill came to 27,060 old francs, and I gave her a dollar check for $77.37. She supplied the blank check but it made no sense to her as I filled it out and there was no one she could ask, but she knew we were acquainted with Dr. Thé and she accepted it. We had to leave my big trunk there until we could send for it, for we could not afford to pay fifteen dollars for excess baggage, nor could we have it about our necks in Paris until we got settled.

For some reason which I do not remember, probably to evade pursuers, I suppose, we did not go direct from Bordeaux to Paris but went through Toulouse, where we changed trains in the middle of the night, standing for hours on the ice-cold platform of the deserted station. We arrived in Paris at about seven o'clock of a cold drizzly gray morning and found the cheap hotels on the Left Bank dark and sleeping at that hour and no proprietor willing to get up for a client. I suggested that we walk about for a couple of hours to keep warm, and we started off from somewhere in the vicinity of Hôtel Michelet, where we had stayed previously, and went through the Luxembourg Gardens, where the police were still huddling in their shelters, down a deserted Rue Bonaparte through a still closed and deserted Saint-Germain-des-Prés and along the Quai Malaquais beside the dirty fetid stinking Seine and passed over the Pont du Carrousel into the Place du Carrousel in front of the Louvre. All the time I had been carrying our two heavy suitcases—Alva's big American suitcase and my black horsehide suitcase, which I kept clean and polished for a status symbol—and Alva had been lugging my typewriter and her big handbag and her ancient Hermes typewriter, which was about to give up the ghost. Alva had about given up the ghost herself by the time we arrived at the Place du Carrousel. So we sat on a stone bench in the cold gray drizzle with visibility almost to zero and looked at the equestrian statue atop the original Arc de Triomphe in front of us.

At nine o'clock we returned to the Latin Quarter and began hotel hunting again. The Hôtel Welcome overlooking the Odéon, a favorite of the young white Americans, set the pattern. They said they couldn't rent to *noirs*; their clients wouldn't like it. The first nine hotels we tried turned us down because I was black. The majority of the proprietors unequivocally gave that as the reason. Afterward I told that to many French persons and no one believed me. Some said that I could have called a policeman, and forced the issue then and there. Others said perhaps I had arrived at a misconception from not knowing the language. It is true I only had Alva's word for it. But I believed her. And in later years a number of Africans also have complained of a color bar in the Latin Quarter, because of the cheap-hotel proprietors' desire to please their white American clients. But on that particular morning I was too weary and dispirited to make a scene, as I would normally have done.

At the hotel Jeanne d'Arc on rue de Buci I went up to the first-floor bureau alone because Alva was too weary to climb the stairs. I was told by an indifferent proprietor the hotel was *complet*. When I returned to the sidewalk where Alva was waiting, on sudden impulse she suggested she go back up alone and see what they'd tell her. Not knowing she was with me, they welcomed her and showed her several available double rooms, one of which she took on the fourth floor at 450 old francs per day. The proprietor turned blood-red when he saw me again returning with our hand luggage, but there was nothing he could do and he had better sense than to say anything at that moment. Later, when Alva went out alone, leaving me in the room, he was very insulting to her. But when I went down and challenged him about it, he made as though he didn't understand what I was talking about and his wife stood around throwing up her hands and giving a performance of spurious indignation.

Alva had used the last of our money to pay the required two weeks' rent in advance. I walked down to the Old Navy Café et Tabac on boulevard St. Germain, in the hope of seeing an acquaintance, and I got talking to a tall, cynical African from Nigeria called Slim, who told me about the nationalized pawnshops, which were known as Crédit Municipal. But the only one he had ever done business with was on the Place de Clichy, two *métro* stops beyond Place de Pigalle. Leaving Alva in our room, I took her diamond engagement ring (which she said had cost $150) and my old Remington portable typewriter, and caught the *métro* at the Odéon. The bureau near Place de Clichy offered to lend me ten thousand old francs (twenty dollars) on Alva's ring, which was the maximum loaned on anything. They did not question my right of possession of the ring, but they informed me that I would have to go to the main bureau of the Crédit Municipal on rue Francs-Bourgeois, one *métro* stop from the Hôtel de Ville, in order to pawn my typewriter. Never before had I been able to converse in French, but I understood what they said to me and they understood what I said to them. I have always maintained that the French will understand foreigners only for profit or in an emergency; otherwise they refuse to admit that a foreigner can speak the French language.

I took my typewriter to the main bureau and was requested to fill out a form, giving the number of my passport, my address in the U.S.A., and the names and addresses of living relatives. After it had been perused by someone in a private office—the director, I presumed—I was loaned 5000 old francs (ten dollars). Finally we had thirty dollars—not very much, but at least enough to keep us alive for a spell.

As soon as I could maneuver, I telephoned Yves. He had given up his "penthouse" on the rue Montparnasse and with the help of friends had bought a large old apartment house for two thousand dollars at 46 rue Lamartine, which he called the bargain of the century. He said he had given the manuscript of *The End of a Primitive* to a publisher who was trying to promote a book club, but he hadn't reached a decision.

I felt that he could have reached a decision already if he had wished. It was the only property that I had and I couldn't wait. He gave me his friend's address on rue du Four, in Saint-Germain-des-Prés, and when I went for my manuscript I discovered it was a bookstore and record shop with editorial offices in the rear.

My sudden and unannounced appearance threw everyone into such a panic that they all disappeared, leaving Alva and me sitting in the store, and one girl who seemed to be deaf and dumb in a glass cashier's cage in one corner. Naturally I thought the worst. It looked like one of those fly-by-night publishing houses for which Paris was noted in those days, and it occurred to me that they were printing my book without my permission. We sat there for two or three hours or more. I was getting angrier by the minute. The girl in the cashier's cage refused to look at us. In reply to Alva's queries as to where everyone had gone, she only shrugged. When closing time came she put on her coat and left. We sat there alone. Then a short time later two men who I thought looked guilty came sneaking in with my manuscript. When I asked what was the reason for the delay, one of them shrugged and said, "*Pas compris.*" I had Alva repeat my question. The other man said the publisher merely asked them to deliver the manuscript to me. Finally we went home. My head was tight enough to explode.

The next day, in desperation, Alva went to the American embassy to apply for a secretarial job. She was given the following memorandum and instructed to return in a week if she could meet the requirements.

TO: AMERICAN JOB APPLICANTS

FROM: PERSONNEL SECTION

The American Embassy in Paris is not authorized to hire citizens. All employment of this nature is done in Washington. The Embassy can, however, submit applications to Washington if the following requirements are met.

1. 21 and not over 25 years of age.

2. An American citizen and have been for at least five years.

3. Willing to accept assignment to any foreign post. Persons who limit their availability to specific locations cannot be considered.

4. If married, to an American citizen.

5. Successfully pass a physical examination based on Army and Navy standards.

If the above requirements are fulfilled, an application (available at the reception desk) may be completed and mailed to the Embassy marked for the attention of the Personnel Office. (Applications will not be accepted in person.) Applications will be screened by the Personnel Office and the applicant advised as to its disposition. If the applicant is acceptable he will be invited to come to the Personnel Office to complete his application for submission to Washington. The applicant will then be subject to a security and suitability examination which involves a delay of at least six months before appointment can be processed.

Again we had to turn to Yves for help in finding a reliable publisher for *The End of a Primitive*.

While we had been in Mallorca, the mountain-climbing expedition headed by Sir Edmund Hillary and Sir John Hunt had scaled Mount Everest and the entire world had become wildly interested in their feat.

Publishers all over the globe were vying with each other to be the first to bring out a book on this adventure. But the Scorpion Press in Paris got a jump on them all. The editors assembled a stack of data and all available material pertinent to the ascent, rented a villa in Switzerland, and employed Yves to go there and write a book about the Tibetan Sherpa in four weeks. The book was to be entitled *Tensing of Everest*. Yves took the material and assembled the book in five weeks, including an interview he had with Tensing in Geneva. Scorpion Press sold the foreign rights, on a fifty-fifty basis with the author, as is customary in France, to publishers all over the world. Little, Brown & Company bought the American rights, and Gollancz the British rights.

Because of the slowness of manufacturing and distributing books in the English-language countries, the book had already been published in most European countries, Japan, and other countries in the Orient before Little, Brown & Company and Gollancz got around to editing the text. Then it was discovered by the editors at Gollancz that some of the material included in the manuscript had been lifted without so much as a change of punctuation direct from the Royal Geographic Society's magazine, and some of the photographs and other quotations which were used had been taken from The New York *Times* and the Associated Press. The Royal Geographic Society brought suit against Scorpion Press and Yves Malartic for plagiarism in the French courts for an astronomical sum. All royalties received from the book were confiscated pending the court's decision.

Under French law the burden of proof lies on the defendant, who is presumed guilty until he proves innocence. Yves had to pay for his own defense. He received no financial aid from Scorpion Press, who had their own worries. At the beginning of the procedure the court ruled itself incompetent to judge and ordered the defendants to employ competent judges from the Académie Française at their own expense. This was a heavy financial burden on Yves, which was the reason he'd had to sell the Villa Madiana in Arcachon.

But despite his financial problems, we found both him and

Yvonne in the good spirits with which the French take all
calamities of life, such as wars, bankruptcy, revolution, death,
and taxes. He apologized for his editor friend who had behaved
so mysteriously with the manuscript of *The End of a Primitive*,
saying he had drunk so much white wine it had destroyed his
brain. He suggested that I submit the book to Gallimard, in
which event he would go with me personally to see the director
of the foreign-book section, a M. Mascolo, with whom he was
acquainted, although he wasn't confident that M. Mascolo would
care to admit it.

We made an appointment with Mascolo and went the same
day to take the manuscript. Yves began to describe the story,
but without speaking I handed Mascolo the manuscript to read,
and we left. As we were leaving Gallimard, Yves said, "Himes,
you'll never be a French writer. A French writer gives his book
to an editor and then takes hours to explain what the book is
all about so that by the time he's finished explaining the editor
doesn't want to read it. You don't talk enough."

Since leaving Margot Johnson I had been without an American
literary agent. My business relationship with Ellen Wright had
come to an end shortly after Alva's appearance, and I had put
The Third Generation into the hands of a young American
agent then operating in Paris who claimed to have handled the
sale of the French rights for James Jones' novel *From Here to
Eternity*. We had intended to stop in the Deux Magots for
coffee, but when I saw him sitting there we hurried past, and
Yves caught a No. 48 bus in front of the Eglise Saint-Germain
and I walked back to our room. This young man hadn't been
able to place *The Third Generation* and I didn't want to have
to listen to the gist of the rejections.

I mailed a copy of *The End of a Primitive* to Victor Weybright of NAL, stating my predicament and asking for a quick
decision, and Alva got a temporary job proofreading from an
ad in the *Herald Tribune*. It was some technical data that was
being translated from French into English and they offered her
150 old francs (forty cents) an hour to proofread the translation. I told her to tell her employers that she had been paid

eight dollars an hour for proofreading in New York and couldn't
do it for less. Her prospective employer was intimidated and as
a compromise offered her four hundred old francs (one dollar
ten cents) an hour, which he assured her was more than he
had ever paid anyone else for the job, but none of us were
happy about it, neither her boss nor herself nor least of all
me. Furthermore, her boss reasoned that if he had to pay
her that exorbitant wage, he might as well get something else
for his money than just her indifferent work. That necessitated
my having to go and bring her home every evening, which was
a bore.

We received a letter at the American Express Company addressed to "Señor y Señora Chester Himes" from Antonio's eldest
daughter, Magdalena, informing us that Carmen, Pedro Tous'
wife, had finally had her baby, after a ten-month pregnancy. She
went on to say how much she missed Alva. Spanish women are
extraordinarily loyal and uncomplicated; very few have any formal education; they don't read, they don't think, they are all good
Catholics, and they marry and have babies. Magdalena had been
engaged for some time to a young businessman in Palma and was
just waiting for Antonio to get together a dowry to get married,
but as I remember she wasn't waiting to enjoy the conjugal bed.
I wondered if I had given Mr. Short my address in Terreno and
whether Antonio's family had learned about the bogus check. I
would have hated for them to know. Matter of pride, I suppose.

On my return to Paris I had sent Annie Brierre, who interviewed me for the journal *France—U.S.A.*, a copy of *The Third
Generation*, and I received the following reply:

Dear Mr. Himes,

I never can tell you how much I admired THE THIRD
GENERATION. It is not only that I enjoyed reading it (which
in itself is saying something, as I am rather blasé about novels).
But I admired every paragraph of it, in every way. It is not only
a very good novel, I am certain it will last as one of the few
great novels of our generation.

France—U.S.A.'s next copy will be entirely for Hemingway.

This is why your interview will be postponed until the next one comes out.

This is also the reason why I have not pestered you about the photograph which perhaps you forgot.

I must send both the article and the photograph before December 15th. Perhaps we could meet again early in December for lunch or tea. Would you telephone one morning when it is convenient for you.

> Until very soon
> Yours very sincerely
> Annie Brierre

I had never introduced Alva to Annie Brierre. It wasn't that I thought they wouldn't like each other, but although she was certainly five or more years my senior, Annie Brierre held a sort of sexual attraction for me, which I didn't want Alva to know.

Then one morning I got a many-page contract for *The End of a Primitive* from NAL, taking all rights, hard-cover, paperback, domestic, and foreign, and offering an advance of one thousand dollars. It was accompanied by a letter from Victor Weybright saying how much better it was for the author to take a small advance on "sizable and continuing accruals" than one big advance which perhaps he'd never earn. Overlooking the bullshit, I signed the contract and airmailed it back and asked that the advance be cabled.

After I received the thousand dollars, everything went incredibly fast. I wrote Doctor Thé and paid the bill:

Monsieur le Docteur Thé
15, Avenue Ste. Marie
Arcachon, France
(*Gironde*)

November 22, 1954

Dear Docteur Thé,

I have received notice from my bank, the Merchants National Bank of Burlington, Vt., U.S.A., that the check I gave you was returned for insufficient funds.

I am very sorry this happened. It is the result of my poor bookkeeping. I sincerely hope that it hasn't caused you any great inconvenience or ill will.

I am enclosing a post check for 30,000 old francs to cover the cost of my bill, which was 27,060 old francs, and to pay for the forwarding of my trunk to the following address:

> CHESTER HIMES
> Hôtel Jeanne d'Arc
> 34, rue de Buci
> PARIS, 6e.

I will appreciate it very much if you will send me the returned check. If there is insufficient money to cover the cost of having the trunk sent *livraison à domicile*, please charge the balance collect; if there is any money left over after shipping the trunk, please give it to your handyman for a tip. At the gare here the baggage clerk said it would cost about 700 old francs for the freight.

I thank you very much.

Mrs. Himes joins me in sending you and Mme. le Docteur Thé and Monsieur Jacques our best wishes. We are going to remain in Paris until after Christmas.

> I remain very sincerely yours
>
> Chester Himes

Within a week the trunk arrived with an understanding letter from Doctor Thé; he gave no indication whatsoever that he knew I had given him a bogus check.

Then I went down to the office of the Holland-America Line on the Place de l'Opéra and bought Alva a second-class ticket to New York departing December 1st. She didn't want to go. She contended that now everything would be all right since we had enough money to maneuver. But I told her she shouldn't think of it as separating. I was just sending her back to America to sell our book, *The Golden Chalice*, and I was depending on her.

We hadn't seen the Wrights, I didn't know whether Dick had

returned from Ghana or not. Nor had I seen any of my other American soul brothers. I hadn't wanted to.

The day before the boat was due to sail, we packed her bags and took them down to the Gare Saint-Lazare and checked them on the boat train. And all that night we made love.

The next morning we had a café crème and croissants at the Brasserie Lipp and afterward took a taxi down to the Gare Saint-Lazare.

We stood very close on the platform and she kept turning to hide her face from the strangers all about us because she was crying. When the conductors blew their whistles for all aboard I took Alva in my arms and kissed her and it seemed to open the floodgates for I had to lift her onto the train. She stood in the open coach door, dangerously, perilously, waving frantically, desperately, until the train had turned the bend way up the track and passed from sight, although I doubted if she could have seen me through her tears.

I went across to a bar on rue Saint-Lazare and had a couple of Cognacs. Suddenly I found myself crying like a baby. Tears streamed down my cheeks. Frenchmen at the bar turned to stare at me. I wiped my eyes and tried to pull myself together. I'm just too emotional, I upbraided myself. My feelings are too intense. I hate too bitterly, I love too exaltingly, I pity too extravagantly, I hurt too painfully. We American blacks call that "soul," I thought deprecatingly.

I had got Alva home safe at last—or at least on the way. That was soul. But in my heart I considered it an achievement, the only valid achievement of my entire life. It had been my supreme ambition ever since I had the controversy with Pedro Canales in Deya to get Alva home safe—not *safely*, but *safe*.

But what about me? I asked myself. Where could I find that was safe?